Euripides and Quotation Culture

Classical Literature and Society
Series Editor: David Taylor

Chaos, Cosmos and Creation in Early Greek Theogonies: An Ontological Exploration, Olaf Almqvist
Classics and the Bible: Hospitality and Recognition, John Taylor
Culture and Philosophy in the Age of Plotinus, Mark Edwards
Homer: The Resonance of Epic, Barbara Graziosi & Johannes Haubold
Juvenal and the Satiric Genre, Frederick Jones
The Myth of Paganism: Nonnus, Dionysus and the World of Late Antiquity, Robert Shorrock
Ovid and His Love Poetry, Rebecca Armstrong
Pastoral Inscriptions: Reading and Writing Virgil's Eclogues, Brian W. Breed
Pausanias: Travel Writing in Ancient Greece, Maria Pretzler
Propertius: Poet of Love and Leisure, Alison Keith
Silent Eloquence: Lucian and Pantomime Dancing, Ismene Lada-Richards
Statius, Poet between Rome and Naples, Carole E. Newlands
The Roman Book, Rex Winsbury
Thucydides and the Shaping of History, Emily Greenwood

Euripides and Quotation Culture

Matthew Wright

BLOOMSBURY ACADEMIC
LONDON • NEW YORK • OXFORD • NEW DELHI • SYDNEY

BLOOMSBURY ACADEMIC

Bloomsbury Publishing Plc, 50 Bedford Square, London, WC1B 3DP, UK
Bloomsbury Publishing Inc, 1359 Broadway, 12th Floor, New York, NY 10018, USA
Bloomsbury Publishing Ireland, 29 Earlsfort Terrace, Dublin 2, D02 AY28, Ireland

BLOOMSBURY, BLOOMSBURY ACADEMIC and the Diana logo are trademarks of
Bloomsbury Publishing Plc

First published in Great Britain 2024
Paperback edition published 2026

Copyright © Matthew Wright, 2024

Matthew Wright has expressed his right under the Copyright, Designs and Patents Act, 1988, to be identified as Author of this work.

Cover image: *The Library of Alexandria*
Heritage Image Partnership Ltd/Alamy Stock Photo

All rights reserved. No part of this publication may be: i) reproduced or transmitted in any form, electronic or mechanical, including photocopying, recording or by means of any information storage or retrieval system without prior permission in writing from the publishers; or ii) used or reproduced in any way for the training, development or operation of artificial intelligence (AI) technologies, including generative AI technologies. The rights holders expressly reserve this publication from the text and data mining exception as per Article 4(3) of the Digital Single Market Directive (EU) 2019/790.

Bloomsbury Publishing Plc does not have any control over, or responsibility for, any third-party websites referred to or in this book. All internet addresses given in this book were correct at the time of going to press. The author and publisher regret any inconvenience caused if addresses have changed or sites have ceased to exist, but can accept no responsibility for any such changes.

A catalogue record for this book is available from the British Library.

Library of Congress Cataloging-in-Publication Data
Names: Wright, Matthew (Matthew Ephraim), author.
Title: Euripides and quotation culture / Matthew Wright.
Other titles: Classical literature and society ; v. 13.
Description: New York : Bloomsbury Academic, 2024. |
Series: Classical literature and society ; vol 13 |
Includes bibliographical references and index.
Identifiers: LCCN 2023055269 (print) | LCCN 2023055270 (ebook) |
ISBN 9781350441170 (hardback) | ISBN 9781350441217 (paperback) |
ISBN 9781350441187 (pdf) | ISBN 9781350441194 (ebook)
Subjects: LCSH: Euripides–Criticism and interpretation. | Euripides–Quotations.
Classification: LCC PA3978 .W76 2024 (print) | LCC PA3978 (ebook) |
DDC 882/.1—dc23/eng/20240304
LC record available at https://lccn.loc.gov/2023055269
LC ebook record available at https://lccn.loc.gov/2023055270.

ISBN: HB: 978-1-3504-4117-0
PB: 978-1-3504-4121-7
ePDF: 978-1-3504-4118-7
eBook: 978-1-3504-4119-4

Series: Classical Literature and Society

Typeset by RefineCatch Limited, Bungay, Suffolk

For product safety related questions contact productsafety@bloomsbury.com.

To find out more about our authors and books visit www.bloomsbury.com
and sign up for our newsletters.

Contents

Preface		vi
1	'Awfully Full of Quotations'	1
2	Quotation Marks and Framing Devices	29
3	How to Quote from Books You Haven't Read	53
4	Quotations in the Theatre	73
5	Quotations in the Classroom	91
6	Quotation as Performance	123
7	Quotations and Life	145
Notes		173
Bibliography		197
Index		207

Preface

I started working on this project in 2011, after discovering *Parole Rubate/Purloined Letters*, the recently established 'international journal of quotation studies', and thinking that more could be done with the topic of quotation within classical studies. The resulting book does not claim to offer the first or last word on the subject but it aims to make an original contribution in several ways. It takes a single author – Euripides – as its main organizing focus but also opens up the concept of 'quotation culture' in a broader sense; it treats quotation as a social activity; it is interested in people as well as texts; it attempts to pinpoint what is distinctive about the ways that ancient quoters deploy quotations in comparison with their modern counterparts; it aspires to a higher level of methodological sophistication than many existing studies of citation or traditional *Quellenforschung*; and it represents a fresh approach to the study of fragmentary tragedy. I hope that this book will be of interest to literary scholars within and beyond classical studies, not just as a timely contribution to an important topic but also as a stimulus to further enquiry.

Many people have helped me during the last twelve years by discussing ideas with me, by reading parts of the book in draft or by offering support and encouragement of other kinds. Particular thanks are due to John Wilkins, Richard Seaford, Chris Gill, Richard Stoneman, David Braund, Lynette Mitchell, David Harvey, Peter Wiseman, Curtis Dozier, Richard Hunter, John Tennant, Alexandra Harris, Steven and Caroline Martin, Tony and Gill Yates, Lily Neal, Hugh Lodder and Katherine Gwynne.

A note on conventions: Greek and Latin texts are cited from the Loeb Classical Library editions where available. All tragic fragments follow the text and numbering of B. Snell, S. Radt and R. Kannicht (eds), *Tragicorum Graecorum Fragmenta* (*TrGF*); all comic fragments come from R. Kassel and C. Austin (eds), *Poetae Comici Graeci* (*PCG*). 'F' denotes a fragment; 'T' denotes a testimonium; 'Σ' denotes a scholion. Any other abbreviations follow the usage of *L'Année Philologique* or *The Oxford Classical Dictionary*. I never abbreviate authors' names or titles because students tend to find this practice off-putting. All Greek and Latin is translated for the benefit of students and non-specialist readers; the English translations are my own.

M.E.W.
Topsham
November 2023

1

'Awfully Full of Quotations'

'Very nice, very nice, but awfully full of quotations...' That notorious description of *Hamlet* might almost have been formulated with Euripidean drama in mind.[1] Euripides' tragedies are full of phrases and passages which were repeatedly quoted by others throughout antiquity, to such an extent that these 'quotable quotes' took on a life of their own. To take just a few examples:

> τί δ' αἰσχρὸν ἢν μὴ τοῖσι χρωμένοις δοκῆι;
>
> *Aeolus* F19
>
> What is shameful, if it does not seem shameful to those who practise it?
>
> αἱ δεύτεραί πως φροντίδες σοφώτεραι.
>
> *Hippolytus* 436
>
> Second thoughts are wiser, I suppose.
>
> ἡ γλῶσσ' ὀμώμοχ', ἡ δὲ φρὴν ἀνώμοτος.
>
> *Hippolytus* 601
>
> It was my tongue that swore; my mind remains unsworn.
>
> οὐκ ἔστιν οὐδὲν κρεῖσσον ἢ φίλος σαφής.
>
> *Orestes* 1155
>
> There is nothing better than a true friend.

Such lines might be quoted for many different reasons – perhaps because they are seen as succinctly summing up profound truths about life, or because they formulate their ideas in a unique manner, or because they encapsulate traditional Greek wisdom in a memorable format, or because they use language in an unpredictable way that transcends cliché, or because they deliberately set out to be provocative or paradoxical. Hundreds of famous verses and phrases from Euripidean drama circulated within the ancient world, even after the plays in which they originally featured became forgotten or vanished completely. Indeed, the majority of Euripides' tragedies now survive only in the form of scattered quotations, otherwise known to us as 'fragments'. This means that studying

Euripidean quotations is, in a sense, a different sort of activity from studying Shakespearean quotations.²

In this book, I attempt to understand Euripides in relation to ancient quotation culture. Who quotes Euripides, and why? Which plays are quoted most? What uses are made of quotation in different contexts, and do they reveal more about the texts being quoted or the people doing the quoting? To what extent are 'book-fragments' (quotations) representative of the plays from which they come? What is the difference between a 'quotation' and a 'fragment'? What can quotations tell us about literary culture and reading habits, in antiquity or in the modern world? How does quotation relate to notions of authorship and authority? Whose voice, words or thoughts are embodied in a quotation? Can quotation be seen as a form of appropriation or rewriting? How can the same words have different meanings depending on the situation in which they appear? What can the study of quotations tell us about cultural memory? Does the habit of quotation develop or evolve significantly over time? In the pages that follow I aim to provide answers to all these questions, with reference to a variety of literary and social contexts throughout Greek and Roman antiquity.

The focus is on Euripides because he is quoted overwhelmingly more often than any other tragedian, and more often than any other Greek author except Homer. The phrase 'quotation culture' – as distinct from 'quotation' pure and simple – is deliberately chosen because it encompasses a plurality of meanings, not all of them purely literary. First, and most basically, it can refer to any formal or functional aspect of the practice of quotation, including any ways in which authors might select or deploy quotations from other writers within their own work. But it can also evoke the intellectual and social milieux within which quotation is practised, the conditions that make quotation possible, the processes that lead to the production of literary texts, the mentality of writers and their readers (as far as this can be accessed or reconstructed), and the whole diverse spectrum of ancient reading practices. A focus on 'quotation culture' as such also emphasizes the historically situated nature of the inquiry. Even though readers at all subsequent periods of civilization have continued to quote Euripides, we are concerned here with the reception of tragedy within the Graeco-Roman world. Attempting to uncover what is distinctive about the ways in which ancient authors of different periods quote Euripides is a valuable activity. Not only does it highlight the changing status and significance of Euripides throughout history, but it also reveals important differences between ancient and modern literary cultures. Of course, many of the questions and approaches discussed here could have a much wider application within modern classical reception studies – but that is a subject for another book.

A chapter-by-chapter summary

In the following sections of this opening chapter I take a single Euripidean quotation or 'fragment' (*Stheneboea* F661) as the starting point for the investigation.[3] Narrowing down the focus in this way can help us to reduce an enormous topic to graspable proportions, making it easier to talk about general tendencies and themes by concentrating on specific details. I look closely at the ways in which this quotation is deployed by those who cite it, and I use this example to illustrate some central aspects of quotation culture that will be explored further in subsequent chapters. Tracing the afterlife of a single quotation through a variety of quoting authors and texts allows us to observe the processes of reception and transmission at work. What emerges very clearly is that Euripides' words are repeatedly manipulated and transformed via quotation. Taken out of their original setting within the tragedy *Stheneboea* and reused in new contexts, their function and their meaning seem to undergo significant changes.

As I shall demonstrate, F661 can be read both in and out of context: that is, it can function both as part of a text and as an independent short text on its own.[4] This inherent quality of doubleness is a highly significant feature of this specific quotation and of quotations more generally. Indeed, the ability of quotations to (as it were) metamorphose in different settings has been noted by various critics and theorists, who have resorted to an intriguingly diverse range of terminology when describing it – including 'the autonomization of language units', 'iterability', 'double coding', 'displacement', 'the dissolve of voices' or 'the Proteus principle'.[5]

Almost any example of a quotation, by any given author, might be seen as having a dual function of this sort, depending on its specific literary context(s) and use(s). Nevertheless, part of my aim in this chapter, and throughout the book as a whole, is to show that there is often something about Euripidean quotations in particular that is extraordinary. Having examined the uses of F661 in the work of other authors, I go on to analyse it as an utterance in its own right, characterized by a formal quality which (following Gary Saul Morson) I call 'quotationality'. Next, I consider the quotation in relation to what is known about reading habits in antiquity, arguing that the decontextualized use of excerpts was more common than one might imagine. Finally, I relocate the quotation in its original setting in the prologue of *Stheneboea* and examine its effect and function there. It emerges that the utterance is formulated by Euripides in such a way that it naturally lends itself to being read both in and out of context. More specifically, the positioning of the quotation as the opening lines of the play can be seen as constituting a framing device analogous to the use of paratextual epigraphs in other types of text. As we shall see, these observations have important consequences for the way in which we understand Euripides' textual strategies, his relationship with his readers and his place within quotation culture.

Subsequent chapters explore these topics in greater detail and depth. Chapter 2 returns to the subject of Euripides' use of framing devices to make selected utterances 'stand out' from the main body of the text. This chapter pays close attention to formal features within the text which may be seen as equivalent to quotation marks, inverted commas or paratextual markers of one sort or another. A comprehensive catalogue of such features is provided, along with discussion and analysis.

In Chapter 3, I survey different types of Euripidean quotation in the work of other ancient writers, arranged by form, function and citational context. I also pose an important but elusive question: 'what are quoting authors quoting *from*?' In other words, I address the difficulty of determining whether any given author was quoting on the basis of first-hand knowledge of a complete text, and I question the extent to which anyone needs to know a play in order to quote from it.

Chapters 4 to 7 survey a wide variety of contexts in which Euripidean tragedy was quoted within antiquity, including both social environments (on the comic stage, at symposia, in lawcourts, in classrooms, in the library) and different literary genres (drama, biography, oratory, philosophy, literary scholarship and criticism, history, anthologies, letters, Christian apologetics). Inevitably, given the huge scope of the topic, these chapters take the form of a representative series of revealing 'snapshots' or case studies rather than a comprehensive survey of all conceivable quoting contexts.[6] Cumulatively these case studies confirm that via quotation culture Euripides' plays were subject to endless transformation. What they also show is how important it is to study not just the quotations themselves but also the surrounding context in the work of the quoting author. The quoted text and the quoting text can be read together as constituting a sort of dialogue, with each participant in the dialogue reflecting on the other. Studying these different authors is illuminating not just for what it reveals about Euripides but for what it reveals about these writers' outlook and quoting practice more generally, since naturally Euripides is not the only author whose works they quote.

The afterlife of a quotation

What happens to texts when they are quoted? This section offers a preliminary answer to that question by selecting just one Euripidean quotation – from the lost play *Stheneboea* – and using it as a test case:

οὐκ ἔστιν ὅστις πάντ' ἀνὴρ εὐδαιμονεῖ.

No man exists who is fortunate in every respect.

Stheneboea F661.1

Many other quotations could have been used for this sort of exercise, but what makes F661 particularly good for illustrative purposes is that it was repeatedly cited by numerous authors at different points throughout antiquity. Indeed, *Stheneboea* was among its author's most quoted plays within antiquity. Apart from the quotation with which we are concerned, there exist ten other fragments, several of which are cited more than once.[7]

It is important to acknowledge that F661 is both a 'quotation' and a 'fragment'. These two terms are often practically synonymous, since the majority of tragic fragments are book-fragments rather than papyrus remains. On a theoretical level, the act of excerption from a complete text could be seen as an act of deliberate fragmentation. The person who selects a portion of the text and makes it into a quotation is, in a sense, transforming or rewriting that text.[8] And yet for a modern scholar, the experience of dealing with the 'fragments' of a lost work is usually not quite the same sort of activity as studying 'quotations' from a surviving text.[9]

What we now refer to as 'F661', following Richard Kannicht's *Tragicorum Graecorum Fragmenta*, was quoted, in slightly different forms, by numerous writers throughout antiquity. The full text of F661 as printed by Kannicht runs to thirty-one lines, which were preserved by the Byzantine scholar Ioannes Logothetes in his commentary on Hermogenes. This passage as a whole, despite a few gaps, represents nearly all of Bellerophon's monologue with which *Stheneboea* opened, and a papyrus Hypothesis to the play confirms that these were the opening lines.[10] In this speech – a typical example of a Euripidean scene-setting prologue narrative – Bellerophon explains how he came to Tiryns as a suppliant, having killed a member of his family in Corinth, and was cleansed of pollution by King

Proetus; he goes on to say that Stheneboea, Proetus' wife, has fallen in love with him and has been attempting to seduce him, despite his resistance. No other source quotes Bellerophon's prologue speech in full. The quotation as it appears elsewhere – in the work of several Greek comedians, as well as Aristotle and Plutarch – is limited to the first three lines of text, or even just the first line on its own, as given above. This fact raises some important questions about textual knowledge and memory. How many people in the comedians' audiences would have recognized the source of the quotation? How many of them knew it as part of a complete text, and how much did they know, or need to know, about the play *Stheneboea* in order to get the point? To what extent does Aristotle or Plutarch's use of the quotation depend on knowledge of its source? How many of these writers, or their readers, knew it only as a quotation? When we try to reconstruct the mental processes of these people, should we be thinking in terms of their memory of tragic performances or their knowledge of books, including books of quotations?

Not all of these questions can be definitively answered, though some plausible explanations suggest themselves. The main points I want to emphasize here are: (i) that this quotation, even as early as the fifth century, obviously became famous *as a quotation* in its own right; and (ii) that the quotation was used in a variety of ways, most of which had nothing to do with the tragedy *Stheneboea* itself. We can tentatively trace a process by which the quotation rapidly became, in effect, an autonomous literary work, acquiring a life and currency independent of its original author and context.

The earliest known quotation is found in Aristophanes' *Frogs* (1215-19). In this scene the character 'Euripides' is reciting portions of his own prologues, in an attempt to prove their superiority to Aeschylean opening scenes, but 'Aeschylus' repeatedly interrupts:

ΕΥ.   ἀλλ' οὐδὲν ἔσται πρᾶγμα· πρὸς γὰρ τουτονὶ
τὸν πρόλογον οὐχ ἕξει προσάψαι ληκύθον·
οὐκ ἔστιν ὅστις πάντ' ἀνὴρ εὐδαιμονεῖ.
ἢ γὰρ πεφυκὼς ἐσθλὸς οὐκ ἔχει βίον,
ἢ δυσγενὴς ὢν –
ΑΙ.   ληκύθιον ἀπώλεσεν.

Euripides: Oh, it won't bother me. He won't be able to attach an oil-flask to *this* prologue: '**No man exists who is fortunate in every respect. Either someone has noble birth but no livelihood, or he is of lowly origin but . . .**'
Aeschylus: . . . loses his oil-flask.

This comedy was produced in 405 BC, within living memory of the original production of *Stheneboea*, which means that some of Aristophanes' audience members, at least, may have remembered that tragedy and its striking opening speech. But it would have made little difference whether or not they did, for no detailed knowledge is necessary in order to appreciate the joke. The whole scene is concerned with Euripides and his prologues, as would have been obvious even to someone who had never heard of Euripides, and no very complicated point is being made. On a literary level, the point of the criticism being directed at Euripides is rather obscure, but it does not seem to depend on any specific aspect of the style, content or meaning of *Stheneboea*. Aristophanes quotes three other Euripidean prologues as well – *Antigone*, *Hypsipyle* and *Archelaus* – and is evidently using all these examples to make a broad, general point (i.e., that Euripides' prologues are all uninterestingly formulaic).[11]

It is significant that *Stheneboea* is not named as the source, because this may imply that the quotation had already assumed some degree of detachability from its source text. It also means that there will have been an extra level of appreciation involved for those audience members who enjoyed quotation-spotting for its own sake. This extra level will not have been much more than the pleasure of recognition or self-congratulation, such as one might get from answering a quiz question correctly, but still Aristophanes can be seen as subtly differentiating between the effects of his play on different types of audience member – the bookish and the not-so-bookish.[12] (Note that none of the other Euripidean prologues in *Frogs* is identified either.) In the same vein, the manner in which the quotation is presented also suggests that Aristophanes is mobilizing the audience's literary knowledge. By supplying this quotation in truncated form, he is implicitly inviting them not just to identify it but also to complete it. The character 'Aeschylus' comes up with his own ludicrous (or perhaps obscene?) ending to the quotation,[13] but the more erudite spectators will no doubt have been mentally filling in the real missing words for themselves.[14] The difficulty of this sort of parlour game would have depended on the length of time that had elapsed since the première of *Stheneboea* and the spectators' power of recall. This tragedy was produced at least eighteen years before *Frogs*, and perhaps considerably earlier.[15] One cannot rule out the possibility of reperformance shortly before 405, but there is no evidence for it. Thus it seems unlikely that the majority of Aristophanes' spectators would have remembered it in detail – unless they had read the script, or part of it, in the form of a book.

In Aristophanes' hands, then, our quotation has not yet become completely autonomous. Even if not universally familiar, it is still being treated as part of a longer Euripidean work. However, the situation changes when we move forward a few decades to look at the quotation's afterlife in fourth-century comedy. The next occurrence comes in a lost play by Philippides (F18, a fragment-within-a-fragment quoted by the anthologist Stobaeus).

ὅταν ἀτυχεῖν σοι συμπέσηι τι, δέσποτα,
Εὐριπίδου μνήσθητι, καὶ ῥάιων ἔσηι·
οὐκ ἔστιν ὅστις πάντ' ἀνὴρ εὐδαιμονεῖ,
εἶναι δ' ὑπόλαβε καὶ σε τῶν πολλῶν ἕνα.

Whenever you find yourself in an unfortunate situation, sir, just remember Euripides, and you'll feel better. '**No man exists who is fortunate in every respect**' – so understand that you are one among many.

The first thing to note is that 'the quotation' has shrunk down to a single, easily memorable verse. After the fifth century, no one ever quotes more than this one line from the opening to Bellerophon's speech, even though the complete text of *Stheneboea* continued to be available to a reading public. Both Philippides and his character seem to be making use of the quotation specifically for its gnomic and consolatory properties: it is being treated purely as a moralizing maxim or piece of general advice for life. This was a very common way of reading extracts from tragedy throughout antiquity, as we shall see, and the majority of the tragic quotations/fragments that we possess are gnomic in nature. Tragedy was commonly used, not just by comedians but by serious writers of all sorts, as a source of moral wisdom or ethical advice, to be dipped into at will whenever help or encouragement was desired.

The fact that the speaker explicitly attributes the line to Euripides shows that its authorship and genre remain important factors when judging its function: the quotation has not yet become simply proverbial. Nevertheless, there is no mention of *Stheneboea*. Perhaps Philippides is playing another 'quotation-spotting' game with his audience, as in Aristophanes, or perhaps the quotation has become decontextualized to such a degree that it no longer matters whether we recognize its exact source. Note also that the quoter leaves it ambiguous exactly what he means when he says, 'Remember Euripides, and you'll feel better.' Exactly what are we supposed to remember, and what is the source of the beneficial effect? Perhaps we are supposed to assume that maxims can have an efficacious or quasi-magical power, almost as one might repeat a mantra; or perhaps we are to imagine that this maxim somehow encapsulates the meaning or message of the play; or perhaps we are supposed to reflect on the figure of Euripides himself, in his capacity as a wise man or moral counsellor; or perhaps the verse that is quoted is merely meant as an *aide-mémoire*, calculated to prompt more detailed recollection of the play *Stheneboea*. This last option might seem the least likely when we recall the unhappy plot of that tragedy[16] – for reflecting on what actually happened to Bellerophon, Stheneboea and Proetus could scarcely make anyone feel much better – but this is a comedy, after all, and no doubt Philippides is trying to be funny.

However we might interpret the specifics of the joke, it is clear that Philippides is explicitly drawing our attention to the habit of selective quotation of excerpts as a topic of interest in its own right. The scene above depends on the premise that this was already a widespread use of tragic quotation during the fourth century.[17] Another comic fragment which contains the *Stheneboea* quotation (Nicostratus F29) is based on the same premise:

οὐκ ἔστιν ὅστις πάντ' ἀνὴρ εὐδαιμονεῖ·
νὴ τὴν Ἀθηνᾶν συντόμως γε, φίλτατε
Εὐριπίδη, τὸν βίον ἔθηκας εἰς στίχον.

'**No man exists who is fortunate in every respect**'... yes, by Athena, that's right! My dear Euripides, how very neatly you have managed to put the whole of life into one line!

Once again, the quotation is treated as a decontextualized soundbite or maxim containing general advice for life; and once again, there is no obvious sense in which *Stheneboea* is being specifically evoked. (Nicostratus could, admittedly, have mentioned the play in the lines that are lost, but the mode of citation and the punchline here suggest that he did not.) Here, however, the comedian seems to go further than Philippides, not only drawing our attention to the practice of excerption but actually making fun of it.[18] The speaker's ironically fulsome or disingenuous tone is clearly intended to challenge the idea that the meaning of a whole play can really be boiled down to a series of pithy one-liners.

A similar tone is adopted by the character Daos in Menander's *Shield* (407-8), who once again quotes the line οὐκ ἔστιν ὅστις πάντ' ἀνὴρ εὐδαιμονεῖ, before immediately adding the words πάλιν εὖ διαφόρως ('Oh yes, jolly well done again!'). We can read this utterance as a self-congratulatory comment on his own apposite choice of quotation, or as a sign of admiration for the playwright who conveniently supplies the *mot juste* for every occasion.[19] Daos is accused of 'spouting maxims' (γνωμολογεῖς, 414), but in fact the function of the quotation is not the same as in the other passages above. Here the Euripidean verse is being quoted not for its gnomic qualities but simply because it sounds tragic. At this point in the plot of *Shield*, the characters are trying to create a 'tragic' situation: Chaerestratos is pretending to be mortally ill in order to bamboozle Smikrines, and Daos is using tragic mannerisms as window dressing in order to create an exaggerated impression of gloom and despair. Daos enters the stage and bursts into a paratragic lament, into which he inserts a series of unconnected (and seemingly random) lines from various tragedians. Some of these lines are gnomic, others are not; some are attributed to specific authors, others are not. According to one commentator on the play, the quotations represent 'popular tags', but even if some were more popular or familiar than others, the point is that they will all have been instantaneously recognizable as generic examples of tragic lines.[20] The overall effect is of a broadly paratragic collage or pastiche. At any rate, the meaning, content, authorship and source of the *Stheneboea* quotation all seem to be irrelevant, since they are ignored by Menander.

But it is also interesting to note who is doing the quoting: Daos, the speaker, is a slave. The same situation is seen in the extract from Philippides above. In both of these comedies it seems significant that the sort of characters who are well versed in tragedy, and who can apply this knowledge effectively to other situations, should be of low social status. It is hard to judge how far this state of affairs is representative of real life, but this comic evidence may have consequences for our knowledge of fourth-century literacy and the extent to which quotation culture permeated different levels of society.[21]

In this respect, it is important to consider these comic texts from the perspective of the audience or reader. Comedians are conventionally seen as purveyors of mass entertainment, aiming their work at the broadest possible audience; but in the passages above, we can imagine that the humorous effect of the quotation will have varied slightly depending on whether or not the audience member(s) could identify the source.[22] The fact that Greek comedy of all periods is full of quotations and literary allusions may imply a high level of literary culture and general knowledge in the average audience member; or it may imply that some of the precise details would have been picked up only by a smaller subgroup of educated people who were capable of appreciating the 'literariness' of comedy in full. Our approach to the problem will depend on whether we tend to privilege the act of going to the theatre or the act of reading books in the formation of literary knowledge. The sphere of quotation culture encompasses both types of activity, as well as word of mouth or the oral tradition more generally. The social contexts for quotation in classical Greece cannot be reconstructed with absolute confidence, but – as I shall show in Chapters 4 to

7 – they would have included schoolrooms, lawcourts, dramatic festivals, symposia, and daily life and conversation, as well as the private reading of books for a privileged minority. Much of what I have to say here is couched in the terminology of texts and readers, but it applies equally well to a world of orality and performance.

Menander's approximate contemporary, Aristotle, is normally seen as writing for a very different sort of audience. His *Rhetoric* is aimed not at the general public but at the educated elite and, in particular, the aspiring politician or rhetor. Nevertheless, at the point at which he quotes *Stheneboea* F661, he is talking about the use of maxims as a rhetorical device, which means that he must have the needs of a general audience in mind, at least in the sense that he is considering how to exert a persuasive effect on the public in the lawcourt or assembly.[23] Aristotle goes on to add that maxims are effective in speeches because of the uncultivated mind of the audience. Most people, he says, enjoy hearing the sort of wisdom that they already agree with, which means that even clichés are permitted. Certainly there is nothing about Aristotle's own use of the Euripidean quotation that is any more sophisticated or complex than what we have seen in comedy:

> καὶ τὸ **οὐκ ἔστιν ὅστις πάντ' ἀνὴρ εὐδαιμονεῖ·**
> καὶ τὸ οὐκ ἔστιν ἀνδρῶν ὅστις ἔστ' ἐλεύθερος. . .
> γνώμη, πρὸς δὲ τῶι ἐχομένωι ἐνθύμημα·
> . . . ἢ χρημάτων γὰρ δοῦλός ἐστιν ἢ τύχης.
>
> Another example [of a maxim] is: '**No man exists who is fortunate in every respect.**' Also, take 'There is no one among men who is free . . .'
> which is a maxim, but when taken together with the line that follows
> ('. . . because he is in thrall to either money or fortune' [= Euripides, *Hecuba* 864-5])
> is an enthymeme.

In this passage, Aristotle includes the *Stheneboea* quotation as an example of a generally applicable maxim, such as a rhetor might use in any situation at all. It seems that by this time the verse has become an autonomous text in its own right. Perhaps Aristotle is not even treating it primarily as a verse from tragedy, but as a disembodied *gnome*. Indeed, we might even consider the *gnome* to be an independent literary genre.[24]

Probably Aristotle is aware that this is a Euripidean line – his next example is also taken from a Euripidean tragedy – but he gives no indication of its provenance. It even seems possible that he is unaware of its precise source. Note that Aristotle is discussing two distinct types of generalization, the *gnome* (maxim) and the *enthymeme* (consisting of maxim plus *epilogos* or 'supplement'). The manner in which Aristotle quotes *Stheneboea* F661, as distinct from *Hecuba* 864-5, shows that he thinks of it as the first type: he treats it specifically as a free-standing single verse, complete in itself. But in fact the full version of the *Stheneboea* quotation does have an *epilogos*: it includes a continuation of the maxim using precisely the same form of words (ἢ γὰρ) as the *Hecuba* example. All this seems to suggest that by the fourth century, οὐκ ἔστιν ὅστις πάντ' ἀνὴρ εὐδαιμονεῖ had developed a life of its own as a one-line maxim – with the result that even such a highly educated man as Aristotle did not associate the line with a particular literary context.

But how did Aristotle know the quotation, if not from his reading of *Stheneboea*? It may be that the verse had attained a quasi-proverbial status in everyday discourse, or it may be that Aristotle was already relying on rhetorical handbooks or collections of maxims. The anthology or *florilegium* is often seen as a relatively late literary development, as exemplified above all by Stobaeus' *Eclogae*, but – as we shall see in the next section – such collections came into being, in some form, as early as the fifth century, and there is quite a large amount of evidence pointing (directly or indirectly) to the use of anthologies at an early date. The tendency of many authors throughout antiquity to quote the same lines over and over again has also been taken as implying the widespread use of anthologies as a source of illustrative, paradigmatic or thematic material.

Anthologies would certainly have been familiar to Plutarch, who quotes *Stheneboea* F661 some centuries later in his *Letter of Consolation to Apollonius* (103a-b). Plutarch treats the quotation in much the same way as the authors whom we have already examined: as a moral generalization and a source of wisdom and consolation. He is writing here about the capacity of sensible men to bear up with fortitude and adopt a becoming attitude towards adversity. Life is uncertain; but one needs must persevere:

οὗτοι τῆς φρονήσεως καὶ τῶν ἄλλων ἀρετῶν εἰσι κανόνες, οἷς πρὸς ἀμφότερα χρηστέον. **οὐκ ἔστιν γὰρ ὅστις πάντ' ἀνὴρ εὐδαιμονεῖ**.

These are the principles of thought and of all the other virtues, which for better or for worse must be followed: '**no man exists**', after all, '**who is fortunate in every respect**'.

It is clear that the quotation was still well known to Plutarch and his readers, some four hundred years after the first production of Euripides' play. But how did they know the quotation, and in what form had they encountered it? Perhaps the quotation had trickled down over the centuries through the oral tradition, as a proverb or motto; but by this date, it is more likely than ever that we have to think in terms of a world of books, readers, textual citation, and anthologies of famous quotations.[25]

It is not impossible that Plutarch or some of his readers might have known *Stheneboea* as a complete play, but there is no sign that this was the case, or that it makes any difference to our understanding of the quotation's function here. The fact that Plutarch even breaks into the quotation with an unmetrical word of his own (γάρ) shows that he is not even treating it primarily as a line of poetry, and implies that he values it more for its content than its form. Like Aristotle, Plutarch quotes the line without mentioning its author or source. This is in line with his normal methods of citation elsewhere, which are fairly unsystematic,[26] but the point to be emphasized here is that no knowledge of the original context is required to make sense of the quotation. The play *Stheneboea* has long ago become irrelevant, whereas the quotation has assumed a status and significance that is apparently timeless and universal.

In the passages above we have seen that the quotation is deployed and manipulated in a variety of ways; but it is clear that it developed a life of its own *as a quotation* from a very early stage in its existence. It is remarkable that the play *Stheneboea* is not cited by name in a single one of these texts, and that Euripides is mentioned only in half of them. Nor does any of these authors indicate who was the original speaker of the words, or whose point of view is represented. It may be that some of them are treating the verse as if it reflected Euripides' own view of the world, but more often the quotation is treated as a disembodied voice of wisdom, a general truism or even a cliché. Nowadays, readers tend to be scrupulous about treating lines from a play as the utterances of a particular character within a particular dramatic context. Indeed, recent scholarship on tragic maxims has been concerned with precisely the sort of effects that arise from the contrast (or ironic dissonance) between content and context, or between the characters' sentiments and their identity or status – a quality of maxims that has been called 'polysemy'.[27] But this sort of distinction does not seem to have played much part in ancient reading habits. It certainly does not appear that any of those who quote F661 knew or cared that these words originally appeared in the mouth of Bellerophon. Whatever special meaning or nuance the quotation may have had in its original dramatic setting seems to have been almost immediately forgotten, if it was ever acknowledged at all.

The eclectic reader

According to Xenophon in *Memorabilia*, among the accusations brought against Socrates in 399 BC was that he was wont to pick out (ἐκλέγειν) the most immoral or provocative verses by the most famous poets and, using such verses as evidence (μαρτύρια), to teach his associates how to behave disgracefully.[28] Xenophon defends Socrates by saying that he did not deliberately set out to use poetry for immoral ends, though the Athenians who condemned Socrates to death seem to have taken a different view.

Whether or not Xenophon is correct in his interpretation of Socrates' aims, this story is significant because it provides good evidence for reading habits among Athenians in more or less the same period as Euripides was producing his plays. Specifically, it shows that the selective excerption of key passages was seen as a normal way of approaching a text. Such passages were prone to be treated as the extractable essence or meaning of a work, as sources of inspiration and moral teaching, or as testimonies of their author's own views. (A close analogy can be seen in the way in which verses from Holy Scripture are quoted within faith traditions.) What landed Socrates in trouble was his specific choice of excerpts and the uses to which they were allegedly put, rather than the method of reading itself, which is seen as unexceptional. Xenophon goes on to attempt to exonerate Socrates by showing that he sometimes did quote edifying verses to his followers (*Memorabilia* 1.2.57-61), and elsewhere in the same work (1.6.14) he depicts Socrates, in conversation with Antiphon, as explicitly advocating this method of reading as a general principle:

> καὶ τοὺς θησαυροὺς τῶν πάλαι σοφῶν ἀνδρῶν, οὓς ἐκεῖνοι κατέλιπον ἐν βιβλίοις γράψαντες, ἀνελίττων κοινῆι σὺν τοῖς φίλοις διέρχομαι· καὶ ἄν τι ὁρῶμεν ἀγαθὸν ἐκλεγόμεθα.
>
> And as for the treasure-trove of the wise men of old, which they wrote down in their books and left behind as a legacy, I unfold it and go through it together with my friends; and if we see anything good there, we excerpt it.

Xenophon himself implicitly endorses the same method by noting its beneficial effects on those who practised it and by calling Socrates 'blessed' (μακάριος). The way in which Socrates is made to describe his activities here might seem to imply a strong connection between the process of interpretation and the materiality of written texts, though it is important to note that the word ἀνελίττων is commonly used in a figurative sense (to denote the explication of a book's contents) as well as a literal sense (to denote the 'unfolding' of a bookroll).²⁹ When Socrates talks about 'going through' the text with others, he is obviously envisaging reading as a social process involving shared discussion and conversation. This reminds us that we need to think in terms of oral culture, not just written words on the page. Similarly, in another work Xenophon portrays eclectic reading as a habit acquired in the classroom, describing Socrates and Critoboulos together as schoolboys 'searching for some passage or other in the same book' (ὅτε παρὰ τῶι γραμματιστῆι ἐν τῶι αὐτῶι βιβλίωι ἀμφότεροι ἐμαστεύετέ τι, *Symposium* 4.27): here again, there is a sense that this is a communal activity.

It is crucial for our purposes to distinguish between two ways of reading. On the one hand, there is the continuous or 'linear' reading of texts in their entirety, and on the other, the discontinuous or 'non-linear' reading of extracts.³⁰ Of course tragedy, like almost any other type of literary text, can be read in either way, and it can be put to many different uses. No doubt Euripides' readers differed greatly from one another in their motives and their individual cognitive processes, not to mention other contextual factors such as social status, education, literacy levels and the availability of books. Such considerations, together with the scarcity of historical evidence, make it difficult to generalize with complete confidence. Nevertheless, it is very striking that when we examine the surviving sources relating to ancient reading practices, at any period from the fifth century BC onwards, we find that almost all of them, like these passages from Xenophon, are concerned with 'non-linear' reading. Plato in his *Laws* (7.811a) explicitly contrasts the 'linear' and the 'non-linear' methods of reading, as practised in the Athenian education system, without concluding which is the better method. A handful of texts, including the influential *Poetics* of Aristotle, are based on the idea that a literary work should be understood as a unified whole. But the overwhelming majority of writers and literary critics in antiquity adopted a more eclectic approach to literature.

This fact has been observed by Richard Hunter, who notes that 'ancient criticism is more interested in the interpretation and application of the individual verse or passage than of overall structure and meaning'.³¹ Hunter explains this tendency, plausibly, as the result of factors including the physical difficulty of reading long bookrolls and the heavy emphasis on rhetorical training within Greek and Roman education. There may be other factors involved as well, including the importance of orality and memory in societies in which ownership of books was relatively rare: the excerption and repetition of short passages can be seen as a practical means of facilitating memorization.

Unfortunately, there is little sign that any Greek or Roman critics were interested in explicitly thematizing the reading process or the activity of quotation as distinct subjects of interest. Nevertheless, as we shall see in later chapters, many ancient writers deploy selective quotation in a way that can be interpreted as a form of metaliterary commentary. From time to time, writers also offer valuable self-reflexive comments on their own reading practices – such as Plato, who advocates learning 'selected highlights' (τὰ κεφάλαια) from poets' work; or Lycurgus, who treats selected verses from tragedy as equivalent to the utterances of an oracle; or Isocrates, who encourages his students to learn 'the best bits' (τὰ βέλτιστα) from poetry and to approach texts in the manner of bees flitting from flower to flower to extract pollen; or Plutarch, who uses the same apiary imagery when warning readers never to neglect a valuable passage in any book they happen to be reading; or Lucian, who likens literary texts to meadows full of flowers ripe for the plucking; or Aulus Gellius, who describes his *Attic Nights* as a fortuitous compilation of key passages culled from his reading and transformed into a 'literary store-cupboard' (*litterarum penus*).[32] Our evidence may be somewhat motley and piecemeal, but it shows that eclectic reading was commonly practised throughout antiquity. Individual readers may have differed widely from one another in their specific aims or intellectual preoccupations, but most of them happily adopted a pick-and-choose approach to literary texts.

It is obvious that many readers, especially in the Hellenistic and Roman periods, were familiar with ready-made anthologies of extracts. These might be used as a convenient aid to study or memory, or as an alternative to reading complete texts. It seems likely that ordinary readers of limited means would have found it easier to consult anthologies than to access extensive libraries; but even professional scholars and critics might have recourse to anthologies on occasion, in the absence of more advanced technologies for the indexing and retrieval of information. Gellius openly admits that in his own research he has relied on other people's anthologies or miscellanies, and he cites several works of this kind with suggestive titles, including *The Muses*, *The Woods*, *The Honeycomb*, *Meadows* and *Flowers*. These anthologies (or *florilegia*) are the distant ancestors of modern reference works such as *Bartlett's* and *The Oxford Dictionary of Quotations*.[33] Many literary references, together with papyrus remains of ancient books, show us that the anthology flourished in the later classical period and beyond. The form reached its apex in the fifth century AD, in the form of the *Eclogae* of John of Stobi (usually known as 'Stobaeus'), an extensive collection of quotations from classical authors organized into sections by theme: this work survived into the modern age more or less intact. It is to Stobaeus, who himself drew on earlier collections, that we owe the preservation of hundreds of verses from lost plays by Euripides (alongside many quotations from extant works).³⁴

As I have already noted, even though the anthology as a literary medium has often been regarded as especially characteristic of Hellenistic and Roman culture, it is clear that the phenomenon was already current, in some form, at least as early as the fifth century BC. A certain amount of indirect evidence is provided by Aristophanic comedy, in which various scenes depend on quotation-spotting or what we might call an 'anthologizing mentality'. This was seen by Eric Havelock, who interpreted the famous contest between Aeschylus and Euripides in *Frogs* as 'a competition of quotations'; Havelock made the plausible suggestion that when the chorus sings that 'each spectator has a book' they are referring specifically to anthologies of quotations.³⁵ Characters in many other comedies quote gnomic verses from Euripides in such a way as to suggest that they had already acquired the status of famous lines or quasi-proverbial tags.³⁶ Another contemporary comedian, Cratinus, seems to be alluding, albeit somewhat cryptically, to the anthologizing mentality – and also making some sort of connection between Aristophanes, Euripides and quotable *gnomai* – when he characterizes a certain type of person as γνωμιδιώκτης ('one who hunts after sententious maxims').³⁷ (See Chapter 4 for further discussion of quotations in comedy.)

Going back somewhat further in time, several scholars have detected signs of the anthologizing tendency in the remains of archaic Greek poetry. Ewen Bowie, for instance, argues that the *Theognidea* was based on a fifth-century anthology of early elegiac verse.³⁸ David Sider believes, on the basis of the surviving fragments and testimonia, that collections of Simonidean epigrams were in circulation in the fifth century.³⁹ Both Richard Hunter and Lilah Grace Canevaro have argued, independently, that Hesiod's *Works and Days*, a work which has often been criticized for its baggy structure or apparent lack of unity, was designed to be read in 'piecemeal' form, as essentially constituting a sort of anthology of gnomic advice for life.⁴⁰

Indirect evidence of this sort is compelling in itself, but we also have some direct evidence for fifth-century anthologies, which is even more significant for our purposes. Xenophon once again proves an invaluable source of information, making his Socrates refer to 'a large collection of the writings of the most prestigious poets and sophists' or a 'treasure-trove of wisdom' that has been amassed by the young student Euthydemus.⁴¹ These descriptions denote a home-made anthology or commonplace book filled with poetic quotations of a general nature. Xenophanes goes on to mention the existence (or perhaps the hypothetical possibility) of other comparable collections organized by subject matter, including medicine, architecture, astronomy and other branches of practical knowledge.

A similar sort of book, though one designed for wider publication, was produced by the sophist Hippias of Elis. This anthology went by the title *Synagoge* ('Compendium') and apparently consisted of a mixture of prose and poetic extracts in a variety of languages. In part of the introduction to this work (preserved by the much later quotation-collector Clement of Alexandria), Hippias describes his own method and rationale:[42]

τούτων ἴσως εἴρηται τὰ μὲν Ὀρφεῖ, τὰ δὲ Μουσαίωι κατὰ βραχὺ ἄλλωι ἀλλαχοῦ, τὰ δὲ Ἡσιόδωι τὰ δὲ Ὁμήρωι, τὰ δὲ τοῖς ἄλλοις τῶν ποιητῶν, τὰ δὲ ἐν συγγραφαῖς τὰ μὲν Ἕλλησι τὰ δὲ βαρβάροις· ἐγὼ δὲ ἐκ πάντων τούτων τὰ μέγιστα καὶ ὁμόφυλα συνθεὶς τοῦτον καινὸν καὶ πολυειδῆ τὸν λόγον ποιήσομαι.

Some of these [extracts] might be sayings of Orpheus; some might be brief *aperçus* from here and there in Musaeus' work; some might be from Hesiod or Homer, some from other poets; others might be from prose writings by writers both Greek and non-Greek. But by compiling from all these sources material that is of a similar nature and especially important, I shall make this anthology original and full of variety.

These programmatic remarks and the self-justifying claim of novelty confirm that the *Synagoge* was designed for other readers rather than for Hippias' own personal use. To judge by this extract, Hippias' aim was to assemble quotations organized by content or theme (if that is what is meant by ὁμόφυλα συνθείς, 'putting together material of a similar nature'). He also seems to have presented extracts from different authors side by side, perhaps in order to demonstrate the influence of the earlier on the later ones, or to compare and contrast the instructive content of different works, or to show that these writers were all connected to one another in a continuous tradition of wisdom. Since the *Synagoge* is lost, we cannot know exactly what it contained, but it is a plausible hypothesis that the 'other poets' represented there would have included Euripides and other tragedians.[43]

It is impossible to know exactly when the first anthologies of Euripidean quotations began to be compiled. The earliest recorded papyrus books containing selected extracts rather than complete playscripts date from the third century BC.[44] Nevertheless, on the basis of the discussion above, it may well be that collections of quotations from Euripides' plays were already circulating during the poet's own lifetime. The first literary reference to a Euripidean anthology can perhaps be identified in Antiphanes' *Carians*, a comedy produced at some point in the middle of the fourth century BC. In this work, now lost, Antiphanes is said to have made fun of a sophist who, among his other activities, compiled κεφάλαια of Euripides' plays.⁴⁵ The brevity of the fragment and the lack of context makes it difficult to decide exactly what is being referred to here: κεφάλαια could mean 'excerpts' or 'selected highlights',⁴⁶ or it could denote plot-summaries or something along the lines of the hypotheses that are transmitted in the manuscript tradition.⁴⁷

Even though we cannot know exactly when Euripides was first anthologized in book form, the purpose of this discussion has been to establish that an 'anthologizing mentality' (in either a general or a specific sense) was current in Euripides' own time and should not be seen merely as a tendency of later scholarship. As we have seen, the evidence for ancient reading habits suggests that the excerption of selected highlights was normal and widespread. I suggest that excerpts may even have been the principal medium, apart from live theatrical performances, through which readers within antiquity encountered tragedy. People might go to watch entire plays in the theatre, but after the performances there is no reason to think that they would have had easy access to complete texts of those works. We do not really know what fifth-century books of tragedy looked like, but it may well be that excerpts were easier to obtain in written form than full playscripts. Excerpts will certainly have been easier to commit to memory and thus to disseminate in non-textual form, via recitation or everyday conversation. At any rate, the main point to be emphasized here is that Euripides himself and his contemporaries were already familiar with the habit of eclectic, 'non-linear' reading. As I shall go on to argue, this fact played a crucial part in the conception and design of the plays right from the start.

The excerptable text

Many works by ancient writers have become fragments; many modern works are fragments right from the time of their genesis.

Friedrich Schlegel⁴⁸

It is easy to feel dismay at the sort of treatment to which Euripides' work has been subjected – whether we are talking about banal over-simplification, selective misinterpretation, the reduction of his plays to a collection of excerpts, or the literal fragmentation and loss that eventually befell most of his oeuvre.

However, it could be argued that certain texts actually encourage their readers to treat them in this way.

It is not just later authors (or critics, anthologists or other sorts of quoter) who make certain portions of a text into 'quotations'. The original author can also formulate or frame parts of his work as 'quotations' right from the start. This is precisely what we see in the case of *Stheneboea* F661, the example discussed earlier in this chapter. It did not simply *become* a quotation in the course of its complex afterlife. Even within its original setting in the play, it was already a quotation. Euripides designed the utterance in such a way that it stands out from its context and is inherently detachable.

The useful term *quotationality* has been coined by Gary Saul Morson to denote the special qualities that certain types of utterance possess (in varying degrees). Quotationality, according to Morson, 'confers on phrases a degree of otherness'; it is said to create an 'aura' or a vague feeling that something is being quoted, even when nothing is literally being quoted as such. Not every utterance that is quoted possesses quotationality (Morson distinguishes between 'quotations' and 'citations' in this respect). But a phrase with this quality will typically be 'short', 'memorizable', 'interesting', 'complete in itself', 'shared' and 'potentially autonomous' (of speaker, author or context); it will also possess an inherent 'doubleness' or ambiguity, either because it can function in or out of context or because it has an implied 'shadowy second speaker, who is not identical to the speaker of the source'.[49]

It could be said that all maxims (*gnomai*) in tragedy conform to this definition of quotationality. They are short and memorable. They have a high degree of iterability. They seem to stand out from the surrounding text. They are conveniently detachable. They have an inherent doubleness about them, allowing them to function both contextually and independently. They are often intertextual in a broad sense, in that they are adapted from earlier texts or the tradition of Greek popular wisdom more generally. They seem to blur the narratological category of voice; they also blur the boundaries between past and present, or between the world of the play and the real world of the audience.[50]

By typically including a large number of maxims in their plays, the Greek tragedians are showing that they are to be taken seriously as poets and custodians of traditional wisdom, along with their epic and lyric predecessors. But more importantly, they are also conferring a high level of quotability on their own work. We can see this not as an incidental outcome but as a central feature of the way in which they aimed to communicate with their audience. The tragedians knew perfectly well that their readers would have mined their work for quotations, and so they are playing along with this tendency. The fact that Euripides' plays contain so many more quotable maxims than other tragedies seems to indicate that he was especially interested in ensuring that he would be quoted in the future.

It is easy to appreciate how the authority or prestige of a literary text may be directly linked to its quotability. The more a text is quoted, the more it will come to permeate popular culture and influence the way people think. The more a text can be mined for its perceived didactic content, its political precepts or its moral wisdom, the more it will lend itself to educational uses. Through repeated quotation, texts are preserved, transmitted, perpetuated, assimilated and absorbed into cultural memory; they gain value and durability with each successive repetition; their distinctive view of the world comes to seem indistinguishable, perhaps, from the accepted truth about life; and thus these texts and their authors gradually acquire the status of classics.

Euripides will have been acutely aware of all this – and because he knew that his readers would be likely to approach his plays by dipping into them and making excerpts, he helped them along in various ways. One of the central claims of this book is that Euripides, more than any other Greek tragedian, *actively* participated in quotation culture by making portions of his plays stand out as 'quotations' right from the start. By going out of his way to ensure that people would quote his works, he can be seen as playing a decisive part in shaping his own subsequent reception. Euripides did indeed achieve the status of a classic author – he became the most celebrated and widely read of all the Greek dramatists – and this achievement came about, I suggest, partly through his own deliberate efforts. The degree to which he was motivated by personal ambition is a matter about which we can merely speculate, since we have no way of knowing what Euripides actually thought. Maybe he hungered for personal status and fame; maybe he hoped that one day his own name would be mentioned in the same breath as that of Homer; maybe he simply wanted to be regarded by his contemporaries as a better tragic poet than Achaeus or Xenocles; or maybe he saw himself as a serious moralist, using excerptable lines as a way of conveying a didactic message to his readers.

No doubt some readers will think that I am going too far by even tentatively attempting to imagine the poet's intentions or designs, but there are many clearly observable formal features of Euripides' work that can be identified in support of my central argument. As I shall demonstrate in Chapter 2, the majority of Euripidean 'quotations' are presented or framed in such a way as to make them stand out from their surrounding context. On the whole, it is hard to avoid the conclusion that Euripides' plays are carefully designed to be susceptible to quotation and selective excerption.

Friedrich Schlegel, whose well-known pronouncements about fragments are quoted as the epigraph to this section, deplored the fragmentation and loss of the bulk of Greek poetry, seeing this state of affairs as a tragic collapse of civilization. This was partly because he viewed classical poetry and drama as paradigmatic of unity, and partly because he was concerned to establish a rhetorical contrast between ancient and modern poetry. Nevertheless, it is important to acknowledge (as Schlegel himself admits) that fragmentary texts possess distinctive aesthetic or intellectual qualities of their own. It is not just that the fragment can be a valid modern literary form for original writing (especially philosophical *pensées*). Ancient fragmentary texts too can exert a curious appeal on certain types of reader. The modern reception of some ancient authors – Sappho and Alcaeus, for instance – has been determined largely by the fact that they are fragmentary and evanescent.[51] But more importantly, the whole post-Aristotelian tradition that has fetishized unity as a criterion for evaluating classical poetry (especially tragic poetry) represents only one possible approach to the material.[52] It would be equally possible to privilege other criteria such as variety, polyphony and open-endedness. This is the view taken by, among others, Theodor Adorno, who sees completeness in art and literature as an inauthentic or illusory quality, since it fails to reflect the reality of human life. For Adorno, works of art are inherently fragmentary, made up of irreconcilable parts that resist our attempts to integrate them into wholes or identify a definitive meaning within them.[53]

Are Euripides' plays coherent wholes? Perhaps not. At least, it cannot automatically be taken for granted that unity, in the sense understood by Aristotle or later critics, was the main or only aim of Euripides when composing his dramas. Given the fact that ancient readers habitually tended to dip into texts and focus on selected extracts, it is more than likely that poet himself planned his work to accommodate this sort of non-unitary reading. It comes to seem even more likely if we bear in mind the form and polyphonic texture of drama, consisting of a dialogue between multiple voices with the notable absence of any explicit authorial voice to impose coherence.

In the section above I distinguished between the 'linear' (complete, consecutive, unitary) and 'non-linear' (disconnected, fragmentary, selective, eclectic) reading of texts. These two modes of reading are probably best seen as complementary rather than mutually exclusive. But Roland Barthes has argued, more provocatively, that the act of reading is always inherently fragmentary. Whenever we 'read' a text, even a complete text which can be shown to possess unity, our interpretation of its meaning is inevitably provisional and incomplete, and we only ever read it, or understand it, or recall it, selectively. No one ever accords exactly equal weight to every single utterance within the text; and even if you and I are both reading the same text, we are bound to interpret it differently, or describe it differently, or remember and quote different portions (i.e. 'fragments'). Perhaps we are not even reading 'the same' text at all.[54] A similar viewpoint is articulated in Wolfgang Iser's cognitive model of the reading process, in which meaning is seen as being created by each individual reader rather than the author. According to Iser, the overall design of any literary work is irrelevant, since no one is capable of perceiving or mentally processing the text in its totality all at once; each reader necessarily adopts a 'wandering viewpoint' and builds their own meaning from the text by idiosyncratically identifying and assembling separate 'segments'.[55] These theoretical insights have important consequences for our understanding of how Euripidean tragedy works, though I suggest that it is desirable to make a slight adjustment to this model of the author–reader–text relationship. Barthes and Iser both assume that a traditional, author-centred interpretation is synonymous with a linear or unitary conception of the meaning of a text (Barthes refers to this as 'the "message" of the Author-God', or 'a single "theological" meaning').[56] But even if we acknowledge that the author of a text may not be able to exert a total, God-like control over its meaning, it is possible to imagine a situation in which the author himself acknowledges this fact and takes it into account when constructing his texts. Far from closing down interpretative possibilities, Euripides can be seen as consciously opening up a range of different meanings, inviting his readers to select their own favourite verses and interactively make their own connections between them.

Whatever one's own perspective on these theoretical matters, it will be clear that the contrast drawn by Schlegel – 'many works by ancient writers have become fragments; many modern works are fragments right from the time of their genesis' – is open to doubt, at least for Euripidean tragedy. It may well be that certain tragedies were conceived of at the time of their origin as, in a sense, collections of fragments, susceptible of being read either consecutively or in the form of excerpts.

Parts, wholes and paratextuality

Bearing in mind these general reflections on the relationship (or tension) between parts and wholes, let us return to our test case (*Stheneboea* F661) in particular. I want to examine a further way in which this utterance stands out from its original context. It not only possesses 'quotationality' and an inbuilt excerptability; it also belongs to a distinct (and rare) category of gnomic lines that are prominently placed right at the beginning of a play.[57] This sort of opening device has been seen as loosely analogous to the *priamel* technique favoured by lyric poets, whereby a discursive argument, a purposely obscure assertion, a list of items or a gnomic generalization is used to provide an arresting opening, especially as a contrast or foil to a main idea that follows.[58] The device has also been discussed in light of the conventions of tragic prologues, and especially Euripides' penchant for 'detached' narrative prologues (in contrast with the more integrated or organic openings seen in Aeschylus and Sophocles): Euripidean prologue speeches often seem to embody 'a microcosm of major themes' or 'resonances' which will be developed later in the play.[59]

I suggest that the opening of *Stheneboea* can be seen as directly analogous to the use of epigraphs in other types of literary work. In this respect, Euripides' technique can be illuminated by Genette's theory of paratextuality, as outlined in his book *Paratexts* (originally *Seuils*, i.e. 'Thresholds'). Paratexts in Genette's sense include all those parts of a modern printed book which affect our reading but are not considered part of the text proper, such as the cover design, the dust-wrapper blurb, the table of contents, the foreword, the footnotes, the index and so on.

> More than a boundary or a sealed border, the paratext is, rather, a *threshold* ... it is an 'undefined zone' between the inside and the outside, a zone without any hard and fast boundary on either the inward side (turned toward the text) or the outward side (turned toward the world's discourse about the text), an edge, or, as Philippe Lejeune put it, 'a fringe of the printed text which in reality controls one's whole reading of the text.' Indeed, this fringe, always the conveyor of a commentary that is authorial or more or less legitimated by the author, constitutes a zone between text and off-text, a zone not only of transition but of transaction: a privileged place of pragmatics and a strategy, of an influence on the public.

Of course one must avoid anachronism, and it is important to remember that tragedies were performances as well as texts; but nonetheless, it seems that much of what Genette says about paratexts can be applied, *mutatis mutandis*, to Euripides. The quotation with which *Stheneboea* begins can be seen as quite literally on the edge or fringe of the text; it is a 'zone of transition and transaction' in terms of the way in which the text communicates with its audience. This is equally true whether we are thinking in terms of a book, in which the quotation might be the first words unrolled by the reader, or of a stage production in the theatre of Dionysus.

Our quotation can be called paratextual in terms of its form and pragmatic function within *Stheneboea*; but what Genette has to say about epigraphs in particular is also highly suggestive in terms of its content. It is suggested that such utterances stand in dialogue with the other portions of the text but are seen as auxiliary or 'heteronomous'.[60] The function of epigraphs is to provide food for thought; to challenge or puzzle us; to be, at times, deliberately evasive; to place us, as readers, in a position in which we have to make connections and do a lot of interpretative work for ourselves:

> The semantic relevance of epigraphs is often, as it were, random; and without the least ill will, one can suspect some authors of positioning some epigraphs hit-and-miss, of believing – rightly – that *every* joining creates meaning and that the absence of meaning is an impression of meaning, often the most stimulating or most rewarding; to think without knowing what you are thinking – is that not one of the purest pleasures of the mind?[61]

Genette's focus is mainly on the epigraph in the nineteenth- and twentieth-century French novel, but (once again) his remarks seem to describe the content and function of Bellerophon's opening lines extraordinarily well.

This will become clearer from a closer examination of the beginning of *Stheneboea*, in an extended version consisting of the first six lines (including 'the quotation' and its continuation). Viewed as an act of communication between author and reader, or as a statement possessing 'semantic relevance', it is ambiguous in several ways:

> οὐκ ἔστιν ὅστις πάντ' ἀνὴρ εὐδαιμονεῖ.
> ἢ γὰρ πεφυκὼς ἐσθλὸς οὐκ ἔχει βίον,
> ἢ δυσγενὴς ὢν πλουσίαν ἀροῖ πλάκα.
> πολλοὺς δὲ πλούτωι καὶ γένει γαυρουμένους
> γυνὴ κατήισχυν' ἐν δόμοισι νηπία.
> τοιᾶιδε Προῖτος <γῆς> ἄναξ νόσωι νοσεῖ ...

> No man exists who is fortunate in every respect. Either someone has noble birth but no livelihood, or he is of lowly origin but ploughs rich farmland; and many who pride themselves on wealth and birth are disgraced by a foolish wife in their house. Such is the affliction which afflicts Proetus, the ruler of this land ...

Let us begin by imagining the effect of these lines on a spectator in the theatre. As is well known, the Greek theatre had no curtain, which means that we always have to think carefully about the exact point at which any play can be said to begin, and about the different ways in which a boundary is established between the real world and the mimetic world of the drama. The speaker of the first lines is simultaneously a character in the play and an actor alerting the spectators to the fact that the play has now begun and encouraging them to settle down and be quiet. The opening words function as a 'raising of the curtain', but are they truly part of the play proper? Did everyone in the theatre audience even hear them? Perhaps not.

Even if we can make out the lines clearly enough, we will be unaware who is speaking them. It is not till much later in the prologue that Bellerophon reveals his identity. Until that time, he is simply a voice – an anonymous and mysterious figure, who could represent anyone at all. Is he fully in the guise of a character? Does he represent some sort of transcendent presence, such as an impersonal 'voice of wisdom' or 'implied second speaker' (to use Morson's term), or might he be some sort of divine, quasi-authorial figure, such as would become so central to the prologues of New Comedy? Note that most Euripidean prologue speeches are delivered by a minor character or a god, rather than a principal participant in the action, which means that we will be unlikely to guess Bellerophon's identity at any rate. These feelings of uncertainty would probably have been common to spectators or readers alike. Modern playscripts provide reader-friendly orientation in the form of cast lists, speaker attributions and stage directions, but it seems unlikely that a fifth-century bookroll would have contained any of these aids to understanding.[62] The speaker's identity eventually becomes known, but for the moment, crucially, we are left dangling on the play's threshold.

A further source of ambiguity presents itself: where does 'the quotation' end? We have seen that in the hands of other authors it was soon reduced to a single verse, but the full version of the maxim might be perceived as occupying the first three or five lines of the play. It seems that there is a deliberate blurring of the cut-off point between the opening maxim and the narrative that follows. (Note also that the narrative proper seems to begin at line 6, but even there the transition is brought about by the pronoun τοιᾶιδε, which initially might seem to refer back to γυνή on line 5.) Not only that, but the expansion of the maxim in lines 2-3 and 4-5 is unnecessary: the development of the idea is slightly odd and inconsequential, and it seems to weaken the overall effect. One could dismiss it as faulty writing, perhaps, but actually this blurring of the general and the specific seems completely in tune with the communicative strategy of the opening scene as a whole. It is deliberately ambiguous, 'an undefined zone between the inside and the outside' (to quote Genette again).

We could also detect ambiguity in terms of the authorship of the maxim, which, in terms of its content, might well be called a 'quotation' in an additional sense. Can Euripides really be considered the author of a sentiment that is so banal and so commonly encountered elsewhere in Greek literature and thought?[63] The tragedian has packaged an old truism in an attractive, memorable format, but he was presumably not regarded as the unique originator of the idea. Here we have a partial explanation why so many of those who later quote the line do not treat it specifically as a Euripidean quotation. Indeed, it is not even clear whether the play is to be read as endorsing the sentiment or offering it as a topic for debate – an embodiment of traditional wisdom which the audience is being invited to reflect upon, or question or modify in some way. We might compare the way in which Deianeira in Sophocles' *Trachiniae* (1-5) begins by quoting a similar maxim, but explicitly distances herself from the maxim by referring to it as 'a well-known old saying' (λόγος μὲν ἔστ' ἀρχαῖος ἀνθρώπων φανείς) which her own experience makes her inclined to doubt.

To sum up: the quotation/fragment F661 in its original context is presented and framed from the very beginning *as a quotation*. Considered either as a maxim or as a paratextual epigraph, it is characterized by ambiguity and doubleness. It is inherently detachable or semi-detached from the main text of the play's prologue. It both is and is not properly part of the scene that follows. It stands in dialogue, or tension, with the rest of the speech in which it appears. It is an undeniably arresting opening device, but it raises unanswerable questions about authorship, voice, function, interpretation and meaning. The experience of listening to the opening words in the theatre or reading them in a book will have been significantly different, of course, but it seems obvious that more or less the same types of ambiguity, and the same sense of hovering uncertainly on the threshold of the text, will have arisen in either case. All these features help to explain how easy it was for the quotation to float free of its moorings in *Stheneboea* and set off on its own long journey through time and space.

Conclusions

This opening chapter has used a single small quotation as a way of posing some much bigger questions about Euripidean tragedy, ancient reading practices and quotation culture. Whether or not the reader is convinced by my suggestion that tragedy can be treated as a collage of quotations or a dialogue composed of multiple fragments, I hope to have made a case, at least, for regarding 'quotationality' as an important formal feature of Euripidean drama, for better appreciating excerption as a common method of reading literature in antiquity and for viewing quotations simultaneously in and out of context. I explore these ideas in greater depth and detail in the remainder of the book.

2

Quotation Marks and Framing Devices

By the late fifth century BC, as we have seen, eclectic reading was a well-established habit. Dipping into texts, excerpting important verses, hunting down memorable phrases or edifying sentiments, identifying portions which might be interpreted as central to the play's meaning, quoting passages and treating them (rightly or wrongly) as embodying the author's own opinions – these were among the most common ways in which Euripides' readers engaged with tragedy and other forms of poetry. In the previous, chapter I made the claim that Euripides was fully aware of these practices and played along with his readers by deliberately highlighting certain verses as 'quotations' right from the start. In what follows, I justify this claim with reference to specific formal features of the poet's work.

The sheer number of excerptable maxims (*gnomai*) in these plays is perhaps the most obvious sign of Euripides' preoccupation with quotability. His penchant for aphorisms was frequently noted by writers during antiquity, usually with approval. Dio Chrysostom, for instance, praised Euripides for 'scattering his plays with maxims that are useful for all occasions', and associated Euripides more than any other tragedian with the use of *gnomai* for moral exhortation; Quintilian recommended Euripides as reading matter for aspiring orators because he was 'bristling with aphorisms' (*sententiis densus*); and Valerius Maximus saw Euripides' maxims as the medium through which he fulfilled his role as 'teacher' to the Athenians.[1] Occasionally we see signs that not everyone admired this tendency – such as the scholiasts who grumble that Euripides superfluously adds maxims where the dramatic context does not require them – but it is obvious that Euripides came to be generally regarded as the classical world's quotable, aphoristic poet *par excellence*.[2] Not only do we find overwhelmingly more *gnomai* in Euripides' extant tragedies than in those of Aeschylus or Sophocles, line for line, but we also possess more quotations, most of them gnomic, from the lost plays of Euripides than the lost plays of any other tragedian.[3] By including such a large number of conveniently quotable verses in his plays, Euripides has, in effect, facilitated their preservation and transmission as 'fragments' via the indirect tradition, even though the complete texts of many tragedies have been lost.

But it is not simply the number of maxims in these plays that marks them out as extraordinary. Straightforwardly quantitative considerations aside, there are two ways in which Euripides invites us to treat selected verses as quotations. First is the manner in which certain utterances are formulated: their language, style or content gives them a special lapidary quality which I have already described as 'quotationality' (see Chapter 1). Euripidean aphorisms are neat, elegant and pithy. They use words in a deliberate and artful way, creating special effects through their vocabulary, word order and sound effects, including assonance and occasional mid-verse or verse-end rhyme.[4] They often fill complete lines of verse, typically between one and five iambic trimeter lines; even when an aphorism begins mid-verse, it almost invariably finishes at a verse-end. Frequently the final trimeter line of a maxim is unresolved, indicating that the metre is being used to give an effect of *decelerando* leading up to a decisive cadence. All these features create the sense that these quotations are compact, self-contained units, complete in themselves. (In this respect it is relevant to consider Friedrich Schlegel's enigmatic, much quoted dictum that: 'a fragment must, like a small artwork, be separate from its surrounding world and complete in itself – like a hedgehog'.[5]) Whether we are thinking of these utterances as parts of a larger work or as autonomous units, they seem to possess a certain unity, coherence and wholeness.

The second significant factor is the context of the 'quotations' within their plays: that is, the precise way in which these quotable lines are positioned or deployed in relation to the rest of the text. As I shall show in this chapter, most Euripidean 'quotations' are presented or framed in such a way as to make them **stand out** from their surrounding context, almost *as if they were appearing within quotation marks.*

Modern authors can of course use a variety of orthographic or typographic conventions, as I have just done in the sentence above, to make key words or phrases stand out in a written or printed text. Inverted commas, italic type, bold type, underlining, indentation, marginal signs, typefaces and other paratextual markers are very familiar to readers in today's world.[6] None of these conventions existed in Euripides' time, but what we will be discussing here is a variety of devices which can be seen as analogous in their function to a greater or lesser degree. Note that I refer to Euripides' *readers* for the sake of convenience, though every time this word occurs it should be understood as a form of shorthand for 'readers and audiences of all kinds'. I happen to believe that Euripides did have a reading audience in mind, even if this constituted a tiny minority, and that he envisaged his work as having a dual existence in performance and on the page. But almost all of the quotation markers I shall be discussing here will have been equally discernible to everyone, whether in the theatre or the library.

Opening lines

The beginning of a play – or any work of literature – will inevitably have a special prominence.[7] Even if the opening words are not particularly remarkable in terms of their content, their position makes us take notice of them. Whether in the theatre, where the actor in live performance must use his first utterance to grab the audience's attention, or in the pages of a book, where the first words are emphasized and thrown into contrast by the blank space that precedes them, openings naturally stand out. It is clear that initial lines were seen as especially memorable by audiences and readers in antiquity. This is shown by, for example, comic parodies and pastiches which rely on the audiences' familiarity with tragic prologues and their recognition of specific source texts;[8] or the frequency with which opening words function as a site of intertextuality and allusion;[9] or by the high proportion of opening lines that are preserved, via quotation, from Euripides' lost plays;[10] or by the fact that ancient scholars (including, notably, the writers of dramatic hypotheses) habitually use the *incipit* as a way of identifying a literary work.[11]

In light of these considerations, it is perhaps surprising how seldom Euripides opens a play with a 'quotation'. His repeated use of the scene-setting narrative monologue, a device which he employs in almost all of his plays, has been seen as a distinctive signature theme.[12] The device is often used to striking effect, and the opening words of his prologues are calculated to make an impact on the audience, but only in a handful of cases do we find a quotable aphorism at the beginning of a tragedy.[13] This means that those examples that exist are all the more conspicuous. One such case (*Stheneboea* F661) has already been discussed at some length in Chapter 1, where I argued that it functioned in much the same way as an epigraph, hovering ambiguously on the threshold of the text. A further example is *Children of Heracles* 1-5:

πάλαι ποτ' ἐστὶ τοῦτ' ἐμοὶ δεδογμένον·
ὁ μὲν δίκαιος τοῖς πέλας πέφυκ' ἀνήρ,

ὁ δ' ἐς τὸ κέρδος λῆμ' ἔχων ἀνειμένον
πόλει τ' ἄχρηστος καὶ συναλλάσσειν βαρύς,
αὑτῶι δ' ἄριστος· οἶδα δ' οὐ λόγωι μαθών.

I have reached this conclusion long ago: by nature some men are just to those around them, but others seem excellent only to themselves; abandoning themselves to thoughts of gain, they are no good as citizens and they are terrible to deal with. This is not a proverb that I have learned; it is personal knowledge.

These five verses, with their universal moral observation, form a neatly detachable, self-contained unit of meaning before the more personal and specific narrative that follows in lines 6-54. Here, as elsewhere in prologue speeches, the speaker (Iolaus) begins by adopting a tone of lofty omniscience. This tone – together with the fact that the speaker's identity is initially unknown to the audience – affects the way in which we read the content of the *gnome*. There is some typical ambiguity concerning voice: are these the personal thoughts of a specific character, or are we encountering the disembodied voice of traditional Greek wisdom? It is hard to decide. The quotation presents itself as the product of mature reflection: this is shown by the words πάλαι . . . δεδογμένον, which tell us that the speaker has lived a long time and had plenty of opportunity for thought.[14] But the final phrase (οἶδα δ' οὐ λόγωι μαθών) also emphasizes the point that the speaker is not simply regurgitating a proverb (*logos*) that he has picked up from elsewhere. No doubt this is a rhetorical strategy to make the *logos* seem more persuasive, though there is something paradoxical about a proverb that goes out of its way to convince us that it is not a proverb. At any rate, this 'quotation' emphatically draws attention to itself by its form and content as well as its position at the start of the text. Its first and last phrases together might be seen as forming, in effect, an additional frame or set of quotation marks enclosing the central content of the *gnome* which occupies lines 2-5. The lines were duly excerpted and anthologized by more than one ancient quotation-hunter.[15]

Quasi-epigraphic opening lines of this type appear to be distilling universal truths about life, applicable to any situation. However, they might also have a more specific programmatic function within their play, announcing an important theme that will be explored in the plot, or stating a proposition that will be tested by subsequent events. The gnomic verses about the effects of wealth at the start of *Phoenix* (F803a) probably fall into this programmatic category, though the fragments of that play do not allow us to reconstruct the plot in detail. Electra's first words in *Orestes* (1-3) can be read either as a general truism about human and divine nature or as a specific reference to the gruesome history of her own family:

> οὐκ ἔστιν οὐδὲν δεινὸν ὧδ' εἰπεῖν ἔπος
> οὐδὲ πάθος οὐδὲ ξυμφορὰ θεήλατος,
> ἧς οὐκ ἂν ἄραιτ' ἄχθος ἀνθρώπου φύσις.
>
> There is nothing that is so dreadful, to tell the tale or to suffer, nor is there any situation sent by a god, of which human nature is not liable to bear the burden.

The unusual syntax and slightly opaque phrasing mean that the reader has to work hard to untangle the meaning of these alliterative lines, but the point, baldly summarized, seems to be that anything at all may happen in the course of life.[16] On the one hand this sentiment is a variation on the conventional theme of the vicissitudes of fortune (a theme encountered many times in Euripides and elsewhere), but on the other hand it can be interpreted as an implicitly self-referential warning of the unpredictable events that will follow. The plot of *Orestes*, which departs radically from previous versions of the myth, comes closer to free invention than any other tragedy known to us. This is indeed a play in which anything at all might happen; it also features other metapoetic signals of the playwright's provocative originality.[17] Thus there are several layers of meaning available in these lines, depending on whether they are read in or out of context. But the crucial fact is that their position combines with their inherent 'quotationality' to facilitate their excerption. They clearly became famous lines in their own right, and were quoted by many Greek and Roman writers, including Dio of Prusa, Lucian and Cicero.[18]

Closing lines

Endings, like openings, naturally stand out. If a gnomic generalization is placed at the very end of a play, it is tempting to read it as a form of summary or conclusion to the events that we have just witnessed. A definitive statement encapsulating the moral of the play might be welcomed as a satisfying way of providing closure – tying up loose ends, suggesting some sort of answer to the intellectual problems that have been raised, or reducing the play's difficult subject matter to an easily digestible meaning or message that we can take away as we leave the theatre or close the book.[19]

Of course, the meaning of a tragedy usually turns out to be more complicated and open-ended than this, and Euripides seldom uses a maxim to close a play. (I discount the anapaestic tailpieces found at the end of *Andromache, Alcestis, Bacchae, Helen* and *Medea*, which are formulaic, interchangeable and almost certainly inauthentic.[20]) Nevertheless, one exception is *Hecuba*, in which the decisive final words, sung by the chorus as they dance off, take the form of a grim proverb: στερρὰ γὰρ ἀνάγκη ('necessity is harsh').[21] Another exception is *Ion*, where the chorus wrap up the action by singing:

> ἐς τέλος γὰρ οἱ μὲν ἐσθλοὶ τυγχάνουσιν ἀξίων,
> οἱ κακοὶ δ', ὥσπερ πεφύκασ', οὔποτ' εὖ πράξειαν ἄν.
>
> *Ion* 1621-2
>
> So in the end the good get what they deserve, while the bad, because of their very nature, could never prosper.

As Francis Dunn remarks on this passage, 'Euripides prefers morals so general that they might fit anywhere'; though he adds that 'the gnomic quality of such reflections does not offer up the truth or the lesson of a particular drama; instead it is a general or generic cue that the play is over and that the time has come to reflect on it as we may'.[22] In other words, the specific relationship of this maxim to the play's plot and themes is less important than its formal dramatic function or its proverbial wisdom in a general sense.

A couple of other plays also end (in effect) with *gnomai* delivered by their leading characters before they exit the stage. These are not quite the final words that the audience hears, since in each case there also follows a perfunctory anapaestic coda from the chorus, but they are the last words that properly belong to the plays' action. At *Heracles* 1422-6, the hero Heracles, distraught after having killed his wife and children, delivers the following lines before going away into exile:

> ἀλλ' ἐσκόμιζε τέκνα, δυσκόμιστ' ἄχη·
> ἡμεῖς δ' ἀναλώσαντες αἰσχύναις δόμον
> Θησεῖ πανώλεις ἑψόμεσθ' ἐφολκίδες.
> ὅστις δὲ πλοῦτον ἢ σθένος μᾶλλον φίλων
> ἀγαθῶν πεπᾶσθαι βούλεται κακῶς φρονεῖ.
>
> Take my children inside, though they are a burden hard to take. I, who have ruined my house by my shame, I who am totally destroyed, shall follow in the wake of Theseus. Any man who prefers wealth or power to good friends is a fool.

The ending of *Phoenician Women* is a more problematic case, since its authorship has been disputed,[23] but it features a similar scenario, with a central character, Oedipus, offering a final piece of wisdom before departing into exile (1758-63):

ὦ πάτρας κλεινῆς πολῖται, λεύσσετ'· Οἰδίπους ὅδε,
ὃς τὰ κλείν' αἰνίγματ' ἔγνων καὶ μέγιστος ἦν ἀνήρ,
ὃς μόνος Σφιγγὸς κατέσχον τῆς μιαιφόνου κράτη,
νῦν ἄτιμος αὐτὸς οἰκτρὸς ἐξελαύνομαι χθονός.
ἀλλὰ γὰρ τί ταῦτα θρηνῶ καὶ μάτην ὀδύρομαι;
τὰς γὰρ ἐκ θεῶν ἀνάγκας θνητὸν ὄντα δεῖ φέρειν.

O citizens of a glorious country, behold! I am Oedipus, here before you – I am he who understood the famous riddle and was the greatest of men, who single-handedly withstood the power of the deadly Sphinx – but now I am cast out of the land, disgraced and pitiable. But why do I lament this situation and vainly weep? A human being must bear the inevitable outcome that the gods bestow.

In both cases, the general truism is presented as if it follows on naturally from the more specific description of the situation in hand.[24] These exit lines have a terrible finality, and they bring the drama to a resounding conclusion. Perhaps they do not altogether satisfy our desire for closure in an intellectual sense. (Could any maxim, however insightful, truly sum up the meaning of an entire play?) It can seem as if Oedipus' last line is little more than a platitude, while the sentiment expressed by Heracles seems inadequate as a summing-up of everything that has gone before (as if the entire plot and conception of *Heracles* had centred on the theme of friendship). In their dramatic context, these maxims will have been accorded a special weight because they are spoken by the plays' central characters, who have suffered calamities and now seem to acquire a new insight into their own condition.[25] But there is nothing about their content or expression that marks them out as belonging to Oedipus or Heracles in particular. They stand out not because of any great originality but because they appear at the end. Quoted out of context, they could be the words of anybody at all.

Position within a scene, speech or song

We might have expected that the identity of the speaker would make a difference – perhaps certain characters within a play could be seen as especially authoritative or trustworthy, or especially prone to making gnomic pronouncements – but on the whole, it is hard to see any pattern at work in any of the extant tragedies.²⁶ A few characters here and there might be said to exhibit a gnomic mentality – Jocasta in *Phoenician Women*, Theseus and Adrastus in *Suppliant Women*, Amphitryon in *Heracles* and Iolaus in *Children of Heracles* perhaps fall into this category – but in most plays maxims are found in the mouths of several different characters, and their distribution, or the specific choice of speaker, is apparently irrelevant. What gives the quotable maxims far more emphasis is their position in relation to the speech or scene in which they appear.²⁷

The principle seems to be that beginnings and endings are a particularly effective place for inserting quotable lines, for reasons that we have already mentioned. In performance, these key verses stand out because they coincide with natural pauses and cadences in the dialogue. On the page, they are more eye-catching and easier to locate, especially for readers who may be quickly scanning the text for 'useful' excerptable content.

Aphorisms are commonly used as the opening words of a character's monologue,²⁸ or the final words of a monologue,²⁹ or the final words uttered by a character before their exit from the stage,³⁰ or the end of a speech just before a new character enters the stage,³¹ or the end of a speech which also coincides with the end of an act or scene.³² Brief choral interjections in between the speeches of main characters typically form self-contained units of two or three iambic lines, which very often have an aphoristic character.³³

While the majority of Euripidean *gnomai* are found in scenes of spoken dialogue, they also feature in choral songs, where we can see the same principle at work. A quotable piece of wisdom may be emphasized by its appearance at the beginning or end of a song.³⁴ In certain cases, an entire strophe of a choral ode may consist of an extended *gnome*: thus the music and rhythm combine with the words to give the sense that the utterance is self-contained and complete.³⁵ Choral odes of this sort would naturally have lent themselves to being reperformed as free-standing songs in other settings such as symposia.

Even though some 'quotations' appear in the middle of a speech or song, the overwhelming majority of them are opening lines or closing lines. This is a hugely important observation because it shows that Euripides consistently aimed to make these soundbites as prominent as possible. Furthermore (as Holger Friis Johansen has demonstrated through comparative analysis), Euripides' practice contrasts strongly with that of Aeschylus and Sophocles, in whose plays gnomic reflections are more thoroughly embedded within the dialogue, and consequently less easily detachable for re-use.³⁶

Maxims introduced by φεῦ

Φεῦ is a word of elastic meaning and variable nuance.[37] Liddell and Scott define it as an exclamation of grief, anger, astonishment or admiration;[38] translators typically render it as 'Oh!', 'Ah!', 'Alas!' or similar. It is utterly characteristic of tragic diction: in the classical period, at any rate, it is seldom found outside tragedy.[39] Sometimes the word may appear *extra versum*, interrupting the rhythm of the dialogue; sometimes it may be repeated (φεῦ φεῦ), probably but not necessarily conveying extra emphasis.[40]

In a significant number of tragic passages, almost all of them by Euripides, the word is used specifically to introduce or emphasize a quotable maxim.[41] In these cases, φεῦ does not usually express a vehement emotion – or indeed any definitely discernible mental attitude – on the part of the speaker. Sometimes, of course, it is hard to deny the presence of emotion, and sometimes the sentiment expressed in the maxim does naturally give rise to grief, sorrow or resignation. This is obviously the case when, for instance, Medea complains about the perils of love, or when Hecuba laments the servile state of humankind:[42]

> φεῦ φεῦ· βροτοῖς ἔρωτες ὡς κακὸν μέγα.
>
> What a great evil love is for mankind!
>
> *Medea* 330

> φεῦ·
> οὐκ ἔστι θνητῶν ὅστις ἔστ' ἐλεύθερος·
> ἢ χρημάτων γὰρ δοῦλός ἐστιν ἢ τύχης
> ἢ πλῆθος αὐτὸν πόλεος ἢ νόμων γραφαὶ
> εἴργουσι χρῆσθαι μὴ κατὰ γνώμην τρόποις.
>
> There is no person who is free: either he is a slave to wealth or fortune, or the multitude or the city's laws stop him from acting as he wishes.
>
> *Hecuba* 864-7

Elsewhere, φεῦ may perhaps indicate an extreme of positive feeling, as in the following lines:

> φεῦ φεῦ· βροτοῖσιν ὡς τὰ χρηστὰ πράγματα
> χρηστῶν ἀφορμὰς ἐνδίδωσ' ἀεὶ λόγων.
>
> How true it is that fine actions always provide people with the basis for fine speeches!
>
> *Hecuba* 1238

Here the speaker is expressing approval of the general principle that good deeds give rise to good speeches, though it is open to doubt whether the tone is really one of vehement emotion.

Other examples of φεῦ-plus-maxim are more neutral or ambiguous in tone. This tends to be especially true of cases where the maxims in question are very conventional in their content – such as *Orestes* 1155-7:

φεῦ·
οὐκ ἔστιν οὐδὲν κρεῖσσον ἢ φίλος σαφής,
οὐ πλοῦτος, οὐ τυραννίς· ἀλόγιστον δέ τι
τὸ πλῆθος ἀντάλλαγμα γενναίου φίλου.

There is nothing greater than a true friend – not wealth, not tyranny – no, a genuine friend has an exchange value that is incalculably large.

In these alliterative and quotable lines, as elsewhere in the same play, Orestes affirms the value of true friendship. The theme of *philia* is undoubtedly important in this tragedy, but the sentiment as expressed here is blandly unexceptional, which means that the exact nuance is hard to judge.[43] Furthermore, it is important to note that neither the exclamation φεῦ nor the maxim itself marks a direct reaction to anything that has already been said. (The lines that immediately preceded were a comment, from the chorus, on Helen's hateful nature.) Thus φεῦ can be proleptic and anticipatory, introducing a new idea rather than, as one might expect, responding to something that has already been said or done.

The same could be said of the following example from *Hippolytus* (431-2):

φεῦ φεῦ· τὸ σῶφρον ὡς ἁπανταχοῦ καλὸν
καὶ δόξαν ἐσθλὴν ἐν βροτοῖς καρπίζεται.

What a good thing is virtue everywhere, and how fine a reputation it enjoys among mortals!

This two-line maxim is delivered by the chorus, and once again it is hard to read this as an outpouring of powerful emotions, despite the repeated φεῦ. (In fact, there is no discernible difference in nuance or degree of intensity between single or double φεῦ, either in this passage or anywhere else.) The maxim might be seen as a very general sort of reflection on the situation in hand, but it is highly conventional both in its content and in its dramatic function. The lines are there chiefly to mark a formal separation or pause between the end of Phaedra's speech and the beginning of the Nurse's speech. Choral couplets of this sort, with or without φεῦ, are an extremely common rhetorical device in Euripidean *agon* scenes.[44]

It would be hard to imagine sentiments more conventional than those expressed in the following lines:

φεῦ φεῦ· βροτείων πημάτων ὅσαι τύχαι
ὅσαι τε μορφαί· τέρμα δ' οὐκ εἴποι τις ἄν.

How many are the accidents, and how many the forms, of human woes: no one could say where they will end.

Antiope F211

φεῦ· τοῖσι γενναίοισιν ὡς ἁπανταχοῦ
πρέπει χαρακτὴρ χρηστὸς εἰς εὐψυχίαν.

How true it is that well-born people are distinguished in all situations by a fine, courageous character.

Danae F329

φεῦ· τοῖσι γενναίοισιν ὡς ἅπαν καλόν.

As far as the well-born are concerned, everything is fine.

incert. fab. F961

φεῦ φεῦ· τὸ νικᾶν τἄνδιχ' ὡς καλὸν γέρας,
τὰ μὴ δίκαια δ' ὡς ἁπανταχοῦ κακόν.

What a fine reward it is when just deeds prevail, and how evil it is in all circumstances when unjust deeds do so.

incert. fab. F1034

Such truisms about human character, the uncertainty of life and the mutability of fortune may strike the reader as either profound or banal, but they are extremely common throughout Greek tragedy.[45] Because these verses are now fragments without a dramatic context, it is even harder than usual to judge the precise nuance. The fact that they have been preserved and handed down in the form of autonomous, universal statements is bound to make their tone seem more authoritative and neutral to a modern reader (perhaps misleadingly so). Nevertheless, given the bland nature of the sentiments being expressed, one suspects that φεῦ is here not as an expression of intense emotion but simply as a way of drawing attention to the maxim.

In a couple of other instances, this signalling function is particularly notable:

φεῦ φεῦ· παλαιὸς αἶνος ὡς καλῶς ἔχει·
γέροντες οὐδέν ἐσμεν ἄλλο πλὴν ψόφος
καὶ σχῆμ', ὀνείρων δ' ἕρπομεν μιμήματα·
νοῦς δ' οὐκ ἔνεστιν, οἰόμεσθα δ' εὖ φρονεῖν.

Aeolus F25

How well the old saying holds true: we old men are nothing except a sound and a shape; we creep along, mere semblances of dreams, and there is no sense in us, though we imagine we are wise.

φεῦ φεῦ· παλαιὸς αἶνος ὡς καλῶς ἔχει·
οὐκ ἂν γένοιτο χρηστὸς ἐκ κακοῦ πατρός.

Dictys F333

How well the old saying holds true: there can never be a good son born of a bad father.

These are not the only tragic passages which explicitly label themselves as maxims.[46] But both of the examples above, extraordinarily, use exactly the same opening line, combining the self-labelling phrase and φεῦ φεῦ to constitute an emphatic marking device. In effect, Euripides is doing the job of a commentator, saying: 'This is a good maxim: take note.' But it is obvious that we are dealing with a conventional formula, which might accompany any general reflection at all.

Tellingly, this 'gnomic' use of φεῦ is never found in the surviving plays of Aeschylus (including *Prometheus Bound*), and only two or three times in Sophocles. The overwhelming majority of examples come from the works of Euripides. The full significance of this fact emerges in the context of all the other quotation markers being discussed in this chapter: it lies precisely in the fact that Euripides' plays, much more than tragedies by other authors, are designed to be susceptible to quotation. It seems clear that this use of φεῦ constitutes yet another framing or highlighting device.

In this specific usage, as we have seen, φεῦ eludes straightforward interpretation or translation. But I suggest that its meaning as an exclamation is less important than its formal function. In the passages cited above, its main use is to act as a signal to the audience or reader, announcing that a gnomic utterance is to follow. In linguistic terms, φεῦ is functioning as a *pragmatic marker* (conventionally defined as 'those constructions that are present in speech to support interaction but do not generally add any specific semantic meaning to the message').[47] Linguistic theorists have observed that interjections can often act as pragmatic markers in a variety of contexts, independent of their primary semantic (emotional) meaning: they frequently act as 'turn-indicators' (that is, they occupy the initial position of an utterance, signalling a contrast or transition between one topic and another), and they can also be an attention-grabbing device.[48] It seems clear that, in its 'gnomic' usage, the interjection φεῦ is to be understood in just this way.

Of course, there are many other cases of detachable maxims where φεῦ is *not* found, but it seems that φεῦ could be used from time to time to add a further level of emphasis, perhaps denoting sentiments which we are invited to regard as especially trenchant or memorable. 'Gnomic' φεῦ is seen exclusively in dialogue rather than lyrics, and in every instance the gnomic utterance consists of one or more complete iambic verses: this allows the lines to stand alone as apparently self-contained, decontextualized quotations. All maxims with φεῦ are also conveniently detachable in the additional sense that they contain no specific reference to speaker, addressee or dramatic context: the same cannot be said of many other tragic maxims. Note also that when used in iambic dialogue (whether in conjunction with a maxim or not) φεῦ always appears at the beginning of a verse or *extra metrum*.[49]

In view of this last fact, it is conceivable that φεῦ or φεῦ φεῦ would have acted not just as an audible signal in performance but also as a visual marker in written texts, assisting readers to locate verses that were particularly ripe for excerption. In this sense, it could be seen, perhaps, as broadly analogous to the various systems of 'gnomic pointing' used in certain papyri, manuscripts and early printed texts.[50] Of course one must beware of anachronism, and (as I have already observed) it is almost impossible to imagine the physical appearance of fifth-century bookrolls, but I assume that Euripides was writing, at least in part, with the needs of a reading audience in mind. The fact that so many surviving examples of 'gnomic' φεῦ have come down to us in the form of fragments – i.e. selected quotations – indicates the frequency with which Euripides' ancient readers took note of these textual signals and duly responded with their scissors and paste.[51]

Apostrophe

The use of apostrophe and other deictic signals can make selected lines stand out. There are two reasons why this is so. First, these signals function linguistically as another sort of 'turn-indicator', in that they attract attention and create a slight pause or separation between the preceding dialogue and the verses that immediately follow. Second, the specific character being addressed at these moments is not the only possible addressee. The use of apostrophe may be natural within the dramatic context, but it can also be seen as an artificial literary device, as part of a performance designed to engage its audience. The speaker can be seen as, in effect, addressing two different audiences simultaneously: an internal audience (the character being apostrophized within the fictional scenario) and an external audience (the spectator or reader in the real world). Whenever we read or watch a play, we undergo a complex cognitive response to it. For the duration of its action, we 'suspend our disbelief'; in our imagination, we enter into its world and experience a sense that we are somehow 'there'. This means that we identify with the characters to some extent, and whenever we hear someone in the play being addressed, it is possible to imagine that the speaker is directly communicating with us. This phenomenon is sometimes called 'triangulated address' – a useful term coined by Jonathan Culler – and it has been widely discussed in relation to lyric poetry.[52]

One can point to a relatively large number of instances from Euripidean dialogue in which apostrophe is used to introduce a general reflection. In many such passages, a specific individual or group within the play is being addressed,[53] but it is possible for the audience to interpret these lines as a form of 'triangulated address' directed at themselves as well. If the utterance in question is removed from its original dramatic setting and repurposed as a free-standing quotation, the fact that it is formulated as an address to *someone* means that it can easily function in a new context as an address to *anyone*. This is true even when the words are notionally addressed to the subject of the *gnome* itself (old age, fortune, love, wealth or similar) rather than to any particular person.[54] However, in several cases, the primary addressee is so vague that the content of the utterance acquires a more universal significance right from the start, as in the following passage from *Hippolytus* (916-20) in which the whole of humanity is addressed:

ὦ πόλλ' ἁμαρτάνοντες ἄνθρωποι μάτην,
τί δὴ τέχνας μὲν μυρίας διδάσκετε
καὶ πάντα μηχανᾶσθε κἀξευρίσκετε,
ἓν δ' οὐκ ἐπίστασθ' οὐδ' ἐθηράσασθέ πω,
φρονεῖν διδάσκειν οἷσιν οὐκ ἔνεστι νοῦς;

O mankind, prone to great error, devoid of purpose! You teach countless arts, and you discover and contrive all manner of devices, but there is one thing that you do not know and have never even sought to understand – why not? – and that is how to teach intelligence to fools.

This sort of generalization is especially effective as a 'triangulated utterance' because there is a natural slippage in meaning between the fictional play-world and the real world. The moral advice being offered here might apply equally to the *dramatis personae*, to Euripides' spectators and readers, or to anyone else.[55]

Even in the original dramatic context there is something artificial about the phrasing, since at this moment the speaker (Theseus) is actually talking to just one person (his son Hippolytus). The 'quotation' appears in the middle of a long scene of angry confrontation between father and son, and no other characters are present on stage (apart from the chorus of young Troezenian women, for whom the vocative ὦ . . .ἄνθρωποι would not be used). Even though Theseus is supposedly talking in private to Hippolytus and upbraiding him for his personal conduct, his outburst at 916-20 suddenly seems to take the form of a speech aimed at a wider public. Is Theseus addressing Hippolytus, or an imaginary audience consisting of the entire human race? Does the actor playing Theseus turn away from Hippolytus at this point and direct his remarks to the spectators in the theatre? It is hard to decide. But as the scene continues it is notable that when Hippolytus responds to his father's criticisms, Theseus repeatedly counter-responds with universalizing references or appeals to humankind (925, 936) rather than addressing Hippolytus directly. Thus it becomes increasingly obvious that he is, in effect, talking to two different sorts of audience at once.[56]

Many of Euripides' tragedies included moralizing passages in which an older character offered advice to a younger one, as in the following examples:

πόλλ᾽, ὦ τέκνον, σφάλλουσιν ἀνθρώπους θεοί.

O child, the gods often make humans lose their footing.

Archelaus F254.1

τὸ γῆρας, ὦ παῖ, τῶν νεωτέρων φρενῶν
σοφώτερον πέφυκε κἀσφαλέστερον,
ἐμπειρία τε τῆς ἀπειρίας κρατεῖ.

O child, old age is naturally wiser and more infallible than the minds of younger people, and experience overcomes lack of experience.

Peleus F619

Such passages, which were frequently collected in anthologies, were particularly ripe for reuse in rhetorical or educational contexts. They can be connected to the view of ancient rhetorical theorists that *gnomai* are appropriate for older and wiser speakers.[57] The majority of these passages are found among the fragments of lost plays. Even though in some cases it is not possible to identify the speaker or the addressee, the use of certain vocative forms – 'O child' (ὦ παῖ, ὦ τέκνον) or 'O children' (ὦ παῖδες) – definitively shows that an older speaker is addressing a young person.[58] By adopting this generalizing form of apostrophe rather than the specific use of a character's name, Euripides can be seen as having facilitated the application of the moral content to other situations.

It is instructive to note that all of these vocative phrases and deictic markers were invariably retained when the lines were excerpted by other writers, even when they could easily have been detached. This suggests that this type of framing device came to be treated as an integral part of the quotation. It seems that in a new context it could even be seen as a useful rhetorical device (i.e. for grabbing a listener's attention or underlining a speaker's didactic stance) rather than as a distracting reminder of the verses' original speaker or dramatic setting.

'Listen carefully…'

An even more emphatic use of apostrophe is encountered in scenes in which a character explicitly instructs the listener to pause and reflect, using an imperative verb or equivalent formula:[59]

> ἄκουσον· οὐ γὰρ οἱ κακῶς πεπραγότες
> σὺν ταῖς τύχαισι τοὺς λόγους ἀπώλεσαν.
>
> Listen! People who fare badly do not lose the ability to speak along with their good fortune.
>
> *Antigone* F165

As in the case of the lines discussed in the previous section, instructions of this type are treated as an integral part of the quotation, and they are usually retained by those who later quote the verses in question as 'fragments'.[60] Spectators and readers may treat such instructions, like other forms of apostrophe, as equivalent to a form of 'triangulated address' applying in part to themselves; but even if they do not, the use of a direct instruction can be seen as a way of highlighting the content of the utterance that immediately follows. Speakers who employ this device are underlining the fact that the *aperçu* that they are about to serve up is especially worthy of our attention.

Sometimes, in an extant play where we are able to read the quotation in its dramatic setting, we can see how the device may be used to stop a speech mid-flow and change topic. In such cases, the instruction and the accompanying *gnome* seem to arise plausibly enough out of the dramatic situation, but a common criticism of such scenes is that the natural development of plot and character interaction is hampered by these rhetorical generalizations.[61] For instance, Theseus in *Suppliant Women* breaks off in the middle of a monologue and exclaims: 'Acknowledge the sins of mankind, you foolish creatures!' (ἀλλ', ὦ μάταιοι, γνῶτε τἀνθρώπων κακα, 549), before launching into a ten-line maxim about the uncertainty of fortune (550-59). Jocasta in *Phoenician Women* (452-3) interrupts a speech by her son Eteocles, saying 'Stop!' (ἐπίσχες) and proceeding immediately to deliver a maxim about the dangers of jumping to hasty decisions.[62] Heracles in *Alcestis*, in the middle of a speech addressed to an old slave, interrupts his own rambling reflections on human nature in order to insert a maxim (781-9):

> ἀλλ' ἄκουέ μου.
> βροτοῖς ἅπασι κατθανεῖν ὀφείλεται,
> κοὐκ ἔστι θνητῶν ὅστις ἐξεπίσταται
> τὴν αὔριον μέλλουσαν εἰ βιώσεται·
> τὸ τῆς τύχης γὰρ ἀφανὲς οἷ προβήσεται,
> κἄστ' οὐ διδακτὸν οὐδ' ἁλίσκεται τέχνηι.
> ταῦτ' οὖν ἀκούσας καὶ μαθὼν ἐμοῦ πάρα
> εὔφραινε σαυτόν, πῖνε, τὸν καθ' ἡμέραν
> βίον λογίζου σόν, τὰ δ' ἄλλα τῆς τύχης.

Listen to me! Death is a debt that all humans must pay; there isn't one mortal who's able to say if he's going to survive for another day. The workings of Fortune are hidden away: they cannot be taught, nor unlocked with a key. Therefore listen to this and learn a lesson from me: enjoy yourself! Have a drink! Accept that today is yours for the living, but the rest of time belongs to Fortune.

This last example is particularly striking, partly because it both begins and ends with the instruction to stop and listen carefully, and partly because the maxim is in rhyming verse (an effect which I have tried to reproduce in the translation above). Line-end rhyme is an extremely rare phenomenon in Greek tragedy.[63] In this passage it has been seen as a stylistic device for emphasizing Heracles' drunkenness, but the occasional use of rhyme in other Euripidean maxims might encourage us to regard it as a way of enhancing the lines' quotationality and their eye-catching oddity.[64]

Universality of perspective

Whose voice are we hearing when we encounter a quotable aphorism? Even though all tragic maxims are uttered by a specific character or by the chorus, it is possible to treat them as the words of the author; and of course many ancient readers did precisely this. Nevertheless, these generalizations do not usually represent the unique thoughts of any individual person; it is probably better to see them as part of a traditional, shared repertoire of 'tragic wisdom'.[65] The voice that speaks to us through a *gnome* – 'the shadowy second speaker', to use Gary Saul Morson's phrase – is a detached and impersonal one.[66] The typical content of a maxim seems to depend on a level of knowledge, experience and insight beyond normal human limits. These quasi-omniscient pronouncements about human life and supernatural powers are presented as if from a universal perspective that transcends time and space.

This quality marks out tragic maxims as different in kind from the more naturalistic, everyday, context-specific utterances of the characters. But in numerous passages, the sweeping universality of perspective is accentuated further by the inclusion of certain key words and phrases. One such word is ἀεί ('always'), which is often used in general statements to imply that the observation functions independently of its context and applies to all imaginable dimensions of time.[67] Even more common are the key words βροτοί, θνητοί or ἄνθρωποι ('mortals'), or phrases such as ἐν βροτοῖς ('among mortals' or 'in this life'). If a speaker refers to 'mortals', or to the whole of life in a general sense, he thereby implies that he is able to distance himself from human activities, stepping back from the action and commenting on it as an external observer – or even a deity – rather than as an ordinary human participant.

> ἐν βροτοῖς
> οὐκ ἔστιν οὐδὲν διὰ τέλους εὐδαιμονοῦν.
>
> *Suppliant Women* 269-70

In this life nothing at all remains blessed all the way up to its end.

> οὐκ ἔστιν οὐδὲν χωρὶς ἀνθρώποις θεῶν·
> σπουδάζομεν δὲ πόλλ' ὑπ' ἐλπίδων, μάτην
> πόνους ἔχοντες, οὐδὲν εἰδότες σαφές.
>
> *Thyestes* F391

In mortal affairs nothing is independent of the gods. Our hopes lead us on to great toils, but because we have no clear knowledge we labour in vain.

> τά τοι μέγιστα πάντ' ἀπείργασται βροτοῖς
> τόλμ' ὥστε νικᾶν· οὔτε γὰρ τυραννίδες
> χωρὶς πόνου γένοιντ' ἂν οὔτ' οἶκος μέγας.
>
> *Ixion* F426

For mortals the greatest victories are won by boldness; neither tyrannies nor extensive property can be acquired without toil.

ὦ θνητὰ παραφρονήματ' ἀνθρώπων, μάτην
οἵ φασιν εἶναι τὴν τύχην ἀλλ' οὐ θεούς·
ὡς οὐδὲν ἴστε, κεἰ λέγειν δοκεῖτέ τι.

Phrixus II F820b.1-3

Oh, the delusions of mortal men, who claim that fortune exists but that gods do not! You understand nothing, even if you seem to have some understanding.

Reflections such as these are common throughout Euripides, extant and lost plays alike, including many of the examples discussed elsewhere in this chapter. Their lofty tone, together with their uncompromising formulation of general rules that admit of no exception, makes them very suitable to be extracted from their setting and quoted as proverbs. Their repeated references to 'mortals' emphasize the fact that these truisms are applicable to almost any situation in life, but they also function as a framing device. On the whole (though not invariably), phrases such as ἐν βροτοῖς tend to appear towards the start of a gnomic utterance, and in many cases they are used (rather like 'gnomic' φεῦ) as a 'turn-indicator', immediately preceding or announcing the main idea of the maxim itself. When we are able to examine such phrases at work within a scene, we can see that they are often used midway through a speech, precisely in order to mark the transition from specific subject matter to general reflection – as in the following example from *Hippolytus* (433-8):[68]

δέσποιν', ἐμοί τοι συμφορὰ μὲν ἀρτίως
ἡ σὴ παρέσχε δεινὸν ἐξαίφνης φόβον·
νῦν δ' ἐννοῦμαι φαῦλος οὖσα, κἀν βροτοῖς
αἱ δεύτεραί πως φροντίδες σοφώτεραι.
οὐ γὰρ περισσὸν οὐδὲν οὐδ' ἔξω λόγου
πέπονθας ...

Mistress, I concede that your predicament gave me a sudden fright just then, but now I realize that I was foolish; and in human life second thoughts are no doubt wiser. After all, it's not as if you have suffered anything excessive or out of the ordinary ...

In this passage the speaker is the Nurse. She begins her monologue by responding to the immediate situation (the effects of Phaedra's deranging passion), then she delivers her piece of wisdom, in the form of a neatly detachable one-liner (436), then she resumes her commentary on the plot (at 437-8, using γάρ to mark another transition).[69] The phrase κἀν βροτοῖς signals a change of direction and a change of tone: it marks the precise point at which the Nurse 'zooms out' to take the broader view as the omniscient voice of wisdom, before 'zooming in' again and returning to her normal voice as a palace servant.

Labels

Certain passages self-consciously draw our attention to their status as the embodiment of ancient wisdom. Many Euripidean characters explicitly describe what they are about to say as a traditional piece of advice. Sometimes, they introduce a general reflection with a verb such as φασίν or λέγουσιν ('people say [that] …') or νομίζεται ('it is thought [that] …').[70] Sometimes, they use the terms αἶνος, λόγος, or μῦθος (or equivalent phrases) as a conspicuous way of labelling the maxim. For example:[71]

> λόγος γάρ ἐστιν οὐκ ἐμός, σοφῶν δέ του,
> δεινῆς ἀνάγκης οὐδὲν ἰσχύειν πλέον.
>
> There is a saying – not my own, but some wise person's, I suppose – that there is no force more powerful than dread necessity.
>
> *Helen* 513-14

> αἱ δ' ἐλπίδες βόσκουσι φυγάδας, ὡς λόγος.
>
> Those in exile feed on their hopes, as the saying goes.
>
> *Phoenician Women* 396

> πάλαι μὲν οὖν ὑμνηθέν, ἀλλ' ὅμως ἐρῶ·
> τὰ χρήματ' ἀνθρώποισι τιμιώτατα
> δύναμίν τε πλείστην τῶν ἐν ἀνθρώποις ἔχει.
>
> This is an old saying, but I shall say it nonetheless: money is the thing that humans value the most, and money has more power among humans than anything else.
>
> *Phoenician Women* 438-40

> ἐγὼ τὸ μὲν δὴ πανταχοῦ θρυλούμενον
> κράτιστον εἶναι φημὶ μὴ φῦναι βροτῶι.
>
> I agree with the adage that is universally well known: that the best thing for a human is not to be born at all.
>
> *Bellerophon* F285.1-2

παλαιὸς αἶνος· ἔργα μὲν νεωτέρων,
βουλαὶ δ' ἔχουσιν τῶν γεραιτέρων κράτος.

There is an old proverb: younger people are possessed by action, but older ones by good counsel.

Melanippe F508

ἄνευ τύχης γάρ, ὥσπερ ἡ παροιμία,
πόνος μονωθεὶς οὐκέτ' ἀλγύνει βροτούς.

Stheneboea F668

Without fortune, so the saying goes, toil on its own is no longer a grievance to mortals.

καὶ τῶν παλαιῶν πόλλ' ἔπη καλῶς ἔχει·
λόγοι γὰρ ἐσθλοὶ φάρμακον φόβου βροτοῖς.

incert. fab. F1065

Many ancient proverbs hold true, for fine words are a medicine to cure mortals of fear.

As we see here, the exact form of wording differs from case to case, but the labelling function of such phrases is obvious. It is not simply that the verses in question are being marked as suitable for quotation in future. These labels also acknowledge that the maxims are *already* quotations – at least in terms of the sentiments that they express. In each of the examples cited above, there is no pretence that the maxim represents an original insight on the part of the character or author; quite the opposite. These speakers are making us acutely aware that what they are saying is the distillation of inherited wisdom, which they themselves are validating by repeating it in a new setting.

This is an important point because it helps to explain how Euripidean maxims came to achieve such a wide currency and influence in antiquity. Euripides, had he wished, could have formulated aphorisms on unfamiliar topics, or asserted his originality by expressing radically new or quirky viewpoints. Other ancient dramatists, including Agathon and Philemon, did just this.[72] Some Euripidean *gnomai*, of course, do display a spirit of idiosyncrasy or paradox, but most of them are entirely conventional in their content. Even though his work can often be conceptually unsettling in other respects, it seems that in his quotable maxims Euripides is not trying to shock us. The effect that he achieves with these maxims is authoritative precisely because the point of view expressed will already have been widely accepted by his readers: it is part of an established tragic tradition. (Aristotle in the *Rhetoric* makes a similar point about the usefulness of *gnomai* to the orator, explaining that audiences like them and accept them as true because everyone already agrees with them.[73]) Nevertheless, Euripides is not simply spouting old clichés. He is reformulating time-honoured content in a new format, making it more likely that his readers will quote his version (rather than someone else's) because of the pithy way in which it is worded and the elegance with which it is framed.

Serial maxims

Perhaps the most striking examples of verses that stand out from their context are to be found in a few rare scenes containing consecutive *gnomai*. For instance, a rapid-fire stichomythic dialogue between Jocasta and Polynices in *Phoenician Women* consists almost entirely of gnomic one-liners, each one delivered in response to the last, without any intervening material (390-407); and Jocasta's monologue later in the same scene begins with a thirty-line series of general reflections, one after another (528-58). A comparable serial effect is created by scenes in which a speech ending with a maxim is followed immediately by a gnomic interlude from the chorus and then another speech beginning with a maxim (as at *Andromache* 177-85, *Hecuba* 1180-94, etc.). It is possible to see such passages as, in effect, ready-made anthologies of quotations in miniature.

The most extraordinary scene of all comes from *Erechtheus*, a fragmentary play which, to judge by its remains, was one of Euripides' most explicitly political dramas. This work, centring on the self-sacrifice of king Erechtheus and his children in order to preserve the city of Athens from foreign invasion, was centrally concerned with Athenian identity and civic ideology.[74] Many of the fragments take the form of sententious soundbites about bravery, duty, wisdom and the love of one's country. The majority of these were preserved and quoted by later writers specifically for their noble sentiments and morally edifying content.[75] One speech in particular (F362), delivered by king Erechtheus to one of his children, seems to have consisted entirely of a string of maxims, one after another. (We may be struck by its uncanny similarity to a scene in *Hamlet* (I.3) in which Polonius offers a series of precepts to his son Laertes, beginning 'There – my blessing with thee, / And these few precepts in thy memory / See thou character', though it is unlikely that Shakespeare will have known the *Erechtheus* fragment.) The speech begins thus:

ὀρθῶς μ' ἐπήρου· βούλομαι δέ σοι, τέκνον –
φρονεῖς γὰρ ἤδη κἀποσώσαι' ἂν πατρὸς

γνώμας φράσαντος, ἢν θάνω – παραινέσαι
κειμήλι' ἐσθλὰ καὶ νέοισι χρήσιμα.
βραχεῖ δὲ μύθωι πολλὰ συλλαβὼν ἐρῶ.

It is right that you should ask me this. But, my child, I wish to give you some advice, since you are capable of thought. I am your father, and if I should die, I want you to preserve these precepts that I am telling you now – a treasure-trove of wisdom, fine and useful for young people. I have a lot to say to you, but I shall sum it up succinctly.

Immediately there follow twenty-nine lines containing eight consecutive maxims, ranging widely in subject matter (the importance of showing gentleness and respect to rich and poor alike; the need for decision between alternative courses of action; the excellence of wealth provided that it is justly obtained; the miseries of poverty; the best sort of acquaintances to cultivate; the dangers of corrupt pleasures and shameful desires; the need to curb the activities of wicked men; the undesirability of excessive displays of emotion). Even though we do not have the whole scene from which this speech was taken, the dramatic context is obvious from the content of these lines. Erechtheus, fearing death may be at hand, is taking the opportunity to pass on some fatherly advice before it is too late. Nevertheless, the content of the advice and the form in which it is presented means that the passage naturally lends itself to being excerpted, copied out, memorized and reused in other contexts. Indeed, Erechtheus expressly tells his son – and the reader – that he wishes these lines to be preserved in future. Perhaps we could also make a connection between these lines and another passage from the same play which refers to 'the voice of writing-tablets, in which the wise are celebrated' (δελτῶν ... γῆρυν ἇι σοφοὶ κλέονται, *Erechtheus* F369). Here, too, Euripides seems to be thematizing the written word as a vehicle for the transmission of wisdom – or even, conceivably, referring to books of anthologies.

Erechtheus' prefatory lines contain several of the 'quotation marks' discussed in this chapter, *viz.* the positioning of key verses at the start of a speech, the use of apostrophe as a frame and attention-grabbing device, the authority conveyed by the voice of an older person giving advice to a younger addressee, the explicit labelling of these maxims as *gnomai* (in the specific sense of precepts or wise sayings), and the metapoetic acknowledgement of the self-contained brevity and concision of the maxim as a form of discourse. But the most suggestive feature here is the description of these gnomic verses as a 'treasure-trove' (κειμήλια). This word is more or less synonymous with θησαυρός, the word used by Xenophon and other writers to denote an anthology of selected excerpts.[76]

Euripides could scarcely have made it any clearer that he is offering his readers a ready-made collection of quotations. The fact that these lines (or constituent portions of them) were repeatedly quoted and anthologized by Stobaeus and others is a sign of how successfully Euripides achieved his aim.[77]

Conclusions

Authors are never in complete control of the ways in which their own texts will be interpreted or the uses to which they will be put. Nevertheless, they can exert influence on their readers and give them a helping hand. One of the central arguments of this book is that Euripides participated actively in the process of his own reception by deliberately highlighting verses as suitable for quotation. In this chapter, I have tried to show exactly how he set about to achieve this aim through the design and verbal texture of his work, with specific reference to features of form and content that are clearly observable either on the page or in performance. Such features are equivalent in their function to speech marks, inverted commas or other similar signals. They act as a 'frame', they give extra emphasis to edifying sentiments and well-shaped expressions, and they help readers to pick out some of the best lines for use in other contexts. Each of the features discussed above works in a different way within its context, and the degree to which the quotations stand out against their background varies from case to case. Some of these 'quotation marks' are extremely prominent and unmistakable, while some draw attention to themselves more subtly. Perhaps not all of them will have been equally clearly recognized by readers. But it is the cumulative effect of all of these features, I suggest, that makes them so striking, together with the fact that Euripides, in contrast to other tragedians, uses them so frequently and so consistently throughout his work. Undoubtedly Euripides wanted to be quoted.

3

How to Quote from Books You Haven't Read

When ancient writers made use of Euripidean quotations in their work, what exactly were they quoting from? This may seem to be a straightforward question, but it is surprisingly difficult to answer. This chapter approaches the problem by looking specifically at quotations of tragedies that are now lost. It asks how much these book-fragments can tell us about the textual knowledge of those who quoted them or the exact sources from which they were quoted.

The title of the chapter is a nod to Pierre Bayard's *Comment parler des livres que l'on n'a pas lus?* (*How to Talk about Books You Haven't Read*), in which it is argued that literary or cultural knowledge is essentially a form of social display based on rhetorical self-projection and pretence. According to Bayard, few if any readers ever fully know or understand a work of literature: we typically rely on a variable mixture of first-hand knowledge, second-hand descriptions, critical opinions that we have heard other people expressing and our own unreliable perceptions and memories. Even if we have read a book attentively, we are unlikely to recall its contents in their entirety, and our own interpretation of it is bound to differ from that of other readers. Indeed, any two given readers of a book may differ from one another so widely in their understanding or recollection of it that it is possible to question whether they know 'the same' book at all:

> We do not retain in memory complete books identical to the books remembered by everyone else, but rather fragments surviving from partial readings, frequently fused together and further recast by our own private fantasies ... This process involves both the disappearance and the blurring of references, and transforms books, often reduced to their titles or to a few approximate pages, into dim shadows gliding along the surface of our consciousness.[1]

Bayard is knowingly exaggerating in order to make his point that *unreading* would be a more apt term than *reading* to describe this process, but he is right to say that literary knowledge is often fragmentary and incomplete. He also makes the valid observation that the intellectual content of our own personal reflections on books we have read differs very little from the accumulated mass of opinion about books that we have not read.[2] In other words, our knowledge of books that we have read may be no less shadowy than our acquired impressions of books that we have merely heard about.

Even though he has nothing to say about quotation as a distinct activity in itself, Bayard provides a suggestive starting point for our discussion here because of his insight that 'it is not even the book that is received, but those fragments of the book that circulate in every conversation or written commentary and come to substitute for it in its absence'.[3] It seems clear that quotations of extracts – along with titles, stray plot details, random recollections and assorted critical comments – constitute part of the haphazard baggage that passes for literary knowledge. To the majority of people, *whether or not they have first-hand knowledge of the texts*, literary works are just repositories of 'fragments' of this sort. This means that 'knowing Euripides' is often tantamount to knowing a few key quotations and other snippets. It also means that one does not need to know a play directly in order to quote from it. One can very easily quote from books that one has never read.

We should never automatically assume, whenever we encounter a reference or a verbatim quotation from Euripides in another text, that the quoting author had first-hand knowledge of the play in question. It is theoretically possible that the later author was relying on his memory of a performance which he had personally attended, or that he was able to consult the script in book form. But it is equally possible that he never watched the play and never saw a copy of the text. Perhaps all of his quotations are really quotations of quotations, culled from intermediate sources such as anthologies, commentaries or other scholarly works. Or perhaps it is unnecessary to see quotations as deriving from texts at all, rather than from the medium of orality, performance and shared cultural memory. It may be that texts of nearly all Euripides' plays survived for many centuries after their first appearance, but alternatively it may be that some of the plays were already lost (or obsolescent, or obscure, or hard to track down) at the time of citation. It is unclear how long any of the plays remained available in book form, or how widely they ever circulated in the form of complete scripts as opposed to selected extracts. Should we assume as a general principle that the later a source is, the less likely it is that the quotation is first-hand? Perhaps so, but there is no basis for such an assumption apart from probability or common sense. It is sometimes thought that readers and scholars up to the Hellenistic period, at least, would have been able to access a wide range of fifth-century literature in its original form, whereas later writers such as Plutarch, Athenaeus or Stobaeus would have been more likely to rely on secondary citations, but in the absence of firm evidence it is impossible to prove this.[4] Even in cases where a playscript did survive in full, in some library or other, it is not clear how many readers (at any period you care to mention) would have gone to the effort of locating the book in its dusty recess and laboriously unrolling it in the hope of finding the right verse, rather than consulting a handy *aide-mémoire*.

A 'minimalist' approach

Since we are not in a position to ask any of these ancient authors about their sources of knowledge, no definite conclusions are possible. It is up to each individual reader how much credulity or scepticism they wish to adopt in relation to the question. It would be theoretically possible to adopt a radically sceptical or 'minimalist' approach and to argue that none of those who quoted Euripides ever had a full text of the play to hand.

Certainly there are several categories of citation which seem to imply only minimal acquaintance with the text being quoted. All of the most frequently encountered types of quotation – the maxim (*gnome*), the opening line (*incipit*) and the lexicographic fragment (maybe consisting of a single word or phrase) – seem inherently likely to have circulated independently of their source text. Furthermore, the manner in which these quotations are handled within other texts can also suggest that the quoting authors were not dealing with complete works of literature.

As already observed in Chapter 1, maxims in particular are designed to be excerptable and free-floating; they require no knowledge of the play as a whole, and those who cite them almost never treat them as lines spoken by a specific character in a specific situation. Those who quote Euripidean maxims regularly do so without giving the name of the play to which they originally belonged, and perhaps they were unaware of this information. Since maxims are typically treated as the poet's own personal thoughts, attribution to an author-figure is generally more of a concern than attribution to a specific play.

All the same, quoting authors often betray an indifference to the origin of the quotation. Many gnomic verses are misassigned; many are attributed to more than one author. Aulus Gellius (*Attic Nights* 13.19) openly acknowledges that attribution of quotations was often contested, and he illustrates the problem with reference to *Ino* F413 and other disputed lines by Aeschylus, Sophocles and

Euripides. Other examples abound: *Antiope* F198 is variously attributed to Euripides and Epicharmus; *Meleager* F529 circulated in different anthologies as the work of Euripides or Menander or Philemon; a much cited extract from *Danae* (F324) was misattributed to *Bellerophon* when it was translated into Latin by Seneca (*Epistle* 115.14); Stobaeus' anthology often includes the same gnomic quotations more than once, with contradictory attributions on each occasion (e.g. F326, cited as from *Danae* but also *Hecuba*, or *Philoctetes* F789a, attributed in different sections either to Euripides or to Sophocles) – and so on (a full catalogue would be very long and tedious). Authors sometimes seem unaware that they are quoting continuous extracts, since consecutive lines may be broken up and presented as several separate 'quotations' rather than as a single passage.[5] In cases where Euripides wrote more than one play with the same title (e.g. *Hippolytus, Melanippe, Phrixus, Alcmeon*), there is often some ambiguity concerning exactly which of the plays is being cited.[6] Authors might quote an extract without making it clear which play they are quoting from, or whether they even knew that there existed more than one homonymous work. Sometimes we even see traces of scholarly discussions and disagreements about whether or not a quotation was taken from a specific text – as in the case of the phrase Λικυμνίαις βολαῖς ('Licymnian thunderbolts'), which is quoted by Aristophanes in his comedy *Birds*. The ancient commentators on the *Birds* passage fail to reach agreement on precisely what the phrase means or where it originally appeared: did it feature in Euripides' *Licymnius* or in some other play, and who spoke the words?[7] The very fact that this scholarly dispute could take place at all shows that these scholars did not have a text of *Licymnius* in front of them in order to check the quotation's source.

A 'maximalist' approach

Another way of approaching the problem is by examining the form or content of quotations and attempting to judge on this basis whether they are inherently more likely to come from complete texts. Can we identify any examples of quotations which might plausibly be seen as deriving from direct access to the *Urtext*? As far as I can ascertain, there is no way of conclusively proving that an author is quoting directly from a text. However, there are certain categories of quotation or testimonia which in theory *might* be taken to imply knowledge of the entire work, or which (at least) might seem to indicate the quoter's familiarity with a greater portion of the work than the extract being quoted.

Sometimes an **accompanying testimonium**, in the form of a descriptive paraphrase or a critical comment of some sort, can be more revealing than a verbatim quotation. For instance, one anonymous marginal commentator on *Hippolytus* makes a detailed comparison between the plots and choruses of *Hippolytus* and *Alexandros*, showing knowledge of the respective plays' structures and the interrelationship of individual scenes.[8] The *Art of Rhetoric* attributed to Dionysius of Halicarnassus quotes a mere two lines from *Melanippe the Wise* but situates them within a discussion of the speech from which they were extracted and the plot of the play as a whole.[9] The Byzantine scholar Johannes Tzetzes not only quotes some choral verses from *Alcmeon in Corinth* but also recognizes them as the opening lines of the *parodos*.[10] The first-century AD rhetorician Dio of Prusa demonstrates his knowledge of Euripides' *Philoctetes* via a mixture of quotation, paraphrase and direct comparison of that play with homonymous tragedies by Aeschylus and Sophocles.[11] The Jewish philosopher Philo of Alexandria, writing in the first century BC, had enough knowledge of Euripides' satyr play *Syleus* to be able to supply the dramatic context and speaker attribution for the five quotations that he discusses in his work *Every Good Man is Free*.[12] The geographer Strabo, writing at about the same period, preserves part of the prologue from Euripides' *Phaethon* (*Geography* 1.2.27 = *Phaethon* F771) along with interpretative background information displaying more knowledge than the quotation itself contains. Elsewhere, Strabo presents a mixture of description, quotation and paraphrase of a Euripidean scene (probably from *Temenus* or *Temenidae*) in a topographic discussion of Laconia (*Geography* 8.5.6); the way in which this long passage intersperses seven consecutive quotations with summary of lines *not* quoted may seem to suggest that Strabo had the full text at hand, though it is slightly suspicious that he does not cite the play's title.[13] Any of these (somewhat miscellaneous) examples, from a variety of periods and contexts, *could* hint at extensive textual knowledge on the part of the quoter. Whenever a citing author provides information that could not have been extrapolated from the quotation itself, it is worth entertaining the possibility that this information comes direct from the source text, even if we can imagine alternative explanations.

Plutarch is a good example of a writer who quotes extensively from poetry and drama but not necessarily on the basis of first-hand acquaintance with the texts: his sources and research methods are generally hard to discern.[14] Sometimes the way in which he uses quotations – for instance, by omitting attributions or serially quoting the same passages in different works – might suggest that he is drawing on secondary sources, but at other times his citational practice may indicate a closer engagement with the source text. When Plutarch in his essay *On Eating Meat* (998e) quotes a line from Euripides' *Cresphontes* (F456), he includes a description of the exact moment in the play when the line was spoken, not only providing the name of the speaker but also giving a sense of the on-stage action and even its thrilling effect on the theatre audience. Indeed, Plutarch has a recurrent interest in pinpointing specific moments of interest in performance and in thinking about drama from the perspective of the audience.[15] We can compare his anecdotes and comments on the reception of other Euripidean plays, such as *Aeolus* (discussed below, p. XXX), *Melanippe the Wise* (where he reports that the play's original opening line so offended the spectators that Euripides was forced to alter it) or *Ixion* (where Plutarch claims that Euripides was compelled to defend himself against accusations of immorality).[16] But it is unclear whether Plutarch is reflecting specific occasions during Euripides' lifetime or his own, or what his sources might have been if he is reporting genuine historical incidents. These intriguing testimonia, combining quotations with anecdotes, do at first glance give the impression that they rely on background knowledge about the plays and their author, but it is still possible that Plutarch lifted this information wholesale from some other source, such as an earlier biographical or critical work. (For further discussion of the combination of quotation, anecdote and quasi-biographical material in ancient scholarship, see Chapter 7.)

Obscure or recondite quotations in ancient scholarship sometimes stand out as a distinct category. In a number of manuscripts, we encounter scholia, i.e. unattributable marginal comments which preserve the remnants of ancient scholarship on the transmitted text. The scholiasts' typical method for commenting on a verse or phrase from a play is to quote another passage that compares or contrasts with it in some way.[17] For example, one of the scholia on Euripides' *Medea* 693 (τί χρῆμα δράσας; φράζε μοι σαφέστερον, 'by doing what? Tell me more clearly') notes that this unmemorable line is actually a self-quotation by Euripides from his earliest tragedy *Daughters of Pelias*: it would have taken an unusually sharp eye to spot such a recherché parallel.[18] Some of the most interesting examples are found in the scholia to Aristophanes, where obscure Euripidean allusions are identified and parodies illuminated by reference to the original tragic text on which they are based.[19] Sometimes, we find one scholar correcting another in a way that suggests superior knowledge or more reliable research methods – such as the Aristophanic scholiast who identifies what he calls an 'obscure' parody of Euripides' *Oeneus* at *Acharnians* 471-2 and adds: 'but Symmachus says this is taken from *Telephus*' (πεπαρῳδῆται ἀσήμως ἐξ Οἰνέως Εὐριπίδου· ὁ δὲ Σύμμαχος καὶ ἐκ Τηλέφου φησίν).[20]

Many of these parallel quotations show a wide knowledge of literature. Commentaries of this sort represent the painstaking labours of early critics who were well versed in Greek drama but who also, crucially, had the means of substantiating their sources and comparing one text with another. Certainly many of these anonymous marginalia derive from Alexandrian scholarship – the oldest ones demonstrably contain material from Aristophanes of Byzantium and Didymus – though it is often impossible to pin down any scholion to a definite date.[21] As Donald Mastronarde observes in a recent survey of the Euripidean scholia, 'we have no idea ... how many stages of anonymous adaptation, filtering and compilation our corpus went through between the second century BC and what we find in the minuscule manuscripts over eight hundred years later'.[22] All the same, whether the material in the margins is early or late in origin, it is obvious that whoever *first* identified these quotations had access to an ample collection of books.

Repeated citation or discussion of certain tragedies sometimes suggests that the works in question were popular for many centuries and remained available to readers. The fact that several ancient writers apparently had access to complete texts may increase the likelihood that other quoting authors did as well. Euripides' *Antiope* is one such work. Some of its surviving book-fragments come from Plato's *Gorgias*, which incorporates plentiful quotation alongside paraphrase and extended critical discussion of the play's content.[23] While it is not very surprising that a fourth-century BC Athenian would have been able to consult a complete script of *Antiope*, it is notable that later authors (including Longinus, Dio of Prusa, Olympiodorus and the scholiasts on *Gorgias*) also quote verses from the play in a way that implies a wider knowledge of its plot and themes.[24] The later sources do not cite exclusively those verses that are found in *Gorgias*, thus suggesting that they had independent knowledge. It may be, of course, that Plato's own influence was a factor in the continuing availability of the play. It may also be that later adaptations or translations of Euripides' plays would have further increased their accessibility to readers. Cicero, writing about Latin dramas based on Greek originals, indicates that Euripides' *Antiope* was still available to be 'enjoyed' alongside the *Antiopa* of Pacuvius, and he implies that some of his contemporaries admired Euripides while professing a contempt for their own Roman literature.[25]

The majority of the Euripidean quotations which we encounter in ancient literature take the form of aphorisms, which are likely to have entered circulation as autonomous short texts because of their inherent 'quotationality'. But other sorts of quotation, by contrast, do not naturally lend themselves to decontextualized excerption. These might be called **'non-quotational' fragments**: i.e. the sort of verse or phrase that might be cited for its information content, or to illustrate a point, rather than to be a 'quotable quote' in its own right.[26] Because such extracts are not especially memorable or complete in themselves, it may be thought more likely that a quoting author would require direct access to a text in order to refresh his memory or check the details.

Such passages might include *Meleager* F530, part of a narrative of the Calydonian boar-hunt, quoted by Macrobius to illustrate the footwear worn by the Aetolian hunters (*Saturnalia* 5.18.17); or *Antiope* F221, an incomplete sentence about the death of Dirce, quoted by Longinus as an example of word order and rhythm (*On the Sublime* 40.4); or *Bellerophon* F310, the dying words of Bellerophon, quoted by Aelian apropos of the songs that swans reportedly sing when close to death (*Nature of Animals* 5.34); or *Cretans* F472, a choral passage about the Cretan cult of Zeus Idaios, quoted by Porphyry as an example of vegetarianism (*On Abstinence from Animal Foods* 4.19). Illustrative citations of this type do not always include complete phrases, which suggests that the factual content is more important than any other aspect of the passage in question, though these authors often quote more than is strictly necessary for the purposes of illustration.

In this category, we might be tempted to place *Philoctetes* F797. This is a four-line extract from a speech cited by the author of *Rhetoric to Alexander* (probably the fourth-century BC orator Anaximenes of Lampsacus) as an illustration of the rhetorical device known as *antiprokatalepsis*, whereby the speaker refutes a challenge by an opponent who has anticipated his own line of argument in advance:[27]

κέχρηται δὲ καὶ Εὐριπίδης ἐν Φιλοκτήτῃ τεχνικῶς τούτῳ τῷ εἴδει διὰ τοῦδε·
   λέξω δ' ἐγώ, κἂν μου διαφθείρας δοκῇ
   λόγους ὑποφθάς, αὐτὸς ἠδικηκέναι·
   ἀλλ' ἐξ ἐμοῦ γὰρ τ' ἅμα †μαθήσῃ κλύων,
   ὁ δ' αὐτὸς αὑτὸν †ἐμφανιεῖ σοι λέγων.
ταῖς μὲν οὖν προκαταλήψεσιν ὡς δεῖ χρῆσθαι καὶ πρὸς τοὺς κριτὰς καὶ πρὸς τοὺς ἐναντίους, ἴσμεν διὰ τούτων.

Euripides has skilfully used this figure of speech in his *Philoctetes,* as follows: 'I shall speak for myself, even if he may seem to have done me an injustice by anticipating my argument and ruining it. Well, you will understand my case when you have heard it, and *he* will set out his own case clearly when he speaks for himself.' Thus from this example we know how we ought to employ the device of anticipation in relation both to the jurors and to our opponents.

The verses in question are quoted purely to illustrate a specific use of language, but they are not naturally memorable or remarkable in their content. Their original function was purely prefatory; the more interesting speech that would have followed them is not preserved. The fact that the quoting author does not mention the speaker or the dramatic context of the quoted speech is not necessarily a significant factor, since these details are irrelevant for his purposes. It may be thought that the author would not have been able to come up with illustrative material of this sort without having to search through a complete text of *Philoctetes*. But on the other hand, it is also possible that the lines were taken from some other source such as a school handbook or a collection of rhetorical models. We can point to other similar snippets from Euripidean speeches that were repeatedly used to furnish examples of specific figures or argumentative tactics – such as *Phoenix* F812 (a 'non-quotational' extract from the *agon* between Phoenix and Amyntor), which was quoted by Aeschines but also by many subsequent rhetoricians who followed his lead, no doubt cutting and pasting the same quotation from Aeschines rather than consulting the original speech for themselves.[28] Even though we have no comparable examples of serial re-quotation of the *Philoctetes* passage, it may be that during the fourth century BC it was already being cited as a standard example by teachers of rhetoric.

Longer quotations constitute a further category of extract (whether 'quotational' or 'non-quotational' in form). Most of the quotations/fragments that are attested consist of a small handful of easily memorized lines – or often just a single line – but more extensive passages from speeches are also encountered. Such examples are, admittedly, very rare. From the lost plays of Euripides we have just a tiny handful of book-fragments that consist of more than a dozen consecutive verses. These are a thirty-one-line extract of Bellerophon's opening monologue from *Stheneboea* (quoted by the Byzantine scholar Ioannes Logothetes), a twenty-two-line extract from the prologue of *Melanippe the Wise* (also quoted by Ioannes Logothetes), two speeches by the title character of *Bellerophon* expressing 'atheistic' views (quoted by Stobaeus and in the treatise *On Monarchy* attributed to St Justin Martyr), a fifty-five-line speech by Praxithea from *Erechtheus* (quoted by the fourth-century orator Lycurgus), the thirty-four-line 'anthology fragment' from *Erechtheus* (quoted by the anthologist Stobaeus); and, from unidentified plays, a thirteen-line description of Aphrodite's cosmogonic powers (quoted by Athenaeus), a thirteen-line necromantic prayer to Zeus or Hades (quoted by Clement of Alexandria) and a sixteen-line speech about marital relationships (quoted by Stobaeus).[29] One notes that these quoting writers vary widely in date and origin.

When they quoted these substantial extracts, did they need to have the full text of the play open in front of them in order to do so? This is a plausible scenario, but it cannot be proved. Alternatively, it is possible that whole speeches were excerpted and circulated in anthologies;[30] we also have evidence that some tragic speeches were memorized in their entirety for educational or recreational purposes.[31]

Just as scarce as long quotations are **quotations from scenes of dialogue**. Almost all quoted passages represent the words of a single speaker. From all the book-fragments of the lost Euripides, I can identify only the following dialogue extracts with more than one speaker: *Alexandros* F45 (Stobaeus 4.49.8); *Alcmeon* F78a (Photius A448); *Andromeda* F129-129a (Diogenes Laertius 4.29); *Auge* F271 (Stobaeus 4.47.1) and 271b (Stobaeus 3.22.7); *Bellerophon* F304a (Aristotle, *Nicomachean Ethics* 1136a13); *Oeneus* F565 (Σ Aristophanes, *Frogs* 71); *Scyrians* F682 (Sextus Empiricus, *Against the Experts* 1.308); *Hypsipyle* F752k.20-21 and incert. fab. F1069 (Plutarch, *Moralia* 20d). We might naturally assume that dialogue portions, being harder to memorize as self-contained units and harder to make sense of when wrenched from their context, are more likely to have been taken from a complete text. This may indeed be true, but it is striking that all the dialogue extracts that we possess are extremely brief: either two or three lines, with just one change of speaker in each case. Tellingly, there is not a single example of sustained quotation from a conversational exchange between different characters. It is also striking that most of the quoting authors in these cases do not even acknowledge that the lines quoted are split between two speakers; it often requires the efforts of modern editors to identify the lines as separate utterances.

On balance, then, even though in theory we can identify several types of extract which have a higher than average probability of being first-hand quotations, in practice every single example *could* nonetheless have been taken from a secondary source.

The portable *Aeolus*

In this section, I examine all the surviving book-fragments from a single Euripidean tragedy, *Aeolus*. This play centred on the incestuous love-affair of Macareus and Canace, two of the children of Aeolus (to whom the gods had granted control of the winds).[32] Dramatic fragments tend to be treated primarily as evidence for the themes of lost plays, or as a basis for plot reconstruction; but here I want to examine these fragments specifically *as quotations*, with particular reference to the quoting authors, their habits of citation and their possible sources. Almost any fragmentary play might have been selected for this purpose, but *Aeolus* serves especially well as an illustration of our difficulties: it is cited relatively often by writers from different periods, and it furnishes examples of several different types of quotation. In each case I discuss salient properties of the fragment as a quotation, and I attempt to judge the likelihood that the quoting writer had the full text of the play in front of him.

F13a: The first line of the play (as in the case of *Stheneboea*, discussed in Chapter 1) consisted of a gnomic statement, which was detached and preserved in a fifth-century AD collection of maxims:[33]

ἦ πολλὰ καὶ δύσγνωστα βουλεύει θεός.

Verily the god's designs are manifold and inscrutable.

The *Florilegium* of Orion included this quotation without attributing it to a specific tragedy, and in early editions of Euripidean fragments it appeared among the remains of unidentified plays. Nevertheless, a second-century AD papyrus first published in 1962, containing the remains of a hypothesis to the play, revealed that the quotation was the opening line of *Aeolus*:[34]

Αἴολος, οὗ [ἀρ]χή·
ἦ δεινὰ καὶ δύσγνωστα βουλ[εύει θεός
ἡ δὲ ὑπόθεσις·

Aeolus, of which the opening is, 'Verily the god's designs are terrible and inscrutable,' and the plot-summary is as follows...

Euripidean hypotheses often helpfully include the first line of the play in question, which they typically quote using the formula [*Title*], οὗ ἀρχή, as in this case.[35] This looks like valuable information, but it is also slightly problematic, since the quotation in the hypothesis is different from the version given by Orion. Did one of these authors misquote the verse? If so, which is correct? Kannicht in *TrGF* prints the version in the papyrus, judging this more likely to be the correct version. There are several reasons why this is so, but it is impossible to be certain. Neither variant (πολλά, 'many', or δεινά, 'terrible') seems inherently better than the other or more likely to have been substituted for the other. The papyrus predates Orion by some centuries, but earlier sources are not necessarily better than later ones. We might reasonably suppose that any author of a hypothesis would need access to a text of the play in order to make an accurate summary of its plot, but this cannot be taken for granted, and in general very little is known about who wrote these hypotheses or what their sources were. It could be that either author got the quotation slightly wrong, or that they were quoting from memory rather than direct access to the text, or that the quotation in either version was accidentally altered in transmission when copied out. Alternatively, it could be that neither author really got it wrong. It is possible that during antiquity, especially in the period before the establishment of a standard text by Alexandrian scholars, the text of *Aeolus* circulated haphazardly in multiple editions with slight variants. Indeed, we can point to other examples of Euripidean tragedies for which the opening verses are quoted inconsistently by different authors, each under the impression that their version was the authentic one.[36]

F14 in Kannicht's edition is a narrative testimonium rather than a quotation. The first-century geographer Strabo, writing about the river Enipeus in Thessaly, discusses the mythical Salmoneus (the father of Tyro) and happens to mention *en passant* that in Euripides' *Aeolus* Salmoneus reigned in Salmone, the region adjacent to the river. This small piece of information is of a sort that might typically feature in a 'scene-setting' Euripidean prologue speech; but it is also the sort of fact that could have been picked up second-hand from any scholarly work, and it does not require any detailed knowledge of the Euripidean play itself. The vagueness of the reference together with the absence of verbatim quotation makes it seem unlikely that Strabo had the text of *Aeolus* in front of him (though it should be noted that Strabo does quote Euripides elsewhere, indicating that he had a good general knowledge of that author).[37]

F15 consists of a generalization that originally appeared in the mouth of Aeolus:

ἴδοιμι δ' αὐτῶν ἔκγον' ἄρσεν' ἀρσένων·
πρῶτον μὲν εἶδος ἄξιον τυραννίδος·
πλείστη γὰρ ἀρετή τοῦθ' ὑπάρχον ἐν βίωι,
τὴν ἀξίωσιν τῶν καλῶν τὸ σῶμ' ἔχειν.

> I wish to see them produce offspring, male children from the male line! The most important thing is a fine appearance, worthy of royalty; for excellence in life is greatest when supported by this, a body worthy of noble qualities.

All four lines were included in Stobaeus' anthology (4.21.1) under the heading 'On Beauty'. The same passage was repeatedly cited by other writers throughout antiquity and well into the Byzantine era (including Athenaeus, Porphyry, the Homeric commentator Eustathius and the encyclopaedist Photius): it evidently acquired the status of a commonplace, apt to be trotted out whenever one was talking about physical beauty in relation to other human attributes.[38] It seems likely that the quotation regularly featured in anthologies arranged by theme, and that all of these quoting authors came across it in such a setting. Apart from Stobaeus and Athenaeus, no one who quotes this *gnome* ever attributes it to Euripides. This shows that it was mostly treated as a free-standing proverb rather than a portion of a specific play. (If they *had* known that the quotation came from *Aeolus,* and that it originally related to the generation of offspring via brother-sister incest, perhaps they would not have been so keen on it.) Everyone except Stobaeus omits the first line, which is more context-specific than the remainder, and some of the citing authors selectively include or omit other parts of lines 2 to 4. This shows that 'the quotation' circulated in different versions and did not always take the same shape.

F16: another *gnome.* Stobaeus quotes three verses, under the thematic heading, 'On Those Who Are Powerful in Politics':

λαμπροὶ δ' ἐν αἰχμαῖς Ἄρεος ἔν τε συλλόγοις,
μή μοι τὰ κομψὰ ποικίλοι γενοίατο,
ἀλλ' ὧν πόλει δεῖ μεγάλα βουλεύοντες εὖ

May they shine both in military combat and in debate – and please don't let them be clever at glib speeches, but rather prudent counsellors in respect to great matters that the city needs.

Presumably the speaker was Aeolus (as in F15), expressing his hopes for fine descendants, though this cannot be known for certain. Centuries earlier, the same passage was quoted by Aristotle in the *Politics* (3.1277a19) apropos of the type of education befitting those who will become rulers:

τὴν παιδείαν δ' εὐθὺς ἑτέραν εἶναι λέγουσί τινες ἄρχοντος, ὥσπερ καὶ φαίνονται οἱ τῶν βασιλέων υἱεῖς ἱππικὴν καὶ πολεμικὴν παιδευόμενοι, καὶ Εὐριπίδης φησὶ '**μή μοι τὰ κόμψ', ἀλλ' ὧν πόλει δεῖ**', ὡς οὖσάν τινα ἄρχοντος παιδείαν.

Some people, indeed, argue that the education of a leader should be different from that of others, just as we see the sons of kings being trained in horsemanship and military exercises, and as Euripides says, '**not glib speeches, please, but what the city needs**' – implying that there exists a particular kind of education for a ruler.

The fact that Aristotle truncates the quotation, together with the way in which he incorporates it into his own argument, suggests that he expects his readers to know it already: he is merely reminding them of a passage that they can call to mind and fill in the missing words for themselves. But whether the passage was familiar as part of a speech from *Aeolus* or as a free-standing quotation (i.e. a gnomic commonplace on the popular theme of words *versus* deeds) is impossible to say. We might assume that a writer as erudite as Aristotle, working in the fourth-century BC, will have known Euripides' play at first hand, but it is still possible that Aristotle (along with his readers) encountered the quotation via the medium of rhetorical education and anthologies of useful extracts.

F17-18: a couple of short sections from a choral passage. Such 'non-quotational', non-iambic fragments are thin on the ground. These examples are preserved by a scholiast commenting on Aristophanes' parody of the Euripidean lines at *Peace* 114-19: the original lines are quoted for purposes of comparison with the comic version. The date of the scholia is (as usual) hard to determine. Whoever first noted these parallels – perhaps a scholar working in the Library of Alexandria – must have had access to the text of *Aeolus* to identify the source of the parody, but all subsequent commentators will have been able to copy and paste the same references repeatedly without going back to the *Urtext*.

F19: τί δ' αἰσχρόν, ἢν μὴ τοῖσι χρωμένοις δοκῆι; ('What is shameful, if it does not seem shameful to those who practise it?') This knowingly outrageous line, probably spoken by Macareus in an attempt to defend his incestuous passion for Canace, became notorious.[39] It is decidedly not the sort of line that would normally appear in a collection of edifying extracts, but it was frequently quoted out of context as an illustration of the principle of moral relativity, or as evidence of Euripides' own immorality. The Hellenistic poet and dramatist Machon (F402-10 Gow), relating a fictional encounter between Euripides and a Corinthian courtesan called Lais, included the line as a typical example of the sort of thing that Euripides might have said, but he made Lais quote it back at its author to excuse her own bad behaviour: thus Euripides is seen to receive an appropriate payback for having conceived of such a shocking sentiment in the first place. Stobaeus does preserve the line in his anthology, but he also provides an accompanying anecdote (attributed to another scholar, Serenus) in order to distance himself from the quotation by conveying the effect that it originally produced. We are told that Plato, having watched the play, went to meet Euripides and exclaimed: 'Oh, Euripides! What is shameful is shameful, whether it seems so or not!' (αἰσχρὸν τό γ' αἰσχρόν, κἂν δοκῇ κἂν μὴ δοκῇ).[40] The anecdote is of dubious historical authenticity, but it is valuable in that it constitutes a form of critical comment on the content of the utterance. It also shows us that this quotation was regarded as shocking, not just at the time of its original airing in the theatre but for centuries afterwards.

A similar impression is given by another quoting author, Plutarch, who includes this notorious line in his essay *How the Young Man Should Study Poetry* (33c).[41] Once again, the quotation is framed within a quasi-historical anecdote designed to illustrate its effect on the theatre audience, and once again an earlier scholar is cited as the source. Plutarch is praising the Peripatetic scholar Antisthenes for his habit of emending texts whenever he did not approve of their moral content:

ὁ μὲν εὖ μάλα τοὺς Ἀθηναίους ἰδὼν θορυβήσαντας ἐν τῷ θεάτρῳ 'τί δ' αἰσχρὸν εἰ μὴ τοῖσι χρωμένοις δοκεῖ;' παραβάλλων εὐθὺς 'αἰσχρὸν τό γ' αἰσχρόν, κἂν δοκῇ κἂν μὴ δοκῇ'.

Antisthenes, observing that the Athenians had reacted with outrage when the line 'What is shameful, if it does not seem shameful to those who practise it?' was heard in the theatre, immediately replaced it with 'What is shameful is shameful, whether it seems so or not.'

One of the most interesting features of Plutarch's citation is that he gives us exactly the same 'improved' version that we find in Stobaeus, but each author attributes it to a different source. Who was actually responsible for the emended version? Was it Plato, Antisthenes, or someone else? Who first recorded – or invented – the anecdote? It cannot have been Serenus, nor can it have been Antisthenes, if Plutarch is right to imply that Antisthenes himself came across the story in an earlier source. Can any of these scholars have had access to authentic details of the reactions of fifth-century spectators in the theatre? These questions are impossible to answer. But the testimony of Plutarch and Stobaeus makes it obvious that scholars throughout the centuries kept repeating the same quotation and kept interpreting it in the same sort of way. Furthermore, it is obvious that these scholars' habits of citation and source attribution were far from rigorous. For their purposes, it does not really matter where the anecdote comes from. Nor does it even seem to matter where the quotation itself comes from, since none of them acknowledges that it was originally a line from *Aeolus*. It seems likely that the notorious quotation was transmitted along with the explanatory anecdote, and sometimes with its inoffensive alternative version, but altogether independently of its play.

Perhaps one of the main reasons why 'F19' became so famous is that it featured in an Aristophanic comedy: *Frogs*, first produced in 405 BC. Here, as so often elsewhere, the comic genre draws attention to quotations and other features of tragedy by parodying them, but it also functions as a medium for popularizing or 'classicizing' the works of Euripides.[42] In *Frogs*, Euripides appears as one of the characters, and at one point he complains to Dionysus that he has been made to undergo 'shameful' sufferings. Dionysus replies by firing back at Euripides his own line, with one significant alteration:

τί δ' αἰσχρόν, ἢν μὴ τοῖς θεωμένοις δοκῆι;

What is shameful, if it does not seem shameful to *the spectators*?

Frogs 1475

The humour relies on the same sort of assumptions that were made by Machon (in the passage cited above) – i.e. that any line from tragedy can be quoted as evidence of its author's real-life character and opinions, that the author of such an immoral sentiment deserves some form of punishment, and that quotations can be weaponized in order to win an argument. By the time that Machon was writing, in the third century BC, the quotation was nearly two hundred years old (and clearly still going strong). But even when *Frogs* was staged, the tragedy *Aeolus* was already about twenty years old, if not older. We happen to know this because Aristophanes had already poked fun at *Aeolus* in his earlier comedy *Clouds* (the original version of which premiered in 423 BC), in which one of the characters describes 'a speech from Euripides about a brother screwing his own sister'.[43] In other words, it is possible that Aristophanes in *Frogs* is parodying a verse that was already very well established as a notorious Euripidean saying. In order for the joke to have its full effect, the spectators have to recognize the line as a Euripidean quotation, but Aristophanes does not label it as such. Perhaps there were more spectators who remembered the famous line than who remembered the play from which it came.

F20: This gnomic utterance, spoken by an unknown character, concerns wealth, a very frequent theme of tragic maxims:[44]

μὴ πλοῦτον εἴπηις· οὐχὶ θαυμάζω θεόν,
ὃν χὠ κάκιστος ῥαιδίως ἐκτήσατο.

Do not talk to me of wealth! I do not admire a god whom even the worst sort of person can easily possess.

These lines evidently attained quasi-proverbial status, and they were widely quoted by authors as diverse as Athenaeus, Plutarch, Sextus Empiricus and Gregory of Nazianzus (the fourth-century AD archbishop of Constantinople) to illustrate the evils of money.[45] Of these authors only Athenaeus attributes the quotation to Euripides, though he does not name the play. Stobaeus' anthology includes the quotation in two separate sections, once attributed to

Euripides' *Aeolus* (4.31.61) and once without any attribution (3.3.31). It seems extremely unlikely that any of these quoting authors had first-hand knowledge of the play.

F21: a seven-line gnomic extract, expressing the view that both rich people and poor are necessary for political stability in a city. Stobaeus (4.1.20) quotes all seven lines, attributed to Euripides' *Aeolus*, under the heading 'On Government'. Other authors who cite F21 include only the third and fourth lines (or parts of them). Plutarch cites these same two lines repeatedly in three different works, without giving the play title:[46] this type of serial citation may indicate that the quotation was transmitted via the medium of anthologies, and that Plutarch drew on such sources rather than consulting a full text.

F22: Stobaeus alone (4.31.24) preserves this five-line *gnome* on the subject of money, attributed to Euripides' *Aeolus*. The passage includes a form of direct address (πάτερ, 'O father …'), which is retained as part of the quotation (as in many cases: see discussion in Chapter 2, pp. 41–4). This suggests that the character who originally spoke the lines was one of Aeolus' children, perhaps Macareus. Even though the speaker is criticizing money and urging his father not to take pride in it, Stobaeus includes the quotation under the heading 'Praise of Wealth' – showing that he does not always pay very careful attention to the content of the lines that he quotes.

F23: like F21, this extract is quoted serially by Plutarch in three separate works, perhaps suggesting recurrent recourse to an anthology; the same lines are also preserved by Stobaeus (under the heading 'Criticism of Old Age').[47] In all cases, Euripides is named as the author, but the lines are treated as a proverb rather than a quotation as such. Indeed, the preserved extract does not even represent a complete sentence:

ἀλλ' †ἤ† τὸ γῆρας τὴν Κύπριν χαίρειν ἐᾶι,
ἥ τ' Ἀφροδίτη τοῖς γέρουσιν ἄχθεται

But †either† people say goodbye to sex in old age, and Aphrodite loathes old men …

The textual problem in the first line makes it hard to see exactly what is going on, but essentially this looks like *half* a quotation (the other half of which would have begun 'or …'). The quotation depends for its effect on the readers' being able to fill in the second half of the meaning for themselves; but it is not difficult to do this by logical inference, even if one has no recollection of the original lines from the play.[48] In other words, there is no reason to suppose that anyone who quoted F23 actually knew the end of the sentence from *Aeolus* or expected their readers to do so.

F24: a three-verse gnomic extract on the subject of marriage, included in Stobaeus' anthology (4.22.111) under the heading 'That in marriage the age of bride and groom is an important consideration.' Its subject matter makes it seem likely that it belonged to the same scene or speech as F23, though Stobaeus, following his normal practice, separates the two quotations and presents them in different sections. The early Christian writer Clement of Alexandria (discussed in Chapter 5) also includes the same extract in his *Stromateis* (6.2.8.4), but he shows no awareness of the source of the quotation, and he even runs the lines together with another Euripidean quotation (incert. fab. F914) as if they formed a single continuous passage.

F24a: a lexicographic fragment preserved in Photius' *Lexicon* and other Byzantine encyclopaedias, all of which, presumably, reproduced the same information via serial citation, without any need to consult the original source text. The fragment – or perhaps 'testimonium', since it may not actually be a verbatim quotation – consists simply of the information that in *Aeolus* Euripides mentioned an ancient ritual known as 'Hermes' lottery'.

F24b: a four-line maxim on the subject of physical strength *versus* the power of the mind, notable because it comes from a choral ode (unlike the majority of gnomic quotations, which are from iambic dialogue scenes):

ἦ βραχύ τοι σθένος ἀνέρος· ἀλλὰ
    ποικιλίαι πραπίδων
δεινὰ μὲν πόντου χθονίων τ' ὀρέων
δάμναται παιδεύματα.

Verily a man's strength is insubstantial, but by the brilliance of his intellect he tames the terrible offspring of the sea and the mountains upon earth.

The passage is quoted serially by Plutarch in two different works (cf. F21 and F23 above).[49] It also features in the anthology of Stobaeus and other late collections of proverbs, but in these anthologies the quotation appears in a mangled and partly incomprehensible form, lacking the third and fourth lines. On this basis it seems very likely that the quotation was known only as an autonomous extract, and that each successive anthologist cut-and-pasted the same lines, together with the same mistakes, from earlier collections. It also seems that those who compiled or copied out anthologies did not always read the passages that they included in order to check whether they actually made sense.

F25, F26: two further maxims, preserved only by Stobaeus (4.50.38, 4.20.1). The first line of F25 – which is identical to the first line of *Dictys* F333 – is φεῦ φεῦ, παλαιὸς αἶνος ὡς καλῶς ἔχει ('How well the old saying holds true!'). This formula is a typical Euripidean framing device, of a type already discussed in Chapter 2 (see pp. 39–40).

F28: a two-line maxim which self-consciously draws attention to its own form and implicitly praises its own author's powers of expression:

παῖδες, σοφοῦ πρὸς ἀνδρός, ὅστις ἐν βραχεῖ
πολλοὺς καλῶς οἷός τε συντέμνειν λόγους.

My children, it is the mark of a clever man to be able to compress many words well in a brief space.

The lines are slightly misquoted by Stobaeus (3.35.3), in an unmetrical form, but the correct version can be restored from Aristophanes, who also quotes the lines (in *Thesmophoriazusae* 177-8, where he puts them in the mouth of Euripides himself). In Aristophanes' play the quotation is 'invisible' in the sense that it is not identified as an extract from *Aeolus*, and the joke does not rely on the audience's ability to recognize the specific source.[50] The point is that this is just the *kind* of thing that Euripides would say, in a general sense; no knowledge of *Aeolus* in particular is required. Stobaeus, unlike Aristophanes, retains the original speaker's use of apostrophe (παῖδες). Even though this context-specific form of address might be thought to reduce the universalizing force of the maxim, it is very common for quoting authors to include 'quotation marks' of this sort (cf. F22 above).[51]

F29-F38a: eleven further gnomic fragments are preserved by Stobaeus but by no one else. All of them apart from the last (F38a) are clearly labelled as coming from *Aeolus*, but (like all other quotations in Stobaeus' collection) they were almost certainly lifted wholesale from earlier anthologies, and apart from this basic form of reference Stobaeus gives no indication that he knew *Aeolus* as a text in its own right. The attribution of F38a is disputed: it is unclear from the manuscripts of Stobaeus whether the quotation is taken from *Aeolus* or another tragedy (such as *Alope* or *Melanippe*), or whether part of the quotation comes from another play or author entirely.[52]

F40, F41: two lexicographic fragments, each consisting of a single uncommon word that is said to have been used in *Aeolus*. The scholars who cite these words probably took them from earlier works of scholarship. Who spoke these words in the play, and in what context, are irrelevant considerations for the purpose of lexicography; no knowledge of the original text is necessary.

Conclusions

On balance, it seems to me that almost every one of these writers who quoted *Aeolus* could have done so without ever having seen or read that play. Among all the sources discussed above, the only author who both quotes from the play and is demonstrably aware of its plot and characters is Aristophanes. Did anyone else really know Euripides' tragedy? Did any of them still have access to the full text? Perhaps not – and yet they are perfectly happy to quote verses from it and redeploy them for a variety of purposes.

But *Aeolus* is not a unique case: far from it. The book-fragments of other lost Euripidean plays tell the same story (*mutatis mutandis*), while ancient writers' citations of the extant plays also show very similar tendencies.[53] What we see in every case is a consistent pattern of citation, one which requires only minimal knowledge of the whole work being quoted. The only type of reference ever supplied is in the format 'as Euripides says [in *Title of play*]', but in many cases even this basic information is omitted. Almost no one who quotes verses from drama ever records exactly where the quotation came within the play, or gives the name of the character who originally uttered the lines in question. I have been unable to find a single example of an extract or fragment which can be *proved* beyond doubt to have been taken directly from a complete text, but conversely (as we have seen) there are many quotations which undoubtedly did come down at second or third hand from intermediate works of literature.

It seems clear that after their original performances, the complete texts of the plays very soon faded into the background, but selected extracts from them continued to circulate. Anthologies were in widespread use; serial citation of the same extracts was common. Even in contexts where full texts remained available, it was not necessary to consult those texts in order to quote portions of their contents. Within quotation culture, extracts assumed the status and function of autonomous short literary works. These could be transmitted and reproduced entirely separately from the original plays themselves, and they were often mediated through other sources – and, no doubt, through oral repetition and performance. Through the process of reception the tragedies of Euripides were transformed, in effect, into repositories of quotations and miscellaneous recollections.

From our perspective, as twenty-first-century readers leafing through the pages of *Tragicorum Graecorum Fragmenta*, the lost plays of Euripides might appear to be mutilated, ruined, incomplete, sadly reduced to mere compendia of quotations. But is our experience really so different from that of ancient readers? Paradoxical though it may seem, the answer is: probably not.

4

Quotations in the Theatre

Some of our best evidence for the early reception of Euripides comes from the comic theatre. Greek comedy reflects contemporary society and culture in a general sense, but more specifically it is a rampantly intertextual art form. Perhaps more than any other literary genre it can be described as 'a mosaic of quotations' (to use Julia Kristeva's phrase).[1] Much of comedy's energy and humour derive from other literary and dramatic works, through a combination of allusion, quotation, parody, pastiche and other forms of reference. Tragedy was an especially frequent source of material, perhaps because tragedy and comedy were performed at the same festivals and could be regarded either as sibling genres or as rivals. Throughout the fifth and fourth centuries, many comedians incorporated tragic material into their plays, demonstrating a broad theatrical knowledge and an extraordinarily detailed familiarity with the works of other dramatists. The type of humour on offer might vary from play to play: often it depended on the recognition or transformation of individual words or phrases; sometimes it involved the extended parody of well-known tragic scenes; sometimes caricatures of tragedians themselves might appear among the *dramatis personae*; or sometimes a comedy might even pretend to be a tragedy in its entirety.[2]

Among the tragedians Euripides was by far the most popular, to judge by the number of detectable borrowings from his work in comedy. This trend began in the poet's own lifetime with Aristophanes, who seems to have had something approaching an obsession with Euripides. Aristophanic comedy is characterized by a recurrent, pervasive engagement with Euripides' work, not just in surviving plays such as *Acharnians*, *Peace*, *Thesmophoriazusae* and *Frogs*, but also, apparently, in fragmentary works including *Aeolosikon*, *Heroes*, *Proagon* and *Women Claiming Tent-Sites*. Even within the fifth century this tendency was acknowledged: Aristophanes' rival comedian Cratinus coined a new word, 'Euripidaristophanism', to describe it.[3] More recently it has been recognized that Aristophanes' special brand of comedy depends on Euripidean tragedy while also defining itself in opposition to it.[4] In addition, Aristophanes helped to establish Euripides' reputation by popularizing his work and creating a strong fan base. But Aristophanes was not unique. Other Greek comedians later picked up the baton, and long after his death Euripides remained extremely popular as a source of comic material. Nevertheless, his status and significance gradually changed over time. During the decades from the fifth century to the end of the fourth, Euripides was transformed from a contemporary theatrical figure, one among many, into a venerated classic author of the past.[5]

This elevation to classic status is reflected in several ways, including the frequency with which Euripides' plays were quoted and parodied. Numerous fourth-century comedies share their titles with Euripidean tragedies – such as Strattis' *Phoenician Women*, Anaxandrides' *Erechtheus*, Amphis' *Alcmeon*, Antiphanes' *Aeolus*, Eubulus' *Auge*, Deinolochus' *Telephus* and others. Even though all of these plays are now lost, their titles and fragments suggest paratragic fun and games on a grand scale. Fragments of other fourth-century comedies feature Euripides in ways that suggest that he was held in high esteem. The poet's huge popularity was reflected by Axionicus and Philippides in comedies entitled *Phileuripides* ('The Euripides Fan'); he was addressed as 'dearest Euripides' in a play by Nicostratus (F28) and as 'Golden Euripides' in Diphilus' *Parasite* (F60); his speechwriting skills were singled out for praise by Philemon (F153); and another of Philemon's characters even declared that he would willingly kill himself if this would give him a chance to meet Euripides in the afterlife.[6]

The continued popularity of Euripides as a theme for comic drama shows that his work remained well known among the Athenian public for many decades. His tragedies will have been kept alive through reperformance, through educational study and (we may presume) through the ongoing availability of texts.[7] The decree of Lycurgus in the 330s or 320s BC was instrumental in achieving quasi-canonical status for Euripides, by officially selecting him alongside Aeschylus and Sophocles as the prime exponents of Athenian tragedy and ensuring that authorized copies of his plays were deposited in the state archives.[8] But comedy itself must be seen as an important medium for keeping Euripides in the public eye, both during his own lifetime and even more so in the decades after the fifth century. Comedy does not simply reflect the tragedian's status as a central figure in Greek culture; it actually helps to create and consolidate that status. It also plays a crucial role in perpetuating knowledge and awareness of the plays' content.

Moments at which characters on the comic stage quote extracts from Euripides' plays can be seen as micro-scale reperformances of those works in front of a mass audience. Within their new dramatic setting these quotations might function in different ways. They can vividly but economically evoke the original tragedies via a sort of dramatic shorthand. They can re-enact tiny portions of them and bring their characters momentarily back to life by a process resembling ventriloquism. They can sometimes evoke memories of specific performances by famous actors.[9] They can activate the audience's existing literary knowledge, by inviting them to take part in a game of quotation-spotting and testing their recognition skills. Alternatively, and more simply, they can act as a reminder or a basic source of information, refreshing the audience's memory of half-forgotten tragedies or introducing them to unfamiliar ones.

In this chapter, I examine a variety of fifth- and fourth-century comic scenes in which Euripidean quotations appear. These scenes are discussed from a number of different angles, but above all I am concerned with trying to ascertain how the audience in the theatre responded to all these quotations. Did they always recognize them? If so, what difference did it make to their appreciation of the comedies? How are the quotations repurposed within their new comic setting? What are they doing there, and why were the audience expected to find them funny? These are crucial questions, but they are very difficult to answer. It is impossible to generalize with confidence about the average spectator's existing knowledge or recall of Euripides' work.[10] (This is equally true whether we are thinking of Euripides' contemporaries or of later audiences.) Since we have no direct access to the relevant information, all we can really do is speculate. But what is certain is that the audience at any given performance will have consisted of a diverse range of individuals, not a completely homogeneous mass.[11] I assume that we have to imagine a fairly wide spectrum of literary expertise among the audiences of comedy. Some of these individuals will have been blessed with retentive memories, but by no means all of them. Some will have been dedicated theatregoers, who avidly followed new plays at the major festivals and sought out revivals or smaller-scale productions in the deme theatres, but others will have attended less frequently. Inevitably they will have differed greatly in their level of education: some will have been illiterate, but others (no doubt a minority) will have been well-educated or scholarly individuals with access to texts.[12] Maybe not every spectator detected every single literary allusion or got the point of every single joke. Nevertheless, the comedians, when they devised their plays, were obviously trying to cater for the varying tastes and temperaments of their audiences at different levels. While some of the intertextual humour is relatively complex, depending on a detailed knowledge and recall of literature, many of the jokes require only a superficial familiarity with Euripides and his work: it is not necessary to know the tragedies inside out in order to enjoy these comedies.

'Invisible' quotations

The crucial fact for our purposes is that comedies (at all periods) feature a range of different types of tragic quotation, deployed in significantly different ways. This suggests that they are calling for a variegated range of responses from the audience. One major difference is between what we might call *visible* quotations (those which are explicitly framed as quotations, or clearly labelled as coming from a particular author or text) and *invisible* quotations (those which are not attributed to a particular source, or not even explicitly identified as someone else's words). The former category is easily spotted by anybody, but the latter might easily go undetected. Some of the more recherché quotations might be especially difficult to spot for spectators during a live performance; it could be thought that some of these examples are aimed primarily at a reading audience, since readers are able to pause, reflect and maybe look up an obscure reference in another book if necessary.

Sometimes a comedian might prefer to mix-and-match quotations of both types, by adulterating a parody of one clearly identified tragedy with unacknowledged verses from other sources – as, for example, in Aristophanes' parody of *Bellerophon* in *Peace*, into which 'invisible' quotations from *Aeolus* and *Stheneboea* are interlarded;[13] or in Strattis' paratragic *Phoenician Women*, ostensibly based on Euripides' tragedy of the same name but also including material from *Hypsipyle*;[14] or in Eubulus' *Medea*, which incongruously contains material from *Orestes*.[15] In such cases, it seems likely that there are two different levels of humour in operation: a basic level, which everyone in the audience would be able to appreciate, and a bonus extra level of enjoyment for those able to spot any material lurking in the 'wrong' place.

It is probable that for the average spectator 'invisible' quotations would have been easier to spot if the tragedy being quoted was a recent production, but in this respect it is difficult to discern any pattern in the comedians' habits of citation. Sometimes they make the quotations visible even when the tragedy in question is a new one, as in the case of Aristophanes' clearly labelled parody of *Helen* and *Andromeda* (412 BC) in *Thesmophoriazusae* (411 BC): this suggests that the comedian wished to make sure that everyone got the broad point of the joke, even if the finer details escaped them. But sometimes quotations are inserted invisibly even when the tragedy is decades old, as in the case of Euripides' *Telephus* (438 BC), still being quoted and parodied without attribution in Aristophanes' *Frogs* (405 BC) and in Alexis' *Eisoikizomenos* (mid- to late fourth century). Such cases may suggest that certain plays remained in the repertoire for a very long period, or else that these allusions were detected by an ever smaller number of spectators with each passing year.[16] At any rate, fifth- and fourth-century comedians alike make frequent use of invisible quotations from tragedies of various dates. For example: a maxim from Euripides' *Antigone* (F170) is quoted or parodied by both Aristophanes (*Frogs* 1391) and Archippus (F47); a quotation from *Hippolytus* 415 is silently incorporated into a speech about prostitution in Xenarchus' *Pentathlete* (F4.22); Demeas in Menander's *Samia* (325-6) opens a speech with an unacknowledged quotation from Euripides' *Oedipus* (F554b); a character in Alexis' *Pannychis* (F181) absurdly addresses his drinking cup using a form of address taken from *Medea* 49; Heracles in Eubulus' *Amaltheia* (F6) irrelevantly, and perhaps almost imperceptibly, quotes *Andromache* 369 when extolling the virtues of well-cooked food;[17] another character from Eubulus (*Nannion* F67) slips a line from *Iphigenia at Aulis* (370) into a speech about courtesans; a cook in Philemon's *Soldier* (F82) unexpectedly quotes *Medea* 57 when boasting about his skill in the kitchen; and so on. In all of these examples, apparently, the quotations are incorporated into the everyday speech of the characters without any explicit signal that an act of quotation has taken place. It is hard to say how well known these tragic lines will have been to ordinary spectators in the theatre. In some cases, perhaps, the comedians will have been quoting tragedies that had been reperformed in recent times, but in other cases they will have been relying on distant memory or detailed textual knowledge. Quotations of this sort can be relatively easily detected by any modern scholar sitting in a library, with a pile of commentaries and the *Thesaurus Linguae Graecae* to hand, but I assume that they went over the heads of many audience members.

Eupolis, though in general he seems to have relied less on paratragedy or intertextuality than his rivals, was clearly an aficionado of the 'invisible' quotation.[18] The scrappy remains of his lost comedy *Demes* (c. 417–12 BC) contain three separate examples of Euripidean quotations hidden within scenes of dialogue. In one scene (F106), the character Miltiades spoke the following lines, which happen to be preserved by Longinus as an example of oath-swearing:[19]

οὐ γὰρ μὰ τὴν Μαραθῶνι τὴν ἐμὴν μάχην
χαίρων τις αὐτῶν τοὐμὸν ἀλγυνεῖ κέαρ.

I swear by the Battle of Marathon – *my* battle! – that
not one of them shall pain my heart and get away with it!

What Longinus does not acknowledge – and nor did Eupolis – is that the second of these lines is a quotation from Euripides' *Medea* (398). The line was spoken by

Medea: it originally referred to her faithless husband Jason and his new wife. But Miltiades gives no indication that the line is Euripidean or that it is a quotation at all: it runs on seamlessly from the previous line, and thus Miltiades' own oath and the quotation together form a single utterance. It is not an especially 'quotational' verse; it is not even a complete sentence. Perhaps many of Eupolis' spectators did not even realize that they had just heard a line from *Medea* – in which case, they would not have missed very much. But those who did spot the quotation will have been rewarded with a bonus extra level of enjoyment from the comic scene. Part of this enjoyment was (I take it) the same sort of feeling that one might get from scoring a point for a correct answer in a quiz: anyone who identified the line could congratulate themselves on their cleverness and superior knowledge. Another part of it probably arose from the inference that they were part of a privileged community or subset within the mass audience, or that they were somehow on the same wavelength as the comedian who had inserted this sort of hidden joke for their private amusement. If any of them not only recognized the quotation but retained a detailed memory of its original source text, they may well have recalled that Medea, like Miltiades, spoke the line just after swearing an oath (to Hecate). In that case, a further extra layer of humour will have arisen from the contrast and incongruity between the two scenarios, since Miltiades' character and situation are so different from Medea's. Some of them may also have been struck by the anachronism, given that the real-life Miltiades could not possibly have known *Medea*, a tragedy that did not receive its premiere till fifty-eight years after his death. The effect would have been rather startling, like that of hearing Gladstone or Queen Victoria quoting lines from *Look Back in Anger*.

Whether Eupolis' Miltiades practised Euripidean ventriloquism at other moments in *Demes* is impossible to say. Maybe this single line was the play's only quotation from *Medea*, or maybe there were further borrowings or allusions in the parts that are now lost. We can probably assume that the 'visibility' of tragic quotations in any comedy would have increased in direct proportion to their quantity, however subtly they may have been incorporated into the new text. But at any rate, the way in which *Medea* 398 is introduced within the character's speech in F106 seems completely unmarked. Furthermore (as Ian Storey notes) it is hard to detect any parodic intent here.[20] Since all we have left of the oath-swearing scene is the lines cited by Longinus, it is difficult to go much further than that.

However, thanks to papyrus discoveries, we possess part of a scene of continuous dialogue from *Demes*, which nicely illustrates Eupolis' practice of inserting Euripidean extracts invisibly within his characters' normal speech. This is F99, a 120-line section incorporating a quasi-parabatic choral passage followed by a long exchange between several characters. Despite significant lacunae, it is clear that this scene centres on the conduct of Athenian demagogues, and combines political criticism and obscene personal abuse; its speaking characters include the play's principal character Pyronides, the dead politician Aristides and a sycophant.[21] When Aristides, who has been brought back to life in order to save the city, salutes the Athenians by saying, 'Greetings, o land of my fathers…' (ὦ γῆ πατρῷα χαῖρε, F99.35), his words might seem perfectly natural in the context, but he is actually quoting the words of Diomedes in the opening line of Euripides' *Oeneus* (F558). Maybe a few of the more bookish spectators picked up the precise reference; maybe a greater number detected a generally tragic flavour, even if they did not know *Oeneus*; maybe others remained completely oblivious to what they had just heard. But no particular attention is drawn to the quotation, and Aristides just goes on speaking in his own words. Later in the scene (F99.100-3), Aristides utters a line from a different Euripidean tragedy during a conversation with the sycophant:

>   AP.   τί τοὺς θανόντας οὐκ ἐᾷς τεθνηκέναι;
>   ΣΥ.   μαρτύρομαι· τι δ' οὐκ ἀγωνι[ο]ύμ[εθα;
>   κα]λέσας με συνδεῖς κἀδικε[ῖ]ς.
>   AP.   ἀλλ' οὐ[κ ἐγὼ
>   ξυνέδησά σ', ἀλλ' ὁ ξένος ὁ τὸν κυκεῶ πιώ[ν.

> ARISTIDES: Why do you not let the dead be dead?
> SYCOPHANT: Witnesses! Shall we not go to trial? You summon me and then beat me and tie me up.
> ARISTIDES: But I didn't tie you up – the foreigner who drank the broth did.[22]

The first line here is a quotation from *Captive Melanippe* (F507). Since Aristides himself has been resurrected from the dead for the purposes of the comic plot, the quotation is – at least on a superficial level – thematically relevant to its new dramatic context, though (as before) the contrast between the tragic and the comic situation will have given rise to humour for anyone who was aware of it. Perhaps this example is more easily detectable than the others just discussed, because the verse encapsulates a typically Euripidean paradox: a couple of jokes in Aristophanes' *Frogs* hint that Euripides became notorious for apparently questioning the distinction between life and death in lines such as these.[23] And yet, just as before, the character who utters the line gives no explicit sign that he is quoting Euripides, and the lines that immediately follow (F99.101-3) show that the sycophant does not treat Aristides' words as a quotation or indicate any awareness that they are out of place.

Even though the characters in *Demes* F99 are slipping rapidly in and out of tragic mode, they do not make it obvious that they are doing so. There are no 'quotation marks' here; in the form of source attributions, breaks in the illusion or any other signals that another person's words are being cited. No doubt the actors could have made the quotations stand out somehow in performance, through changes in vocal delivery or other mannerisms, but the written text, at least, gives no indication of where the tragic quotations begin and end. These blink-and-you'll-miss-them quotations are seamlessly incorporated into the otherwise naturalistic dialogue, which carries on without interruption. (Of course the term 'naturalistic' needs careful qualification, since we are dealing with stylized verse drama, not everyday speech; but it is precisely because both genres use iambic trimeter that it is possible to run together tragic and comic lines in this way.[24]) As in F106, no obvious parodic tone is detectable, nor does there seem to be any special significance in quoting these particular tragic lines rather than any others. The quotations are taken from two unrelated tragedies, both of which seem equally irrelevant to the immediate dramatic context in *Demes* or to the theme of the politics and personal habits of Athenian demagogues. The point of the humour seems to lie simply in the pleasure of spotting obscure literary references, combined with the absurdity of hearing Euripidean words in the mouths of the 'wrong' characters. But how many of Eupolis' spectators even noticed?

Comedians on the habit of quotation

One valuable contribution of comedy is that it not only deploys tragic quotations but also thematizes the activity of quotation as a subject of interest or source of humour in itself. In this respect, as in other ways, the comedians can be seen as among the earliest literary critics.[25] Several fifth- and fourth-century comedies provide excellent evidence for the early popularity of selective excerption as a reading habit, and some comedians seem to be implicitly commenting on the practice or poking fun at it.

Several Aristophanic scenes depend on the idea that tragedies are widely treated as repositories of quotable material. In *Frogs*, a good poet is defined specifically as one who can give voice to a 'noble phrase' (ῥῆμα γενναῖον, 96-7); in other comedies, Euripides is characterized as a collector or maker of 'little phrases' (ἐπύλλια, *Acharnians* 398-400, *Peace* 531-2), while another tragedian, Agathon, is also described as a 'forger of maxims' (γνωμοτυπεῖ, *Thesm.* 55). Characters sometimes refer to the habit of performing selected extracts or copying out favourite speeches from tragedies, as if this was an everyday activity (*Wasps* 597-80, *Clouds* 1371, *Frogs* 151). When the chorus in *Wasps* (1051-9) urge the audience to collect poets' ideas and preserve them in boxes, this too can be taken as an allusion to the practice of copying out quotations for future use.[26] Maxims by Euripides are frequently cited, along with jokes based on the premise that such verses represent the poet's own thoughts and opinions.[27] When Euripides appears as a character in *Thesmophoriazusae*, he is portrayed as quoting his own maxims in conversation (177-8 = *Aeolus* F28). Mica, another character in the same play (411-13), complains that certain readers have come to a bad end specifically because they have treated excerpts from Euripidean tragedy as equivalent to the 'moral' of the play or as general advice for life:

ὥστ' οὐδεὶς γέρων
γαμεῖν ἐθέλει γυναῖκα διὰ τοὔπος τοδί·
'δέσποινα γὰρ γέροντι νυμφίωι γυνή.'

As a result, no old man is willing to marry because of that saying of his:
'Any woman who marries an elderly husband becomes his owner'.

Phoenix F804.3

Of course this claim is a ludicrous exaggeration, but there is also a grain of truth in it, because this genuinely does reflect the way in which many people interpreted tragic texts. Furthermore, the fact that many of the Euripidean quotations in comedy are 'quotable quotes' of this sort is significant. These are precisely the sort of lines that would have been excerpted and memorized, and which could have passed down into popular culture orally, whether or not those who quoted them had read the texts of the plays from which they were taken.

In fourth-century comedy, we see even more explicit focus on quotation as a noteworthy activity or as a target of ironic humour. For instance, the following extract from a scene in Menander's comedy *The Shield* (407-15) features a slave, Daos, who is attempting to trick another character, Smikrines, into believing that a death has occurred in the household. In order to create a 'tragic' sort of impression, Daos bombards Smikrines with gnomic quotations from tragedies by Euripides and other authors:

(ΔΑ.) 'οὐκ ἔστιν ὅστις π[άντ' ἀνὴρ εὐδαιμονεῖ.'
πάλιν εὖ διαφόρως. ὦ πολ[υτίμητοι θεοί,

ἀπροσδοκήτου πράγμα[τος] καὶ ἁ[
(ΣΜ.)   Δᾶε κακόδαιμον, ποῖ τρέχ[εις;]
(ΔΑ.)   καὶ το[ῦτό που.
'τύχη τὰ θνητῶν πράγματ,' οὐκ εὐβουλία.'
ὑπέρευγε. 'θεὸς μὲν αἰτίαν φύει βροτοῖς,
ὅταν κακῶσαι δῶμα παμπήδην θέληι.'
Αἰσχύλος ὁ σεμνά—
(ΣΜ.)   γνωμολογεῖς, τρισάθλιε;
(ΔΑ.)   'ἄπιστον, ἄλογον, δεινόν.'
(ΣΜ.)   οὐδὲ παύσεται;

DAOS: 'There is no man who is fortunate in all respects'. Once again, excellently expressed! Oh, ye greatly honoured gods, what an unexpected event, and [...]
SMIKRINES: Daos, you wretch, where are you running off to?
DAOS: ... and then there's this one: 'Chance, not planning, governs human affairs'. Absolutely brilliant! 'The god sows guilt in mortal men, whenever he wishes to destroy a house utterly'. That one's from Aeschylus, the one who solemnly—
SMIKRINES: Quote maxims, will you? Thrice-wretched creature!
DAOS: 'Incredible, irrational, terrible'...
SMIKRINES: Won't he ever stop?

In this scene (which has been discussed in Chapter 1),[28] the quotations are functioning in more or less the same way as theatrical props: they are being used as set-dressing in order to pull off the deception and to create a mood. The verses that Daos quotes here are non-consecutive and unrelated to one another; they are also irrelevant to the comic plot at this point, apart from the simple fact that they are tragic and intended to be instantaneously recognizable as such. Whether they were recognized more specifically as extracts from Euripides (*Stheneboea* F661.1), Chaeremon (*Achilles Thersitoktonos* F2), Aeschylus (*Niobe* F154) and Carcinus (F5b) is less important. It is striking that most of these tragic soundbites are not identified or attributed to an author: clearly Menander is tantalizing his more literary-minded spectators by posing them the familiar challenge of 'spot the quotation'. Nevertheless, recognition is only part of the fun on offer, and it would not have mattered very much if no one in the audience had correctly matched up any of the verses with a specific source. What really matters is that the quotations are seen as typical of tragedy in a general sense. Another equally important aspect to the humour is that these verses, loosely clustering round the subject of human suffering, look remarkably like a ready-made collection of thematic extracts from a gnomic anthology. This fact is deliberately emphasized by the use of the verb γνωμολογεῖν ('to collect maxims'): this word has evidently become a quasi-technical term to denote a familiar type of activity. Smikrines may be a character of somewhat limited intelligence, but he is perfectly able to see that Daos is treating tragedy in the same way as many other readers, *viz.* quoting it for his own purposes, which have nothing to do with those of the tragic poets or their characters. The original meaning of the quotations has become almost irrelevant.

A short passage of dialogue that survives from Diphilus' comedy *Synoris* (F74) provides a trenchant illustration and critique of the habit of quoting Euripidean verses out of context and distorting their meaning. This scene derives much of its humour from ironically pointing up the contrast between selective excerption and the complete sequential reading of a text. The tragic text in question is Euripides' *Antiope*, and the person quoting from it ('character A') is obviously a parasite:

(A.)   οὐκ ἄν ποτε
Εὐριπίδης γυναῖκα σώσει· οὐχ ὁρᾶις
ἐν ταῖς τραγωιδίαισιν αὐτὰς ὡς στυγεῖ;
τοὺς δὲ παρασίτους ἠγάπα· λέγει γέ τοι
'ἀνὴρ μὲν ὅστις εὖ βίον κεκτημένος
μὴ τοὐλάχιστον τρεῖς ἀσυμβόλους τρέφει,
ὄλοιτο νόστου μήποτ' εἰς πάτραν τυχών.'
(B.)   πόθεν ἐστὶ ταῦτα, πρὸς θεῶν;
               (A.)   τί δέ σοι μέλει;
οὐ γὰρ τὸ δρᾶμα, τὸν δὲ νοῦν σκοπούμεθα.

(A.) Euripides would never save a woman: don't you see how he hates them in his tragedies? However, he really likes parasites! Why, indeed, he says: 'The man who is in possession of a good livelihood but doesn't feed at least three folk who can't pay their own way, let him perish on his journey home and never manage to get back to his native land.'
(B.) Where the hell are those lines from?
(A.) What is it to you where they're from? We're not looking at the play but at the sense.

The maxim is being used specifically to illustrate the difference between these two different modes of textual engagement. Reading 'the play' is contrasted with – or even diametrically opposed to – reading 'the sense' of an isolated excerpt. The parasite is appropriating the quotation for his own ends, which involve persuasion or manipulation. He wants a free meal, and he is using Euripides in an effort to obtain one, but he is utterly unconcerned with Euripides' original meaning. The joke here (as in many other cases) works by activating the audience's knowledge of literature. Even though the quotation is not identified by Diphilus, those who were well read in tragedy will have recognized it as deriving from *Antiope*; but they will quickly have become aware that the parasite has misinterpreted the Euripidean lines and partially rewritten them to suit his own interests.

Even though *Antiope* is now lost, the original quotation (F187) is preserved by a couple of other ancient writers who correctly cite it:

ἀνὴρ γὰρ ὅστις εὖ βίον κεκτημένος
τὰ μὲν κατ' οἴκους ἀμελίαι παρεὶς ἐᾶι,
μολπαῖσι δ' ἡσθεὶς τοῦτ' ἀεὶ θηρεύεται,
ἀργὸς μὲν οἴκοι κἂν πόλει γενήσεται,
φίλοισι δ' οὐδείς· ἡ φύσις γὰρ οἴχεται,
ὅταν γλυκείας ἡδονῆς ἥσσων τις ἦι.

The man who is in possession of a good livelihood but ignores matters in his house and neglects them, delighting in musical activities and constantly pursuing them instead, will become idle both at home and in the city, and to his friends and family he will cease to exist – for a person's nature is lost whenever he is overcome by sweet pleasure.[29]

The comic effect of Diphilus' version depends for its full effect on the audience's memory of the Euripidean original. These lines were spoken by the character Zethus, in the course of a moralizing speech arguing that one should *not* abandon oneself to self-indulgence and idle pleasure. Thus anyone who recalled this speech in detail will have found it bizarrely incongruous that an idle parasite should be justifying his way of life by quoting it. It may also have occurred to some of them that even in its original context the maxim was not presented neutrally as a universal moral principle. Rather, it was a provocative contribution to an unresolved debate: Zethus represented social and political activism (*pragmosyne*), in opposition to his brother Amphion, who advocated leisure and artistic pursuits. The contrast between these two ways of life seems to have constituted the thematic heart of the play. As the other fragments demonstrate, both brothers tended to articulate their diametrically opposed viewpoints in the form of maxims (*Antiope* F183-9, F193-8).

Only the first verse from F187 is retained in the comic version. The second verse is a paratragic pastiche representing the parasite's own thoughts and the third verse is 'invisibly' inserted from a different Euripidean play (*Iphigenia among the Taurians* 535). Diphilus has run together several sources to produce a seamless tragicomic mash-up or 'cento', which (just about) makes sense on its own terms but is utterly bizarre. He then challenges his audience to identify the source, or rather sources, of the quotation, by making character B ask πόθεν ἐστὶ ταῦτα, πρὸς θεῶν ('Where the hell are those lines from?'). Essentially, as in the scene from Menander discussed earlier, this is a quiz question to which no answer is supplied: it is left up to individual spectators or readers to fill in the blanks for themselves. Whatever their precise response to the lines may have been, the crucial point is that quotation culture is being treated here, in a sophisticated and multi-layered manner, as a subject of humour in its own right. Diphilus is making his audience hyper-aware that those who quote Euripides have a tendency to exploit his lines for their own purposes or interpret them in decidedly eccentric ways.

These same traits – the quotation and subversion of tragedy, the ostentatious deployment of literary knowledge and the ironical attitude towards decontextualized quotation – can be seen to underpin the humour in Nicostratus F29:

'οὐκ ἔστιν ὅστις πάντ' ἀνὴρ εὐδαιμονεῖ'·
νὴ τὴν Ἀθηνᾶν συντόμως γε, φίλτατε
Εὐριπίδη, τὸν βίον ἔθηκας εἰς στίχον.

'No man exists who is fortunate in every respect'. Yes, by Athena, that's right! Dearest Euripides, how very neatly you have managed to put the whole of life into one line.

Here Nicostratus' character is quoting, without attribution, a verse from Euripides' tragedy *Stheneboea* (F661.1). As we have seen (in Chapter 1), this verse had already become famous within antiquity as a free-floating maxim. The original source of the line and its sentiment are apparently irrelevant in its comic setting. What matters is the speaker's obvious sarcasm and the underlying attitude that it denotes. The idea that the meaning of life can really be summed up in a single verse of poetry is made to seem dubious, even ludicrous. But the joke relies on the fact that lots of people – not just silly asses in comedy, but real-life readers, critics, philosophers and many others – really did treat Euripidean quotations in this way, *as if* a single verse could encapsulate eternal verities about human life.

The comedian Strattis, whose fragmentary plays abound in paratragic motifs,[30] not only alludes to the fondness of readers for quoting soundbites, but also highlights Euripides' own penchant for framing his detachable maxims with prominent 'quotation marks' (as discussed in Chapter 2). In Strattis' comedy *Phoenician Women*, which seems to have presented itself *in toto* as a parodic version of Euripides' tragedy of the same name, Jocasta is made to utter the following lines (F47):

παραινέσαι δὲ σφῷν τι βούλομαι σοφόν·
ὅταν φακῆν ἕψητε, μὴ 'πιχεῖν μύρον.

I wish to give you both a wise piece of advice:
whenever you are cooking lentil soup, do not pour myrrh into it.[31]

This is a parody of a scene in Euripides' play in which Jocasta offered guidance and admonishment to her warring sons Eteocles and Polynices (*Phoenician Women* 460-64):

παραινέσαι δὲ σφῷν τι βούλομαι σοφόν·
ὅταν φίλος τις ἀνδρὶ θυμωθεὶς φίλωι
ἐς ἓν συνελθὼν ὄμματ' ὄμμασιν διδῶι,
ἐφ' οἷσιν ἥκει, ταῦτα χρὴ μόνον σκοπεῖν,
κακῶν δὲ τῶν πρὶν μηδενὸς μνείαν ἔχειν.

I wish to give you both a wise piece of advice:
whenever one friend or relative comes
face to face with another in anger,
he should consider just one thing – the specific cause of the dispute –
and not call to mind anything ill that happened in the past.

Strattis' version is amusing because it completely alters the substance of the 'wise advice', turning Jocasta's heartfelt plea for moderation into practical instructions for use in the kitchen. On its most obvious level, the humour derives from the transformation of solemnity into silliness, and from the intrusion of everyday domestic concerns (the typical subject matter of comedy) into the austere world of tragedy. But Strattis also clearly recognizes that the effect of the original scene came from its sententiousness, and that the introductory line παραινέσαι δὲ σφῷν τι βούλομαι σοφόν represents a typical Euripidean framing device. Crucially, these 'quotation marks' are the only part of the original quotation that Strattis retains in his comic version. What he is parodying is not the *meaning* of Euripides' words but rather their *function*, or, more specifically, the way in which Euripidean maxims are typically introduced by their speakers.

In some of these comedies, the humour depends not just on the habit of quotation but on the question of attribution. In Diphilus F74, as we have just seen, one of the characters questions the authenticity of a supposedly Euripidean quotation, and the full effect of the joke depends on whether the audience can detect the true source(s) of the quoted lines. Elsewhere we find similar jokes, as in Theopompus, *Odysseus* F35, where an untragic-looking maxim is doubtfully attributed to Euripides:

Εὐριπίδου τἄριστον, οὐ κακῶς ἔχον,
τἀλλότρια δειπνεῖν τὸν καλῶς εὐδαίμονα.

That excellent maxim of Euripides, which really isn't bad: that the truly fortunate man dines out at other people's expense.

Euripides probably never said this (even if he might have said something resembling it), but the point of the joke is that he is just the sort of figure to whom 'quotable quotes' habitually become attached.[32] That is to say, Euripides was so firmly associated in the popular imagination with verses of this sort that practically *any* gnomic line might be said to be a 'Euripidean' maxim – rather like the miscellaneous apocrypha collected by Kannicht under the heading 'doubtful or spurious fragments' (F1107-32). In much the same way, anthologists in later antiquity assembled a huge collection of maxims under the umbrella title 'One-liners of Menander' (*Menandrou Monostichoi*), even though fewer than a quarter of these quotations are actually the work of Menander himself – and some, indeed, are taken from plays by Euripides.[33]

Another comparable scene occurs in Antiphanes, *Traumatias* F205, where two characters argue about whether a quotation comes from Euripides or Philoxenus:

(A.)   μὴ μεστὰς ἀεὶ
ἕλκωμεν, ἀλλὰ καὶ λογισμὸς εἰς μέσον
παταξάτων τις, καί τι καὶ μελίσκιον,
στροφὴ λόγων παρελθέτω τις. ἡδύ τοι
ἔστιν μεταβολὴ παντὸς ἔργου πλὴν ἑνὸς
<   > παραδίδου δ' ἑξῆς ἐμοὶ
τὸν ἀρκεσίγυιον, ὥς ἔφασκ' Εὐριπίδης.
(B.)   Εὐριπίδης γὰρ τοῦτ' ἔφασκεν;
                         (A.)   ἀλλὰ τίς;
(B.)   Φιλόξενος δήπουθεν.
                         (A.)   οὐθὲν διαφέρει,
ὦ τᾶν· ἐλέγχεις μ' ἕνεκα συλλαβῆς μιᾶς.

(A.)   Don't let's always be tossing back full cups, but let's have some conversation rattling round between us, and let a little bit of singing issue forth, and some

badinage to boot. After all, 'change is invariably a nice thing', except in one respect, of course ... And then in turn pass me the 'limb-strengthener', as Euripides put it.
(B.) What? Did Euripides say that?
(A.) Who else?
(B.) Surely it was Philoxenus.
(A.) My dear chap, it doesn't make the slightest difference. You're trying to catch me out because of one syllable.

Character A is being deliberately provocative by mixing together a genuine quotation or paraphrase of Euripides, *Orestes* 234 (μεταβολὴ πάντων γλυκύ, 'change in all things is a pleasant thing') with a confusing addition of his own (which may or may not derive from Philoxenus). Possibly the original Euripidean quotation will have been familiar to many in Antiphanes' audience: it is cited as a free-standing aphorism by other fourth-century writers, including Aristotle and Plato, and in general *Orestes* was one of Euripides' most popular plays throughout antiquity.[34] But we cannot be sure that everyone recognized the source or realized that the quotation had been altered. Whether they did or not, they may still have found the scene amusing, because this comic character, like so many others who quoted Euripidean lines, is adapting the proverb to his own situation, as if it really had been formulated by its author as a guide to sympotic etiquette. *Plus ça change, plus c'est la même chose.*

Conclusions

All of these comic scenes, despite their differences, have one key feature in common. They are obviously aimed at audiences who enjoy tragedy (especially Euripidean tragedy) and see tragic quotations and parodies as an almost endless source of entertainment. The chronological range of the examples discussed in this chapter, covering more than a century, tells us that Euripides was enormously popular among Athenian theatregoers not just during his lifetime but for several generations afterwards. The comedians themselves undoubtedly knew Euripides' plays intimately, since their plays feature a large number of abstruse or unexpected quotations alongside more famous lines. Though we can never be certain about the spectators' level of literary knowledge or theatrical competence, it seems inevitable that some Athenians will have been more enthusiastic Euripidophiles than others, and that some of them will have been better than others at spotting quotations and appreciating their effect in their new context. This means that the deployment of quotations in comedy can be seen as a way of differentiating between subgroups within the mass of spectators and a strategy by which the comedians could negotiate their relationship with their own target audiences.

Sometimes, as we have seen, these quotations are entirely visible and obvious; sometimes they are relatively hard to spot. Sometimes, the jokes are very broad; sometimes, they are sophisticated and subtle. In many cases, we can perceive the humour as operating on two or three different levels simultaneously, offering variously nuanced effects to people with different levels of knowledge or critical acuity. The fact that the comedians explicitly acknowledge and play around with the concept of eclectic reading shows that they were well aware that some of their contemporaries would have encountered Euripides primarily through the medium of selected highlights. Indeed, much of the fun in these comic scenes is perfectly accessible to those who know just a few extracts and not much more. But even if we make the reasonable assumption that not everyone noticed or fully appreciated every single quotation, it is still probable that the majority of the comedians' spectators must have had a fairly good level of familiarity with Euripides and his work. If they did not, it is hard to imagine that they would have endured, year after year, this succession of comedies full of Euripidean material. On the whole, then, we must conclude that during the long period in which these comedies were being staged at large public festivals, quoting Euripides was not (as we might have imagined) an exclusively highbrow activity restricted to a small coterie of literati; it was very much a part of popular culture.

5

Quotations in the Classroom

Apart from live performances, one of the main ways in which people would have encountered Euripides was in the classroom. Euripidean quotations featured at every stage of Greek and Roman education. Verses were copied out by young pupils almost as soon as they had learned the alphabet; maxims were repeated and memorized for their edifying sentiments; extracts were studied and commented upon as literature by more advanced students; and key passages were used as models for aspiring orators because of their rhetorical style.[1] Knowledge of carefully selected quotations could play an important part in the formation of a young person's intellect, character and powers of expression. In societies in which relatively few people were literate or educated to a high level, even a superficial acquaintance with the works of Euripides (and a few other classic Greek authors such as Homer and Menander) could be seen as a marker of culture and status.[2] As Raffaella Cribiore puts it, 'these bits of knowledge were coveted talismans of culture, magical formulas that could open doors'.[3]

This chapter discusses Euripidean quotations in educational settings from a variety of periods and places. It begins by examining evidence for elementary education, including papyrus texts illustrating school practices in Egypt as well as material from authors such as Plato and Quintilian. Subsequent sections discuss Plutarch's *How the Young Man Should Study Poetry*, Longinus' *On the Sublime*, and finally a writer within the early Church, Clement of Alexandria, who via selective quotation set out to transform Euripides into a Christian theologian or moralist. As in the other chapters, emphasis is placed upon key factors such as the gnomic mentality, the prevalence of 'eclectic' reading, the relationship between quotation and classic status, and the question of the extent to which anyone had knowledge of the plays that they quoted.

Learning the basics

It is impossible to write a comprehensive history of Greek and Roman education, partly because of the limitations of our evidence and partly because there never was a single standard educational system in operation: the topic encompasses a variety of practices in different contexts and periods. Nevertheless, those few texts which preserve details about primary education give the impression that the same basic methods and materials were consistently employed by teachers throughout the classical world.[4] This impression is backed up by archaeological evidence from Hellenistic and Roman Egypt.[5]

Children whose families were wealthy enough to send them to an elementary schoolteacher (*grammatistēs*) would begin by learning the alphabet. Next they would progress from letters to syllables; then from syllables to short words; then from short words to longer words; then to the reading of continuous passages, including proverbs, maxims and quotations from literary texts. To judge by the evidence of papyri, the authors most frequently adopted as examples for this purpose were Homer, Euripides and Menander.[6] Twenty surviving school exercises (dating from the third century BC to the fifth century AD) quote Euripidean verses, and *Phoenician Women* (which remained one of the author's most widely read tragedies throughout antiquity) was an especially popular choice, featuring in six of these exercises.[7] Other papyri, writing-tablets and potsherds feature quotations from *Bacchae, Women of Troy, Electra, Hecuba, Aegeus, Alcestis, Andromache, Helen, Medea, Hippolytus, Telephus, Hypsipyle* and *Ino*, often in a wobbly scrawl littered with mistakes.[8] These documents give clues to the teaching methods typically employed in Egyptian schoolrooms (and no doubt elsewhere). A teacher might dictate verses for pupils to transcribe, or he might neatly write out a model quotation for a pupil to copy. The goal was accurate reproduction, in written or spoken form, through frequent repetition.

The main focus of this section is a fragmentary papyrus book (P. Cairo 65445) published in 1938 by O. Guéraud and P. Jouguet under the title *Un Livre d'Écolier*.[9] Dating from the third century BC, this happens to be one of the earliest surviving Greek books. Written in a neat and accomplished hand, therefore not the work of a young pupil, it is obviously a schoolteacher's collection of model exercises. What makes it so revealing is the fact that it is designed for use in the classroom with pupils at different stages of their educational progress, and that these stages correspond precisely to descriptions of elementary education found in Greek and Roman texts.

The contents of this exercise book are incomplete (only the bottom portion of the bookroll survives), but what survives is arranged in nine sections: (1) a collection of individual syllables arranged by the sounds they make; (2) a list of Greek numerals; (3) a selection of monosyllabic words; (4) a list of the names of Olympian gods; (5) a list of the names of rivers featured in Homeric epic; (6) a list of disyllabic names; (7) a list of other names, increasing in length to five syllables; (8) a short anthology of quotations from Euripides, Homer, epigrams and elegiac poetry; and (9) a selection of mathematical exercises. In all the linguistic and literary material the main emphasis seems to be placed on spelling or pronunciation rather than content or meaning. The separate syllables at the start of the document (lines 1-20) are meaningless and purely offer practice in handling different vowels and consonants; most of the words in the other lists are typical of epic and tragedy but have evidently been chosen because they are difficult to pronounce. All the words included here have been broken up into their constituent syllables, and in nearly all cases the division is clearly marked with a dicolon (:) to assist the learner. Thus the name Odysseus appears as O: ΔYC: CEYC: and so on.

For our purposes, the most important part is the anthology of quotations (lines 115-215). The beginning of this section, probably coinciding with the start of a new column in the bookroll, is missing,[10] but it appears that the first quotations, from Euripides' *Phoenician Women* and *Ino*, follow on immediately from the list of five-syllable names at the end of the previous column. The presence of section headings elsewhere in the text – ONOMATA ΔIC[Y]ΛΛABA ('disyllabic names', line 67) and EΠH ('verses from epic', line 130) – suggests that these Euripidean quotations would have been introduced by a brief description of this type. What survives, at the bottom of one column (lines 115-25), is most of a gnomic passage from *Phoenician Women* 529-34, originally part of a speech by Jocasta addressed to her son Eteocles. Here is the passage as it appears in a modern edition (Kovacs' Loeb text):

ἀλλ' ἡμπειρία
ἔχει τι λέξαι τῶν νέων σοφώτερον.
τί τῆς κακίστης δαιμόνων ἐφίεσαι
Φιλοτιμίας, παῖ; μὴ σύ γ'· ἄδικος ἡ θεός·
πολλοὺς δ' ἐς οἴκους καὶ πόλεις εὐδαίμονας
ἐσῆλθε κἀξῆλθ' ἐπ' ὀλέθρωι τῶν χρωμένων.

Experience has the ability to speak more wisely than youth. Why, child, do you pursue Ambition, the worst of gods? Better give her up! She is unfair, this goddess. She has entered many households and cities that were once happy, but then abandoned them to their destruction.

But in the schoolbook, the same passage appears as follows:

```
   ]I[   ]P[
  ]ΛE: ΞAI: [
  ]NE: ΩN: CO: ΦΩ [
  ]THC: KA: KIC: TH [
ΔAI: MO: NΩN: E: ΦI: E: CAI
ΦI: ΛO: TI: MI: AC ΠAI: MH: CY: ΓE:
A: ΔI: KOC: HΘE: OC
ΠOΛ: ΛOYC: ΔE COI: KOYC: KAI
ΠO: ΛEIC: EY: ΔAI: MO: NAC:
EI: CHΛ: ΘE: KAI: EIC: HΛ: ΘE:
E: ΠOΛE: ΘPΩI: TΩΓ: XPΩ: ME: NΩN:
```

To present-day readers, this mode of presentation ('EX: PE: RI: EN: CEHAS: THE: A: BI: LI: TY: TO'...) is bound to look strange. Even if we bear in mind the conventions of Hellenistic book design (such as the absence of lower-case letters, accents, breathings and spaces in between words), it is unusual. Laid out in this way, the passage resembles prose rather than poetry. The irregular line breaks correspond more closely to the column width than the ends of verses. Even though the syllabic division of the words shows that pronunciation was the main focus of the teaching, it does not seem that the metre was observed, since some elisions are ignored. But essentially the passage is neither rhythmical verse nor prose. It has become simply a succession of separate syllables. This is fragmentation taken to its ultimate limit.

After the *Phoenician Women* extract there is a lacuna, followed (at lines 126-9) by a passage from *Ino*; it may well be that one or two additional Euripidean quotations originally filled the gap. The *Ino* lines, like the others, are split up into their constituent syllables:

```
O: PAIC: [            ]A: MA: KPΩ[
ΩC: MI: KPA[          ]TA: KAI: CTI: Γ[
Y: ΠO: ΠTE[           ] ΠΛOY: TOC: OIC: ΓAP[
E: ΞEΛ: ΠI: Δ[        ]ΠI: ΠTON: TAC: Y: ΠTI: O[    ]PΩ:
```

By contrast, the Homeric quotations that follow (from line 130) are not syllabified but are written out in the more conventional way, without syllable or word breaks. This may indicate a gradual progression through the stages of education – i.e., that the student, having gained experience by practising the Euripidean pieces, is now expected to deal with *scriptura continua* for himself – but maybe we could infer that Euripides' Greek was judged to be harder to pronounce without artificial aids.

Although none of the quotations is identified by the writer, the Euripidean passages are easy to recognize. One of them comes from an extant play, and both of them were quoted by other writers within antiquity (including Plutarch, Dio Chrysostom and Stobaeus).[11] It seems likely that these were popular anthology pieces even as early as the third century BC, and that the schoolteacher chose them for this reason.[12] Nevertheless, the quotations in this book are slightly different from the versions found elsewhere. Here are those verses from *Ino* in their guise as 'F420' in the standard modern edition (*TrGF*), substantially the same as they appear in Stobaeus' anthology (4.41.1):[13]

ὁρᾶις τυράννους διὰ μακρῶν ηὐξημενους
ὡς μικρὰ, τὰ σφάλλοντα καὶ μί' ἡμέρα
τὰ μὲν καθεῖλεν ὑψόθεν, τὰ δ' ἦρ' ἄνω.
ὑπόπτερος δ' ὁ πλοῦτος· οἷς γὰρ ἦν ποτε,
ἐξ ἐλπίδων πίπτοντας ὑπτίους ὁρῶ

When you observe tyrants whose power has long been growing, do you notice how mere trifles can cause their downfall, and a single day casts down the mighty from their seat and exalts the humble? Wealth can take flight: I see those who once possessed it lying prostrate, dashed from their hopes.

Despite the gaps in the papyrus, it is obvious that the schoolteacher was quoting a different version of the second verse. Instead of the phrase 'a single day' (which would have appeared in 'syllabic' form as MI: H: ME: PA:), he wrote a word or phrase beginning CTI: Γ[. As it happens, this alternative version can be filled in from another source. In the *Consolation to Apollonius* formerly attributed to Plutarch (*Moralia* 104a-b), we find the following discussion:

ὅθεν ὀρθῶς ὁ Φαληρεὺς Δημήτριος εἰπόντος Εὐριπίδου
"ὁ δ' ὄλβος οὐ βέβαιος ἀλλ' ἐφήμερος"
καὶ ὅτι
"μίκρα τὰ σφάλλοντα, καὶ μί' ἡμέρα
τὰ μὲν καθεῖλεν ὑψόθεν, τὰ δ' ἦρ' ἄνω"
τὰ μὲν ἄλλα καλῶς ἔφη λέγειν αὐτὸν βέλτιον δ' ἔχειν ἄν, εἰ μὴ "μίαν ἡμέραν" ἀλλὰ "στιγμὴν" εἶπε "χρόνου".

So Demetrius of Phaleron [F79 Wehrli] was quite right in his opinion concerning a saying of Euripides:
   'Wealth is not constant but ephemeral' [*Phoenician Women* 558]
and another one:
   'Mere trifles can cause downfall, and a single day
   casts down the mighty from their seat and exalts the humble' [*Ino* F420.2-3]

Demetrius said that it was very well expressed, but that it would have been better if Euripides had said not 'a single day' but 'a single moment of time'.

Demetrius of Phaleron, well known for his political activities, was also a Peripatetic scholar and pupil of Theophrastus, noted for the quantity of his writings on topics including history, philosophy, law, rhetoric and literary criticism.[14] It is not known which of his works is being cited here, though one of the books attributed to him was entitled *Chreiai* (denoting anecdotes accompanied by quotations) and he is said to have assembled 'compilations' (συναγωγαί) from other people's work.[15] The work in question seems to have been a literary-critical discussion, including textual criticism (of a sort) based on the principle that tragic verses may be emended or rewritten in order to improve their quotability or piquancy. (As we shall see, a similar principle underpins Plutarch's use of quotations in *How the Young Man Should Study Poetry*.) It seems that Demetrius had an influence on subsequent anthologists, either through his choice of quotations or because someone or other incorporated his editorial suggestions into the text when recopying the verse. However it may have come about, our schoolteacher was obviously quoting Demetrius' 'improved' version, with στιγμὴν χρόνου at its end, rather than the alternative (putatively original) form. This demonstrates the fluidity of the textual tradition of Euripides in the fourth and third centuries BC, before the establishment of the authoritative Alexandrian critical edition. The schoolteacher's source, whatever it may have been, represents a different branch of the tradition from the version transmitted in other sources. It is clear that excerpts from Euripidean texts could undergo big changes within the medium of the anthology tradition, independently of the fate of complete texts in the direct tradition.[16]

Scholars (both ancient and modern) have thought that a major incidental benefit of studying literary maxims as models is that such passages can inculcate sound moral values in a young pupil's mind.[17] This view was put forward by Plato (*Protagoras* 326a) in relation to fifth-century BC Athenian education:

οἱ δὲ διδάσκαλοι τούτων τε ἐπιμελοῦνται, καὶ ἐπειδὰν αὖ γράμματα μάθωσι καὶ μέλλωσι συνήσειν τὰ γεγραμμένα, ὥσπερ τότε τὴν φωνήν, παρατιθέασιν αὐτοῖς ἐπὶ τῶν βάθρων ἀναγιγνώσκειν ποιητῶν ἀγαθῶν ποιήματα καὶ ἐκμανθάνειν ἀναγκάζουσιν, ἐν οἷς πολλαὶ μὲν νουθετήσεις ἔνεισι, πολλαὶ δὲ διέξοδοι καὶ ἔπαινοι καὶ ἐγκώμια παλαιῶν ἀνδρῶν ἀγαθῶν, ἵνα ὁ παῖς ζηλῶν μιμῆται καὶ ὀρέγηται τοιοῦτος γενέσθαι.

The schoolteachers put a lot of effort into this instruction, when the pupils have learnt the letters and are on the point of understanding the written words (not just the spoken, as before), they place before them the works of good poets to read aloud as they sit on their benches. They compel them to learn by heart these verses, in which there are many words of advice, together with much detailed description, praise and admiration of great men of the past, and they do this so that the child may emulate and imitate them and strive to become like them.

An almost identical viewpoint was expressed by Quintilian (*Institutio Oratoria* 1.1.35-6) when discussing elementary education in first-century AD Rome:

> ii quoque versus qui ad imitationem scribendi proponentur non otiosas velim sententias habeant, sed honestum aliquid monentis. prosequitur haec memoria in senectutem et inpressa animo rudi usque ad mores proficiet. etiam dicta clarorum virorum et electos ex poetis maxime (namque eorum cognitio parvis gratior est) locos ediscere inter lusum licet.

> Those verses that are given to the pupil as a model for handwriting practice should not, in my view, be pointless maxims, but ones that offer sound ethical guidance. These verses remain in our memory into old age, and they make an impression on the unformed mind that will aid moral development. Furthermore, the pupil may also amuse himself by thoroughly learning the deeds of famous men and, especially, selected extracts from the work of poets (since small children especially enjoy knowing these).

This sounds good, and it can easily be applied to the quotations in the *Livre d'Écolier*, with their trenchant observations on tyranny, ambition, wisdom and the mutability of fortune. But perhaps (we may suspect) the reality did not always match up to these admirable ideals. How much did young children really understand of these verses as they laboriously copied them out on their wax tablets or falteringly recited them, syllable by syllable? It has been thought odd that this apparently widespread system of teaching literacy should involve such an enormous leap, from basic alphabetic and syllabic literacy straight to literary quotations written in difficult and stylized poetic language.[18] (It might also seem odd that no one in the ancient world ever developed children's literature as a special genre of writing.[19]) Probably many pupils struggled to make much of these lines beyond the letter sounds and shapes. The type of mistakes that we find in handwriting exercises on papyri and potsherds strongly suggest that novice scribes had little grasp of the meaning of the verses that they copied.[20] Even their teachers' own grasp of the material may have been shaky in many cases – including that of the owner of the *Livre d'Écolier*. The handwriting in this book is confident, but there are several mistakes and omissions in the copying of both Euripidean quotations. In the *Phoenician Women* extract, there is a spelling error (gamma for nu) in the last line, and a phrase is nonsensically repeated in the penultimate line (EI: CHΛ: ΘΕ: ΚΑΙ: EIC: ΗΛ: ΘΕ:, 'entered and entered', for ἐσῆλθε κἀξῆλθ', 'entered and abandoned'). In the *Ino* fragment, an entire verse is omitted, rendering the quotation partly incomprehensible. These errors are troubling, given that they appear in the 'model' versions of the quotations. They not only indicate that this teacher was more concerned with the sound than the meaning of the passages; they also imply that he did not fully understand them.

Plutarch on the educational use of poetry

The works of the philosopher and polymath Plutarch of Chaeronea (*c*. 45–120 AD) include quotations from an impressive array of Greek literature. Plutarch's quoting habits and his knowledge of literature in general have been widely discussed.[21] This section narrows the focus to *How the Young Man Should Study Poetry* (*Moralia* 14e-37b).

This essay takes the form of a letter to Marcus Sedatus, a friend whose son Cleander is the same age as Plutarch's own son Soclarus (probably between ten and fifteen years old).[22] Plutarch is writing specifically about the use of poetry at the intermediate stage of education, a topic in which he and Sedatus have a personal as well as a theoretical interest. He describes a milieu in which growing adolescents continue to read extracts from classic works, just as they had done at the elementary level of schooling. As their intellect and powers of expression develop, they are more able to engage with the poetry's content for themselves and interpret it as literature. They are still not quite mature enough to cope with serious philosophical works, but Plutarch's view is that poetry, if chosen and approached in the right way, can serve as an attractive introduction to philosophy later on (14e-15f; 37b). In addition, *How the Young Man Should Study Poetry* grapples with the difficulty of treating poetry and drama as didactic media, in light of the Platonic view – which Plutarch partly accepts – that all poetry, as a form of *mimesis*, is essentially deceptive and false.[23] The difficulty can be circumvented, he suggests, by keeping a close watch over the boys' reading and by teaching them selective reading habits in order to separate true content from false (16a):

προφιλοσοφητέον τοῖς ποιήμασιν ἐθιζομένους ἐν τῶι τέρποντι τὸ χρήσιμον ζητεῖν καὶ ἀγαπᾶν· εἰ δὲ μή, διαμάχεσθαι καὶ δυσχεραίνειν. ἀρχὴ γὰρ αὕτη παιδεύσεως,

ἔργου δὲ παντὸς ἥν τις ἄρχηται καλῶς,
καὶ τὰς τελευτὰς εἰκός ἐσθ' οὕτως ἔχειν
κατὰ τὸν Σοφοκλέα.

They should use poetry as a preliminary exercise to philosophy, by training themselves in the habit of seeking out and embracing the useful content in that which gives pleasure, but rejecting and fighting against it if there is nothing useful there – for this is the start of true education:

'In every task, if one starts off well,
it is likely that one will also end well,'

as Sophocles says. [incert. fab. F831]

This, the first tragic quotation in the essay, is inserted without comment, but presumably it counts as an example of what is true or useful, since it echoes and amplifies Plutarch's own point (and indeed it is hard to imagine how anyone could disagree with such a bland sentiment). But not all tragic maxims are equally acceptable. Although eclectic reading was widespread throughout antiquity, Plutarch cannot be regarded as an entirely typical reader. Whereas most other readers went through texts picking out what they judged to be the best bits, Plutarch's method is specifically designed as a prophylactic method of avoiding portions that are positively harmful.

In other ways, too, Plutarch combines typical and atypical traits. Any literary-critical views that he expresses are conventional and derivative of earlier scholarship.[24] The glimpse that he gives of current classroom practices corresponds to what we know from other Greek and Roman literary texts, and the range of authors cited follows predictable tendencies. Homer features most often (with over a hundred quotations), followed by Euripides (twenty-six); other tragedians are well represented (with fourteen quotations from Sophocles, four from Aeschylus and ten from unidentified plays), as are Hesiod, Pindar, Menander and others. As usual, the question of whether these extracts are quoted directly from the texts or from secondary sources is difficult to answer for certain (see Chapter 3). It has been thought that some of the quotations, along with some of the content of *How the Young Man Should Study Poetry* in general, may have been lifted straight from a work along the same lines by the Stoic philosopher Chrysippus.[25] Plutarch's repeated use of the same quotations (or clusters of quotations) to illustrate stock themes has been seen as a sign that he relied, at least in part, on anthologies or personal notebooks; but then so did many other classical writers and scholars, and so, no doubt, did Plutarch's own readers.[26] The quotations that he includes are of the same type favoured by others: i.e. lines chosen for their moralizing, gnomic or paradigmatic content. What he does with these quotations, however, is more unusual.

In three key respects Plutarch represents a more thoughtful and nuanced approach to quotation than many other ancient readers and critics. First, he is anxious that the student should not be 'in thrall' (καταδεδουλωμένος, 26b) to every word written by classic authors just because prevailing opinion values these figures so highly. Homer, Euripides and others may be widely regarded as 'heroes', but what matters, he says, is the content of specific verses rather than the reputation of the poet. Second, he acknowledges that all lines quoted from drama were spoken by specific characters and therefore cannot be treated as the sentiments of the author himself (18d-f). For instance, some 'wicked and fallacious' lines on the subject of tyranny from *Phoenician Women* (524-5) are quoted, but Plutarch is quick to point out that these are Eteocles' words, not a general principle that Euripides is commending. Third, Plutarch explains that verses from poetry should not simply be swallowed whole, memorized and accepted as the truth. Instead, young readers should be taught to examine them carefully, question their meaning and reject them if necessary. Plutarch illustrates this procedure (28c) by presenting (among other examples) two Euripidean maxims which he implies are famous verses, widely quoted by the majority of people (οἱ πολλοί):

τῶν δὲ μειζόνων ἀβασανίστως δέχονται τὴν πίστιν, οἷα καὶ ταῦτ' ἐστὶν·
  δουλοῖ γὰρ ἄνδρα, κἂν θρασύσπλαγχνός τις ἦι,
  ὅταν συνειδῆι μητρὸς ἢ πατρὸς κακά,
καὶ
  σμικρὸν φρονεῖν χρὴ τὸν κακῶς πεπραγότα.
καίτοι ταῦτα τῶν ἠθῶν ἅπτεται καὶ τοὺς βίους διαταράττει, κρίσεις ἐμποιοῦντα φαύλας καὶ δόξας ἀγεννεῖς [. . .]

In very weighty matters they accept things on faith, without submitting them to interrogation, such as the following lines, for example:
  'Even a bold-spirited man is enslaved if he learns of the ills of his mother or father' [*Hippolytus* 424-5]
and
  'He who fares badly must aim his thoughts low' [incert. fab. F957];
and yet these thoughts influence our characters and disturb our lives, by instilling in us petty judgements and ignoble opinions [...]

Plutarch goes on to condemn as foolish those who unquestioningly accept these maxims, comparing them to people who are blown along by the wind. In contrast, he praises any reader who 'confronts and resists' such passages (ὁ ... ἀπαντῶν καὶ ἀντερείδων, 28d), and he advises young students to practise formulating their own maxims in response to those that they encounter in drama.

This, according to Plutarch, is the correct use of poetry in education, enabling children to benefit from what is good but avoid being harmed by what is false. They should not simply read or reproduce selected verses but 'interrogate' them – an unusual metaphor, deriving from the use of torture in legal cases to extract testimony from slaves, and not seen elsewhere in connection with literature except in Aristophanes' *Frogs* (which Plutarch may be recalling here).[27] One way of 'interrogating' a quotation, Plutarch says, is to juxtapose it with another quotation from the same play or author in order to detect inconsistencies.[28] Three pairs of examples from Euripides are cited to support this point (20d):

ὅπου μὲν οὖν αὐτοῖς τὸ τιθέναι σύνεγγυς ἐκφανεῖς ποιεῖ τὰς ἀντιλογίας, δεῖ
τῶι βελτίονι συνηγορεῖν ὥσπερ ἐν τούτοις·
 πόλλ, ὦ τέκνον, σφάλλουσιν ἀνθρώπους θεοί.
 τὸ ῥᾶιστον εἶπας, αἰτιάσασθαι θεούς.
καὶ πάλιν·
 χρυσοῦ σὲ πλήθει, τούσδε δ' οὗ χαίρειν χρεών.
 σκαιὸν τὸ πλουτεῖν κἄλλο μηδὲν εἰδέναι
καί
 τί δῆτα θύειν δεῖ σε κατθανούμενον;
 ἄμεινον· οὐδεὶς κάματος εὐσεβεῖν θεούς.

Wherever a comparison of passages exposes contradictions, we ought to advocate the better cause – for instance:
(A.) Gods often trip up mortals, my child.
(B.) By blaming the gods you have resorted to the easiest explanation.
[*Archelaus* F254]
And again:
(A.) You may take pleasure in much wealth, but these men may not.
(B.) To be rich but not to know anything else is foolish. [incert. fab. F1069]
And:
(Hypsipyle) Why then should you make sacrifices when you are about to die?
(Amphiaraus) It is better thus: respecting the gods is no effort. [*Hypsipyle* F752k.20-21]

Since all of these examples come from tragedies that are now lost, it is impossible to be sure what effect these verses had within their original context. Plutarch does not name any of the plays, or attribute the quotations to Euripides or any of his characters, but it seems likely that each pair of lines represents the utterances of two different speakers within the same play. This is true of the third pair: a papyrus has shown these to be consecutive lines from a scene in *Hypsipyle* (spoken by Hypsipyle and Amphiaraus, respectively) in which Amphiaraus foresees his own death. Maybe all three examples, similarly, belonged to stichomythic dialogue scenes in which the interlocutors argued with one another in the form of mutually opposing aphorisms.[29] Whether or not that is true, it is clear that each of the six lines was (or could easily be) quoted as an free-standing monostich; some of them actually appear as such in other sources.[30] Did Plutarch or his readers know these lines primarily as self-contained soundbites via the anthology tradition, or as parts of familiar dramatic dialogues? It does not really matter either way. The point that Plutarch is establishing is that each verse makes sense on its own but takes on a different colouring when juxtaposed with another verse. The exact circumstances in which the juxtaposition takes place are unimportant: it can be an author himself or his readers who places the inconsistent verses side by side. What troubles Plutarch is that these contradictory statements can be encountered *anywhere at all* within the body of literature that a young person might read. Indeed, Plutarch goes on to cite mutually inconsistent verses from different works by a single author (including further examples from Euripides at 20f-21a); he even proposes that if an objectionable verse is detected in one author, it should be juxtaposed with a preferable verse from a different author entirely (21d-22c).

After the process of interrogation, if the student finds that he does not like what these verses say, he can reject them – or even rewrite them. Plutarch has previously suggested that they should compose their own maxims in reply to those of the poets (28c); now he commends the methods of scholars such as Antisthenes, Cleanthes and Zeno, who alter the words of selected verses to create new versions (33c). These versions are called 'corrected editions' (παραδιορθώσεις), produced via 'emendation' (ἐπανόρθωσις, 34b) – terms taken from the technical vocabulary of Alexandrian textual criticism.[31] But it is clear that these scholars, like Plutarch himself, are interested in the verses' moral content, not their textual authenticity. The first example of this practice involves a notorious verse from Euripides' *Aeolus* (F19) which we have already discussed in an earlier chapter (pp. 66–8):

ὁ μὲν εὖ μάλα τοὺς Ἀθηναίους ἰδὼν θορυβήσαντας ἐν τῷ θεάτρῳ 'τί δ' αἰσχρὸν εἰ μὴ τοῖσι χρωμένοις δοκεῖ;' παραβάλλων εὐθὺς 'αἰσχρὸν τό γ' αἰσχρόν, κἂν δοκῇ κἂν μὴ δοκῇ'.

Antisthenes, observing that the Athenians had reacted with outrage when the line 'What is shameful, if it does not seem shameful to those who practise it?' was heard in the theatre, immediately replaced it with 'What is shameful is shameful, whether it seems so or not.'

Further examples follow, including *Electra* 428-9, *Iphigenia at Aulis* 29-31, *Chrysippus* F841, and other tragic and comic aphorisms which were popular within the anthology tradition. All are presented in both their original and their 'corrected' versions, for purposes of comparison. In effect, these are what we might call *interactive* quotations, in the sense that their author is no longer seen as solely responsible for creating meaning; the reader too is encouraged to have a hand in the process. Thus the reader – or quoter – is empowered to an extraordinary degree.

In this respect, David Konstan has argued that Plutarch should be seen as a precursor to Roland Barthes, who provocatively argued (in 'The Death of the Author') that readers, not authors, are responsible for writing texts.[32] The resemblance between the two critics is superficially striking, perhaps, but it should not be overstated. This is not (or not only) because of the problem of anachronism, but because Plutarch undoubtedly retains a strong sense of The Author as a figure to be reckoned with. Furthermore, Plutarch, unlike Barthes, holds a clear and straightforward conception of truth: he is not claiming that Euripides' words can mean whatever we declare them to mean. But even if we prefer not to treat him as a quasi-postmodern theorist, Plutarch can certainly be seen as a provocateur. Within his own historical context, he stands out as unusual in placing so much emphasis on the role of the reader, and in presenting quotations as interactive objects rather than inert gobbets of text. He is not completely original in his views, and he openly acknowledges his debt to other critics, but (perhaps for that very reason) he is a valuable case study for our purposes, providing a fascinating glimpse into quotation culture among the educated elite of the Roman Empire.

Longinus' museum of quotations

In this section we turn to *On the Sublime*, a hugely influential document of ancient criticism which continues to shape modern debates about aesthetics.[33] It is included here because it presents itself as a didactic work – or, more specifically, as a set of 'technical precepts' (τεχνικὰ παραγγέλματα, 2.1) constituting a course of 'advanced study' (χρηστομαθεία, 44.1).[34] It is aimed at the young adult who has passed beyond the elementary and intermediate stages of his education and is now undertaking the type of literary and rhetorical training seen as suitable for a career in public life. Though it is obviously designed for a wider readership, its primary addressee is a young Roman named Postumius Florus Terentianus, who is said to be 'well acquainted with culture' (παιδείας ἐπιστήμονα, 1.3). The author refers in the preface (1.1) to a previous occasion, seemingly a private tutorial, during which he and Terentianus were studying Caecilius' *On the Sublime* together. The current work, which pointedly adopts the same title as Caecilius' treatise, might be seen as a transcript of the sort of lecture or discussion that could have taken place in a classroom setting. The teacher/author figure delivers his lecture as if Terentianus were there beside him, frequently including Terentianus' name and other forms of direct address (e.g. ὦ νεανία, 'young man', or ἑταῖρε, 'my companion') along with second-person or first-person plural verbs.[35] The rhetoric creates an illusion of intimacy with the reader as well as a vivid sense of the author's presence and pedagogic style. But the work's authorship and date are hard to pin down.[36] Traditionally *On the Sublime* was ascribed to Cassius Longinus, a Neoplatonist scholar who taught in Athens during the third century AD, but this attribution is widely questioned. It would probably be more accurate to refer to '[Anon.]', but I retain the name Longinus here because it is a convenient and familiar label.

Our author, whoever he may have been, is remarkably well read. His aim is to teach his student to appreciate true greatness in literature, a quality which he calls τὸ ὕψος ('the sublime' or 'the height of excellence'). In the course of his argument he draws on an extensive collection of quotations, nearly all of which are explicitly presented as 'examples' (παραδείγματα) or 'evidence' (τεκμήρια) of sublimity. The author's text has the function of a frame, providing explanation and critical discussion, but the quotations are the main focus of attention. There are 125 quotations in all, from the work of over thirty poets and prose writers. As might have been predicted, Euripides is one of the most cited authors (with nine quotations), though even more examples come from Homer, Plato, Herodotus and Demosthenes.[37] What strikes us is the range, depth and detail of Longinus' literary knowledge, a level of knowledge that he also seems to take for granted in his young reader. The specific choice of quotations is equally striking, in that Longinus does not, on the whole, include 'quotational' passages or aphorisms of the type that typically featured in anthologies. He quotes extracts on the basis of some specific aspect of their style, or some more abstract quality that he discerns in them, rather than because of their content or some prominent key word (e.g. πλοῦτος, 'wealth', or τύχη, 'fortune').[38] In general, he gives the impression of knowing his texts inside out; and in this respect he differs from many other quoting authors.

Cassius Longinus, a man famed for his erudition, was nicknamed 'the living library and walking museum' (Eunapius, *Lives of the Sophists* 4). This description seems to fit the author of *On the Sublime* very well indeed (whether or not he really was Longinus). It also suggests a way of approaching this text. Perhaps we can grasp the overall conception and purpose of *On the Sublime* if we think of it as a sort of museum. The quotations, taken from great authors of the past, can be seen as 'exhibits' on display, and the quoting author can be seen as combining the roles of collector, curator and scholarly guide. Apart from a few quotations adduced in Chapters 3–5 as examples of faults in literature, what Longinus offers his student is a carefully curated collection of prize specimens, representing (in his opinion) the peak of artistic achievement. He leads Terentianus by the hand, as it were, through the museum, viewing the artefacts together with him and describing his own reactions to them as a way of shaping the student's own critical response. Each 'exhibit' is intended to provoke a feeling of wonder in the viewer,[39] but it is also arranged and displayed in such a way as to emphasize special qualities that the student can be taught to appreciate for himself.

The analogy between literature and visual artworks was a well-established mode of thought by the time that Longinus was writing.[40] Throughout his work, Longinus exploits this analogy in a number of key passages. He argues that statues and other artefacts, like literary texts, imitate the fine character of their models (13.4); he discerns the contrasting effects of 'light' and 'shade' in both literature and paintings (17.2-3); he describes passages from Archilochus and Demosthenes as being 'built' like architectural structures (10.7); and he discusses technical artistry with reference to the Colossus at Rhodes and Polyclitus' 'Spear-Carrier' (36.3). More generally, Longinus has a penchant for passages containing colourful imagery or *ekphrasis*, and he often uses visual language when describing the effect produced by great literature. For instance, he talks about the 'apparition' that a Hesiodic passage conjures up in the mind's eye (εἴδωλον, 9.5), and the 'images' seen in a Homeric theomachy (φαντάσματα, 9.6); he repeatedly refers to viewing (as opposed to reading or hearing) features of literary style (e.g. 9.13, 14.1, 34.1); and he pauses to ask Terentianus: 'Do you behold [it], my friend?' (ἐπιβλέπεις, ἑταῖρε; 9.6), just as if the two of them were standing side-by-side contemplating the text as an artefact. A substantial section (15.1-7) is devoted to 'visualization' (φαντασία) or 'image-making' (εἰδωλοποιία) as a distinct sub-topic. As Longinus explains, this concept refers to places where a writer uses language in such a way that 'you think you are seeing the scene and placing it in view of the audience' (ὅταν βλέπειν δοκῇς καὶ ὑπ' ὄψιν τιθῇς τοῖς ἀκούουσιν, 15.1). The function of this 'visualization' is to elicit awe-struck wonder – an effect that is illustrated by two quotations from Euripides (*Orestes* 255-7 and *Iphigenia among the Taurians* 291) which contain vivid evocations of the Furies:

> ἐνταῦθ' ὁ ποιητὴς αὐτὸς εἶδεν Ἐρινύας· ὃ δ' ἐφαντάσθη, μικροῦ δεῖν θεάσθαι καὶ τοὺς ἀκούοντας ἠνάγκασεν.
>
> Here the poet himself saw the Furies, and what he visualized he virtually compelled his audience to behold.
>
> 15.2

Longinus treats Euripidean tragedy not as a script for performance but as a literary text which creates 'images' of a purely conceptual or metaphorical nature via the words on the page. Its theatrical origins have been forgotten or ignored. But there is a direct parallel here between Euripides and Longinus himself in terms of their relationship to their readers. Just as Euripides is said to be compelling his audience to gaze at the Furies, so Longinus is compelling Terentianus to gaze at the Euripidean exhibits on display in his museum.

Connections between the spheres of art and literature are central to Carolyn Higbie's study of art collectors, scholars and forgers in antiquity. Higbie, discussing a range of contexts throughout the Graeco-Roman world and beyond, observes that collection and display – of objects, of texts, of knowledge – generally go hand in hand. The act of collecting in itself can be seen as a form of appropriation, while displaying one's collection to others can be an inherently hierarchical act or a demonstration of superiority.[41] A prime example of 'competitive collecting' for Higbie is the Mouseion of Alexandria, in which the Ptolemies' acquisition of books and antiquities is seen above all as a means of displaying the founders' wealth, power and mastery over rival cultural centres in the Hellenistic world. It is important to bear in mind that the Mouseion and other ancient libraries and museums were designed to display books *and* artworks side by side.[42]

In cultural-sociological terms, the symbolic significance of the items in a collection is just as important as the actual identity, subject matter or content of these exhibits. Collecting valuable items – or, more precisely, knowing how to select the 'best' items for one's collection – can be seen as a marker of social status, or, to use Pierre Bourdieu's vocabulary, an 'embodiment of cultural capital'.[43] Judgements about the quality of literature or art may seem to rest on abstract aesthetic principles, but they can also be interpreted as competitive bids for social status and power.[44] The act of collecting beautiful things – of decorating one's surroundings with artworks, or decorating one's prose with quotations – gives a signal of the collector's scale of values, which can be measured against the values of other people within the social hierarchy. To quote Bourdieu again: 'Taste classifies; and it classifies the classifier.'[45]

It is widely acknowledged that *On the Sublime* is a combative and polemical work.[46] From the outset, as noted, it sets itself up in direct competition with Caecilius' book, even adopting the same title. Caecilius is criticized for his lack of judgement, for confusing or misunderstanding the main points at issue, and for cheapening his subject matter. Elsewhere throughout the book (e.g. 2.1, 8.2, 12.1), other unnamed rival critics are similarly dismissed and vilified, while Longinus imagines his own work being competitively judged in a metaphorical courtroom or theatre (14.2-3). Literary criticism is seen as a contest in which the critics themselves, not just the works of literature being criticized, are competing for status. What is at stake is the degree to which each critic is able to recognize true quality. Longinus repeatedly makes it clear that not everyone who claims this ability actually possesses it. The ideal critic, in his view, ought to be equipped with an exquisitely refined taste and acutely well-developed critical antennae in order to discriminate between the good, the bad and the genuinely sublime. What is being described is a highly exclusive form of elite connoisseurship, which Longinus claims to be able to teach – though not everybody is naturally capable of acquiring it.[47]

Thus Longinus' use of quotations is inherently competitive, in that his selection and deployment of these 'exhibits' is intended to demonstrate that his sense of taste is superior to that of anyone else. For a broadly similar outlook we might compare *The Ignorant Book Collector*, a satirical essay by Lucian dating from around 170 AD. In this work, Lucian savagely criticizes a collector who has enough money to assemble a library of what he thinks are the finest books but lacks the education (*paideia*) to be able to discern their true quality. In other words, amassing a large collection or displaying a lot of knowledge is not enough in itself. Quality, not quantity, is what matters; education is therefore essential. Longinus, like Lucian, draws our attention to his *exclusion* from the collection of items which less discerning critics misguidedly value. This is a sign of the austerely rigorous standards that Longinus is adopting, and it is a rhetorically powerful strategy for presenting himself as the best judge and teacher. It is especially significant that one of the criticisms aimed by Longinus at Caecilius is that he used too many quotations in his own *On the Sublime* (1.1). Elsewhere Longinus writes in a disparaging vein about literary quotations which are superficially impressive but not genuinely sublime (7.1-2). As Glenn Most has piquantly observed, 'like sweaters, canons have an inherent tendency to shrink: it is, after all, an observed fact that social elites tend to form smaller elites within themselves by the narcissism of small differences'.[48]

With all this in mind, let us narrow the focus to the Euripidean exhibits in Longinus' museum. Generally speaking, the treatment of Euripides is not qualitatively different from that of other authors. All these extracts exemplify fine writing and justify Longinus' credentials as an arbiter of taste. There is no special acknowledgement that Euripides' work is drama, designed for performance in a theatre: it is simply treated alongside other works of literature. Nor does Longinus supply Terentianus with any source references beyond the poet's name. Either he regards the source text as irrelevant, or he assumes that his student will already be familiar with the works in question, even when the passages that he cites are relatively recherché.

The first couple of Euripidean quotations (15.2), included to illustrate the technique of 'visualization', have already been mentioned. One of these passages (*Orestes* 255-7, from a famous scene featuring Orestes' madness) seems to have been better known than many of the quotations that Longinus includes: extracts from this scene are cited by numerous ancient authors, and it has been thought that this is 'a somewhat trite example'.[49] After discussing Euripides' quasi-visual language, Longinus adds that the poet works hard at depicting madness, and argues that even though Euripides lacks natural greatness, he forces himself to take risks (ἑαυτὸν ὁ Εὐριπίδης κἀκείνοις τοῖς κινδύνοις προσβιβάζει, 15.3; cf. 15.5). This is a revealing comment for two reasons: first, because Longinus is trying to convince us that he has a privileged insight into the creative process and the poet's inner thoughts; and second, because it shows us that just a single quotation can embody sublimity, even if its author is not invariably great by nature.[50] Longinus continues:

> καὶ παρ' ἕκαστα ἐπὶ τῶν μεγεθῶν, ὡς ὁ ποιητής, "οὐρῆι δὲ πλευράς τε καὶ ἰσχίον ἀμφοτέρωθεν μαστίεται, ἓε δ' αὐτὸν ἐποτρύνει μαχέσασθαι."
>
> In each place where greatness is needed, Euripides 'urges himself on to battle, using his tail as a whip to lash his ribs and flanks on both sides' – as the poet puts it.

'The poet' here is Homer, and this additional quotation is taken from *Iliad* 20.170-1 (where it was part of a simile comparing Achilles to a wounded lion). Unlike the Euripidean extracts, which illustrate the main point under discussion, this passage seems to be purely decorative in its function. It is not an example of 'visualization', nor is it especially apposite as a description of Euripides; Longinus is simply showing off his erudition. Nevertheless, the Iliadic passage seems to set off an associative train of thought in Longinus' mind, for he immediately goes on to cite a couple of consecutive extracts from Euripides' *Phaethon* (F779.168-70,

171-7) in which Phaethon snatches the reins of Helios' chariot and whips the flanks of its winged horses.

After presenting these verses, Longinus invites Terentianus to imagine that when Euripides composed them, his soul mounted the chariot along with Phaethon and took on wings (15.4):

> οὐ γὰρ ἄν, εἰ μὴ τοῖς οὐρανίοις ἐκείνοις ἔργοις ἰσοδρομοῦσα ἐφέρετο, τοιαῦτ' ἄν ποτε ἐφαντάσθη. ὅμοια καὶ τὰ ἐπὶ τῆς Κασσάνδρας αὐτῶι, ἀλλ, ὦ φίλιπποι Τρῶες
>
> [His soul] would never have been able to visualize such things unless it had been borne aloft equally in that celestial enterprise. In the same way, in his Cassandra scene: 'Come now, horse-loving Trojans...'

Note the way in which Longinus keeps jumping from one exhibit to another, even when the connection is far from obvious. The topic under discussion, 'visualization', is conceptually abstract and broadly defined, which means that examples from very different texts can be deployed as illustrations. As elsewhere, no references or titles are given, and the 'Cassandra scene' cannot be identified.[51] The abbreviated form of quotation here implies that Longinus expects his student to recognize the passage on the basis of a brief reminder and to supply the rest of the passage from his own memory. But no other source quotes this extract, and it is too brief to give us any real clue about which play it comes from or what it depicts. Cassandra was repeatedly depicted in tragedy as raving, so perhaps we should treat the *Phaethon* extract as a digression, after which Longinus is now returning to the theme of Euripides' portrayal of madness. However, Longinus immediately jumps to another quotation, from Aeschylus' *Seven Against Thebes*, which he presents as an example of 'heroic visualization' (15.5). This new exhibit, describing the sacrifice of a bull and the swearing of an oath, has nothing to do with madness, and seems to have nothing in common with the earlier quotations beyond its use of bold and vivid imagery. Further quotations from Aeschylus, Sophocles and Euripides follow in rapid succession, culminating (15.8) in an additional extract from the 'mad scene' of *Orestes* (264-5). This last quotation, linking back to the other *Orestes* passage at 15.2, looks like an example of ring composition to bring the 'visualization' sequence to an end, though the section actually concludes with an extended extract from Demosthenes (15.9-10). Even a gifted student might find Longinus' argument difficult to follow. The range and variety of exhibits may be impressive, but it is sometimes easy to feel that we have accidentally wandered into the wrong room in the museum.

Longinus returns to Euripides in a later section on word arrangement (39.1-43.6). As before (cf. 15.3-5), he emphasizes a point which may surprise us: that in his opinion Euripides is *not* naturally a sublime poet. Of the tragedians, only Sophocles seems to be treated as incontestably sublime (33.5) – though in that case we may wonder why Longinus quotes him so infrequently.[52] Nevertheless, it is easy to appreciate the rhetorical force of this heterodox belief in relation to Longinus' elitist stance. Devaluing a poet to whom the world at large unquestionably awarded classic status is yet another way in which Longinus demonstrates his superior discernment and exclusivity. He quotes two verses (*Heracles* 1245 and *Antiope* F221) in support of the assertion that Euripides is 'a poet of word order more than thought' (τῆς συνθέσεως ποιητὴς ὁ Εὐριπίδης μᾶλλόν ἐστιν ἢ τοῦ νοῦ, 40.3), arguing that passages such as these, despite their mundane vocabulary, are elevated above banality by skilful arrangement of words. Once again, the choice of 'non-quotational' examples rather than obvious anthology pieces implies wide knowledge and impressive powers of recall. And again we are invited to acknowledge that this hard-to-define quality of sublimity can reside in a single line of poetry; it should not be seen as characterizing a poet's entire oeuvre. This means that Longinus is making difficult demands of his students, expecting them to read with scrupulous attention to detail and to think for themselves rather than lazily accept received opinion (the same point that Plutarch made in *How the Young Man Should Study Poetry*).

The first of the exhibits in this section on word arrangement is another example – like the Homeric quotation at 15.3 – of a 'decorative' quotation or tag rather than an illustration of the main topic. Maybe our author is deliberately showing off, but maybe he is ventriloquizing Euripides without conscious effort because this tragic phrase had entered the language as part of the ordinary vocabulary of a cultured person. Longinus at this point (39.2) is explaining the power of music to move the listener even against his will:

ἀναγκάζει βαίνειν ἐν ῥυθμῶι καὶ συνεξομοιοῦσθαι τῶι μέλει τὸν ἀκροατήν, **κἂν ἄμουσος ἦι** παντάπασι

It compels him to step in rhythm and join in with the tune, 'even though he be a stranger to the Muse' altogether.

The highlighted phrase comes from Euripides' *Stheneboea* (F663, given here as it appears in *TrGF*):

ποιητὴν δ' ἄρα
Ἔρως διδάσκει, κἂν ἄμουσος ἦι τὸ πρίν

So love is a poet's teacher, then, even though he be a stranger to the Muse previously.

Like the 'Cassandra' example at 15.4, Longinus' version is only a half-quotation, possibly designed to challenge the student to recognize it and fill in the rest for himself. But this time there is no explicit signal that the phrase is a quotation at all, and it is not essential that the student should acknowledge it as such. Indeed, even Longinus himself may not be treating it specifically as a quotation. It seems that this Euripidean fragment early on in its history passed into circulation as a quasi-proverbial phrase (rather like F661, that other famous extract from *Stheneboea* discussed in Chapter 1). It is frequently quoted by writers from Aristophanes and Plato onwards, all of whom treat it as a neat way of expressing the commonplace idea that a person may change their mind under any strong influence (not necessarily love or the Muse).[53] Most of these authors, like Longinus, include only part of the quotation, and each of them presents it in a slightly different version or paraphrased form, which makes it difficult to be confident about what the original words actually were.[54] Only a few of them attribute the words to Euripides, and the only source to identify them as coming from *Stheneboea* is a marginal commentator on Aristophanes. We do not know who originally spoke these words or in what context, and this information is irrelevant for the purposes of Longinus and all other quoting authors. 'These lines ... are a very hackneyed quotation indeed,' writes Donald Russell.[55] Quite so. But it may be that few if any of these writers were consciously *quoting* as such – just as (say) few people nowadays who casually speak of the 'green-eyed monster' are purposely quoting Iago's words in *Othello* (III.3) or even realize that they are doing so. Famous phrases of this sort have a tendency to enter normal language and everyday speech because they encapsulate some familiar aspect of human experience in an appealing way; their connection to a specific author or text is easily forgotten.[56] We also need to consider the possibility that the phrase κἂν ἄμουσος ἦι τὸ πρίν (or some variant on it) was already a proverb even before Euripides incorporated it into his play.

The final quotation in *On the Sublime* (44.12) is also a 'throwaway tag' of this sort:[57]

κράτιστον εἰκῆι ταῦτ' ἐᾶν, ἐπὶ δὲ τὰ συνεχῆ χωρεῖν

'Best to leave these things be' and move on to the next topic ...

Again, this obviously has the status of a proverbial expression or cliché rather than an example of sublimity. The phrase appears in Euripides' *Electra* (379) as part of a speech in which Orestes talks about the difficulty of making correct judgements. It may be that Longinus remembered the phrase's original context and quoted it because the motif of correct judgement is so relevant to his own agenda.[58] But the same phrase also featured in Euripides' *Auge*, according to Diogenes Laertius (2.33), who reports that when *Auge* was first performed Socrates was so displeased by the utterance that he walked out of the theatre. It may be that Diogenes (whose anecdotes are often apocryphal or of questionable provenance) got the title wrong,[59] or it may be that the line in *Electra* represents an interpolation,[60] but it is equally possible that Euripides used the same phrase in two different plays, in each case repackaging an existing commonplace.[61] The question cannot be definitively answered; but 'best to leave these things be' and move on to the next topic.

Christian education and pagan texts

Euripides' status as a classic author and source of wisdom extended beyond the boundaries of traditional Greek and Roman education. Perhaps surprisingly, the tragedian's work continued to be read and taught within the early Church, and we find his work being quoted and discussed by Athenagoras, Eusebius, Theophilus, Basil and other Christian writers ranging from the second to fifth centuries.[62] This section discusses one such figure: Clement of Alexandria (Titus Flavius Clemens), scholar, apologist and head of the Alexandrian catechetical school *c.* 200 AD. Clement's works illustrate the challenges faced by a Christian convert previously educated to a high level in the literature and culture of classical Greece. What attitude should a Christian reader adopt towards pagan myth and polytheistic religion? Can there be any value in texts written by authors who did not acknowledge the divine Word as revealed in the person of Jesus Christ? Should the writings of the ancients be discarded? Is their moral content and traditional wisdom entirely null and void? Selective quotation, together with oblique methods of interpretation, could be seen as providing a way around these problems. Clement demonstrates a way of reading Euripidean tragedy (and other classic Greek literature) in such a way as to render it acceptable to the Christian – or even to present it as entirely compatible with Holy Scripture, improbable though this may seem.

Clement's three major surviving works – the *Protrepticus* ('Exhortation to the Greeks'), *Paedagogus* ('Tutor') and *Stromateis* ('Patchwork' or 'Miscellanies') – have been interpreted as a trilogy of texts designed for the education of young Christians.[63] Together the three works can be seen as constituting a progressive course of instruction: the first sets out to contrast the delusions of ancient religion with the shining truth of the Gospel, the second is mainly concerned with moral precepts and the care of the soul, and the third is a loosely structured compendium of wisdom and assorted learning, with distinct similarities to other works in the classical miscellany tradition (such as Aulus Gellius' *Attic Nights*, Athenaeus' *Deipnosophists* or the Elder Pliny's *Natural History*).[64] Clement uses various direct and indirect methods to emphasize the didactic function of his writings. He addresses his own readers as pupils (*Paedagogus* 1.2.4.1); he recommends that his work should be read in the presence of a teacher or guide (*Stromateis* 1.1.14.4); he repeatedly compares readers to children (*Protrepticus* 10.89.1; *Paedagogus* 1.4.10.1, 1.5.12.1-2; *Stromateis* 7.16.99.2); he describes the teacher's job as that of guiding the soul to true knowledge of God (*Paedagogus* 1.1.2.3); and he describes the content of the *Stromateis* as deriving from the lecture notes that he himself took down from his own teachers (1.1.11.1-2). Clement evidently regards quotations as crucial tools for performing this didactic function. All three works include a large number of extracts from other texts, but the *Stromateis* – which often resembles an annotated anthology more than a text with a clear structure or argument of its own – contains by far the most. The majority of the quotations, predictably, come from the Bible, but there are also many from classical authors. Among Greek poets Homer is cited most often (207 times), followed by Euripides (119 times).[65] These figures reflect a typical pattern which is paralleled in nearly all quoting texts throughout antiquity, including other Christian writers.[66]

In his introduction to *Stromateis* (1.1.11.2), Clement, in common with many other scholars and anthologists, describes readers as like bees flitting from flower to flower in a meadow – an image that would surely have been so familiar by his day as to constitute a cliché.[67] Perhaps we are to infer that he has personally gathered all the extracts which he quotes from complete texts; or perhaps we should assume that some or all of them have been taken, along with the bee metaphor itself, from intermediate sources. Modern scholars have tended to disagree on this point. Some see Clement as a profoundly erudite figure with a wide knowledge and recall of texts from disparate literary traditions, while others prefer to dismiss him as a superficial show-off whose first-hand acquaintance with Greek texts was minimal.[68] As usual, the debate cannot be definitively settled. Even if it could be proved that Clement sometimes or always relied on anthologies, he would scarcely come across as unusual, since so many other Greek and Roman readers obviously did likewise. But for our purposes, what matters is not the nature of Clement's sources so much as the way in which he deploys these quotations.

Clement's overall project is to demonstrate that pagan literature, despite its evils and falsehoods, can nonetheless be used for educational purposes. There are two reasons for this belief. The first is that Greek literature furnishes many examples of error and sin, and thus its shortcomings can usefully be pointed out and refuted by the true Word of God (*Protrepticus* 1.2.2-4, *Stromateis* 1.2.19-20). Several passages from Euripides (among others) are quoted to this end. For instance, *Bacchae* 918-19, from a scene depicting Pentheus hallucinating under the spell of Dionysus, is cited twice, first to show that the worship of idols is a delusion (*Protrepticus* 12.118.5), and later to warn against the evils of alcohol (*Paedagogus* 2.24.2-3). *Iphigenia at Aulis* 71-7, from a description of Paris and Helen, is quoted to illustrate sexual immorality as a counterexample to correct behaviour (*Paedagogus* 3.2.13.1-2). Lines from *Chrysippus* (F840) and *Medea* (1078-9) are presented as examples of the sins that may result from giving in to one's passions (*Stromateis* 2.15.63.2-4). These and other passages function in a simplistic manner as negative paradigms, which by contrast point the way to true Christian belief and morality.

The second, more unexpected reason why Clement treats pagan literature as educative is that it can be shown to contain some genuine insights. He argues that Greek poets can sometimes bear witness indirectly to the Gospel truth, even if they are not fully aware of it (*Protrepticus* 7.74.7). Perhaps this knowledge came to them accidentally, or by a form of divine inspiration or by entirely inexplicable means (*Protrepticus* 6.71.1, 6.72.4; *Stromateis* 1.2.19-20, 5.11.70.1-7). In order to persuade his readers that this is so, Clement is obliged to use quotations in a strategically ruthless manner. He employs four main tactics. First, he radically limits his choice of extracts, ignoring many passages cited by other quotation-collectors and choosing passages which are not representative or typical of the work cited. Second, he omits almost all mention of the plots, characters and other key details of the works in question. Third, he exploits natural ambiguities in the verses quoted. Fourth, he creates further ambiguities by truncating phrases or ignoring contextual details from the passage being quoted. Even if Clement relied on anthologies as his main source, these citational tactics might seem rather eccentric. But if he did know the complete plays at first hand, he must be seen as deliberately misreading them, using quotation, in effect, as a means of falsification. Either way, this mode of (mis-)reading can work *only* with decontextualized fragments. If each fragment were viewed within its original setting as part of a dramatic scene, the quoting author's Christianizing interpretation could not be sustained. It is for this reason, no doubt, that Clement suppresses relevant background information about the fragments that he presents to his pupils.[69] When quoting Euripidean excerpts, he almost never tells us the name of the speaker, and never describes the situation in which the words were originally spoken. He normally attributes the quotations simply to Euripides (or, more vaguely, to 'the poet' or 'the tragedian'), treating them as the author's personal sentiments. He mostly conceals the plays' titles from us, perhaps fearing that we may use this information to track down the texts for ourselves and thus be in a position to refute his version of their meaning.

It is opportune for Clement that Euripides' characters often express a questioning attitude towards their gods and social conventions. Such opinions have often been interpreted, by ancient and modern readers alike, as evidence of the playwright's own heterodoxy or atheism (though the reality is more complex).[70] Clement eagerly seizes on passages which can be read as critical of the Greek gods, treating the words as if they were being delivered from the perspective of an enlightened Christian denouncing pagan religion. For instance, lines from *Alcestis* (3-4) are discussed as if Euripides wrote them expressly in order to question the divinity of Asclepius (*Protrepticus* 2.30.2-3), and a portion of *Iphigenia among the Taurians* is paraphrased and taken as proof that Euripides wished to denounce the gods' cruelty (*Protrepticus* 3.42.3). Several thematically related passages in which characters complain about the behaviour of Apollo and Heracles (*Orestes* 591-6, *Alcestis* 755-6, *Ion* 442-7, incert. fab. F907) are presented as evidence that Euripides somehow perceived the truth of Christianity and despised his audience for not doing so (*Protrepticus* 7.76.1-6). Elsewhere, Euripides' *Antiope* F210 is quoted approvingly alongside snippets from Bacchylides, Cleanthes, Sophocles and others, all of which are interpreted as veiled denunciations of idolatry (*Stromateis* 5.14.110-11):

οὔκουν ἔτι κατὰ τὴν τῶν πολλῶν δόξαν περὶ τοῦ θείου ὑποληπτέον·
οὐδὲ γὰρ λάθραι δοκῶ
φωτὸς κακούργου σχήματ' ἐκμιμούμενον
σοὶ Ζῆν' ἐς εὐνὴν ὥσπερ ἄνθρωπον μολεῖν,
Ἀμφίων λέγει τῆι Ἀντιόπηι.

Thus popular opinions about the divine should be rejected:
 '... nor do I believe that Zeus secretly
 imitated the shape of a wicked beast
 and came to your bed just like a human,'
as Amphion says in *Antiope*.

In the play, Amphion was expressing scepticism about the story that Zeus impregnated Antiope in the form of a satyr,[71] but here Clement affects to believe that Euripides wrote the lines because he personally rejected the Greek concept of anthropomorphic gods. Underlying all of these examples is the principle that any specific comment about individual gods or myths expressed by a character can be interpreted as a general statement of belief on the part of the poet.

Sometimes it is asserted that the moralizing content of Euripidean tragedy is compatible with Christian ethics. Gnomic generalizations on the well-worn topic of truth *versus* falsehood – such as *Iphigenia in Tauris* 569, quoted at *Protrepticus* 10.101.3, or the series of quotations from *Phoenician Women* 471-2, *Alexandros* F56, *Hippolytus Veiled* F439 and *Antiope* F187 assembled at *Stromateis* 1.8.40.3-41.5 – can seem to transfer easily enough from one context to another, provided that we do not look too closely into the details or the specific cultural reference points. Extracts from drama may be presented side by side with quotations from Scripture – as in the following passage from *Paedagogus* (3.8.41.4), which quotes Euripides at the beginning of a section that also includes verses from Hesiod, Jude, Saint Matthew's Gospel and Isaiah:

οὐ γὰρ μικρὰ ῥοπὴ εἰς σωτηρίαν τὰ ὑποδείγματα. ὅρα· φησὶν ἡ τραγῳδία,
    Ὀδυσσέως ἄλοχον οὐ κατέκτανε
    Τηλέμαχος· οὐ γὰρ ἐπεγάμει πόσει πόσιν,
    μένει δὲ ἐν οἴκοις ὑγιὲς εὐναστήριον.
ὀνειδίζων τις μοιχείαν ἀσελγῆ καλὴν εἰκόνα σωφροσύνης ἐδείκνυεν φιλανδρίαν.

These examples are of no little importance in the path to salvation. Behold! It says in the tragedy:
   'Telemachus did not kill the wife of Odysseus,
   for she did not take another husband as well as the husband she already had,
   and the marriage-bed remains pure within the house.'
Reproaching foul adultery, he displayed the fair image of spousal chastity.

These lines, from an argument between Orestes and Tyndareus concerning the killing of the adulterous Clytemnestra (*Orestes* 588-90), are treated as equivalent to an exhortation to chastity or a testimony supporting fidelity within Christian marriage. In order for them to be interpreted as a general statement of doctrine, the inconvenient fact that they were uttered in self-defence by a matricidal madman must be ignored. Whether or not Clement was aware of this information, he attributes the verses simply to 'the tragedy', omitting its title and the name of the speaker. A similar approach is adopted in the case of other Euripidean quotations which are treated as universal ethical precepts, such as extracts from another unnamed play repeatedly cited as paradigms of wifely virtues (*Stromateis*

4.8.63.2-3; 4.20.125.1-126.4).[72] Did Clement realize that these quotations came from *Oedipus*, and that the chaste and devoted marriage in question was actually the incestuous union of Oedipus and Jocasta? If so, he deliberately kept quiet about it; but perhaps he simply inherited these quotations from elsewhere, unaware of their source. Two of them also appear in Stobaeus' anthology, which suggests that they were in circulation as free-standing quotations independent of their source text (though Stobaeus does in fact name the author and title).[73]

Often the original meaning of an utterance is distorted by the manner in which it is quoted, in order to create the misleading impression that Euripides' characters are talking about the same thing as Clement himself. For instance, Clement claims (*Stromateis* 1.24.163.5-6) that when Euripides describes a 'pillar festooned with ivy for Bacchus' (κομῶντα κισσῶι στῦλον εὐίου θεοῦ, *Antiope* F203), he is making the same point as Christian and Jewish writers who hold that God himself cannot be portrayed. At *Stromateis* 1.8.40.3-41-5, several quotations concerning the power and potential dangers of words (*logoi*) – a favourite theme of Euripides, reflecting the influence of sophistic rhetoric – are interpreted as if they somehow relate to the Christian concept of God as the true Word (*Logos*). In a number of places, Clement exploits the natural slippage in meaning between different senses of the singular noun θεός (which in classical usage can refer vaguely to 'some god or other' or to a particular named god). When Clement quotes passages that contain this word, he pretends that it refers to the one true God of monotheism (e.g. *Protrepticus* 6.68.3-4, 7.74.1; *Stromateis* 5.11.75.1-3, 5.14.137.2).

Elsewhere, more provocatively, Clement frames an extract from *Bacchae* in such a way as to make it appear that the 'rites' being described are the rituals of the church rather than the mysteries of Dionysus:[74]

αὐτὸς οὖν ἡμᾶς ὁ σωτὴρ ἀτεχνῶς κατὰ τὴν τραγῳδίαν μυσταγωγεῖ,
    ὁρῶν ὁρῶντας καὶ δίδωσιν ὄργια.
κἂν πύθηι·
    τὰ δὲ ὄργια ἐστὶ τίν' ἰδέαν ἔχοντά σοι;
ἀκούσηι πάλιν·
    ἄρρητ' ἀβακχεύτοισιν εἰδέναι βροτῶν,
κἂν πολυπραγμονῆι τις ὁποῖα εἴη, αὖθις ἀκουσάτω·
    οὐ θέμις ἀκοῦσαί σε, ἔστιν δ' ἄξι' εἰδέναι·
    ἀσέβειαν ἀσκοῦντα ὄργι' ἐχθαίρει θεοῦ.
ὁ θεὸς δὲ ἄναρχος, ἀρχὴ τῶν ὅλων παντελής, ἀρχῆς ποιητικός.

Thus the Saviour himself simply initiates us into his mysteries, as the tragedy says: 'Face to face he bestows on us his rites'; and if you ask: 'These rites, what form do they take?' you will hear once again the reply: 'It is forbidden for those humans who are uninitiated to know'. But if someone tries to ferret out what form they take, let him hear this: 'It is not lawful for you to hear this, though the rites are worth knowing; the god's rites are inimical to him who practises impiety'. God, who is without beginning, is the perfect beginning of all that is, and he made the beginning ...

Stromateis 4.25.162.3-5

The quoted extracts come from a scene of dialogue between Pentheus and Dionysus (*Bacchae* 469-76):

ΠΕ. πότερα δὲ νύκτωρ σ' ἢ κατ' ὄμμ' ἠνάγκασεν;
ΔΙ. ὁρῶν ὁρῶντα καὶ δίδωσιν ὄργια.
ΠΕ. τὰ δὲ ὄργι' ἐστὶ τίν' ἰδέαν ἔχοντά σοι;
ΔΙ. ἄρρητ' ἀβακχεύτοισιν εἰδέναι βροτῶν.
ΠΕ. ἔχει δ' ὄνησιν τοῖσι θύουσιν τίνα;
ΔΙ. οὐ θέμις ἀκοῦσαί σ', ἔστιν δ' ἄξι' εἰδέναι·
ΠΕ. εὖ τοῦτ' ἐκιβδήλευσας, ἵν' ἀκοῦσαι θέλω.
ΔΙ. ἀσέβειαν ἀσκοῦντ' ὄργι' ἐχθαίρει θεοῦ.

PE. Was it during the night or in waking sight that he compelled you?
DI. Face to face he bestowed on me his rites.
PE. And these rites, what form do they take?
DI. It is forbidden for those humans who are uninitiated to know
PE. Do they confer any benefit on those who perform them?
DI. It is not lawful for you to hear this, though the rites are worth knowing.
PE. What a misleading answer, well calculated to make me more curious!
DI. The god's rites are inimical to him who practises impiety.

Clement is quoting the original lines accurately enough, apart from a small grammatical alteration (ὁρῶντα in line 470 is changed to ὁρῶντας, in order to make it seem as if the words are addressed to *us*, i.e. Clement and his readers). But he gives a seriously misleading impression of their meaning and context. His vague reference to 'the tragedy' conceals the fact that the lines come from *Bacchae*; by omitting Pentheus' lines, he fails to reflect that this is part of a dialogue scene; and he disingenuously implies that Christ himself, not Dionysus, is the speaker of the verses quoted. Clement's purpose in using the quotation in this way is hard to judge for certain. Is he pretending that Euripides was really describing Christian religion all along without realizing it, or does he want us to reflect on the structural parallels between the two religions? It might strike us as odd that Clement should be drawing attention to any resemblance between Christianity and Dionysiac mystery-cult, given that his aim is to expose all pagan worship as evil and misguided (cf. *Protrepticus* 2.12.1-23.1, 12.118.5-121.1); but perhaps we are meant to interpret the comparison in a figurative rather than literal sense. As Christoph Riedweg has shown, Clement (in common with other classical writers and philosophers) often uses mystery-cult terminology as a metaphor or an allegory for the process of acquiring esoteric knowledge: it may well be that he is using a familiar image in order to make Christianity seem more acceptable or intellectually graspable to his readers.[75]

A similarly bold, but more baffling, misreading of Euripides is seen at *Stromateis* 5.11.70.1-7. Here Clement quotes some verses from Christ's Sermon on the Mount – 'Blessed are they which do hunger and thirst after righteousness, for they shall be filled' (*Matthew* 5.6) – and immediately goes on to claim that Euripides was making the same point, quoting lines from an unidentified tragedy (incert. fab. F912):

πάνυ θαυμαστῶς ὁ ἐπὶ τῆς σκηνῆς φιλόσοφος Εὐριπίδης τοῖς προειρημένοις ἡμῖν συνῳδὸς διὰ τούτων εὑρίσκεται, πατέρα καὶ υἱὸν ἅμα οὐκ οἶδ' ὅπως αἰνισσόμενος·

σοὶ τῶι πάντων μεδέοντι χοὴν
πέλανόν τε φέρω, Ζεὺς εἴτ' Ἀίδης
ὀνομαζόμενος στέργεις· σὺ δέ μοι
θυσίαν ἄπορον παγκαρπείας
δέξαι πλήρη προχυταίαν.

ὁλοκάρπωμα γὰρ ὑπὲρ ἡμῶν ἄπορον θῦμα ὁ Χριστός. καὶ ὅτι τὸν σωτῆρα αὐτὸν οὐκ εἰδὼς λέγει, σαφὲς ποιήσει ἐπάγων·

σὺ γὰρ ἔν τε θεοῖς τοῖς τοῖς οὐρανίδαις
σκῆπτρον τὸ Διὸς μεταχειρίζεις
χθονίων τ' Ἀίδηι μετέχεις ἀρχῆς.

Euripides, the philosopher of the stage, is found to be most wonderfully in harmony with these words when he cryptically alludes – I know not how – to the Father and the Son, saying:

'To thee, the Lord of all, I bring
a libation and a grain offering, whether you prefer to be called
Zeus or Hades; I pray that thou accept from me
this unburnt offering of all fruits, poured forth in abundance,'

for Christ is a whole burnt offering and rare sacrifice on our behalf. And Euripides shows clearly in his poetry that he is unwittingly talking about the Saviour himself, when he adds:

>   'for thou wieldest the sceptre of Zeus among the heavenly gods,
>   and thou hast a share, along with Hades,
>   of the rule of those within the earth.'

As before, Clement wilfully misses the point of Euripides' words in an attempt to assimilate them to the Christian message. The Euripidean lines are clearly part of a necromantic prayer addressed to Zeus Chthonios or Hades, god of the Underworld.[76] Contrary to his practice elsewhere, Clement retains the direct references to pagan deities, but he nevertheless maintains that Euripides is 'cryptically' (αἰνισσόμενος) alluding to God the Father and Jesus Christ. At the same time, he seems to identify Christ as the god to whom the offering is made *and* as the offering itself. His train of thought is confused, and it is hard to see why Clement thinks that these tragic lines are 'wonderfully in harmony' with Christ's words. They seem to be entirely unconnected to the Gospel verse cited, nor do they have anything in common with what Clement discusses in this chapter immediately beforehand (true knowledge of God) or afterwards (the importance of purification in mystery-cult). It seems that in this case Clement has not properly read or understood the words that he quotes. His confusion illustrates the sort of problems that may arise when one tries to hack away at texts in order to uncover meanings that are not really there.

On the whole, then, Clement struggles to convince us that Euripides was a Christian apologist *avant la lettre*. Nonetheless, his attempt to do so is fascinating because it is a prime example of what Antoine Compagnon has called 'la fonction créatrice de le citation'.[77] Clement shows how the act of quotation can be used as a way of appropriating and rewriting a text, transforming its original meaning into something different. Readers unacquainted with tragedy may find Clement's version of Euripides easier to swallow. But if – as seems likely – Clement's target audience consists of educated people with prior knowledge of the plays, he has a harder task to pull off, for in that case he is not simply rewriting the texts but, more ambitiously, attempting to bring about a cognitive transformation. In effect, he is trying to revise his readers' memories and destabilize their beliefs, persuading them that classic texts which they *think* they understand are radically unfamiliar.

The rewriting may not be entirely successful, but it is notable that Clement performs this 'creative' task without changing Euripides' own words. In this sense he provides a significant contrast with Plutarch, who (as we have seen) sometimes emends or deletes parts of the texts that he quotes in order to make them more suitable for his purposes. Clement demonstrates that *verbatim* quotations, if selected and presented in a certain way, can still constitute a form of rewriting. In other words, meaning does not reside purely in the words themselves; it depends in part on context and use.

Not just the content but the speaking voice or perspective of these quotations is also ambiguous.[78] Who is imagined as uttering the words in question? As I have noted, they are almost never attributed to the character who actually delivered the lines in the play, whether or not Clement had access to this information. Sometimes, Clement, like almost all other quoting authors, treats the quoted verses as equivalent to the personal opinions of Euripides. Sometimes, he presents them in a ventriloquial manner, either blurring them together with his own authorial voice or implicitly attributing them to an impersonal, abstract voice of wisdom.[79] On occasion, he even implies that they represent the revealed Word of God.

Bearing these considerations in mind, we might wonder why Clement bothered to quote Euripides at all. Apparently, he has no interest in Euripides' own ideas, or in the plays' qualities as literature. Why did he not simply expound his own thoughts, rather than attributing them to another writer who did not actually share them? Why was it so important to quote this non-Christian poet in a work of Christian apologetics? The explanation lies in the symbolic value of classic authors. What is being said may be less important than who is saying it. Euripides' enduring status as the most popular and widely admired Greek poet after Homer, together with his reputation as a moralist or 'the philosopher of the stage',[80] meant that his name carried enormous authority and cultural prestige. Such qualities could be used by Clement to his own advantage. As others have noted, certain types of text function as 'authoritative' when quoted: these typically include legal documents, academic research papers, biblical verses, and so on.[81] At first glance, Clement seems to be treating Euripidean quotations in precisely this manner: they are quoted side by side with scriptural quotations, and they are ostensibly presented as authoritative testimonies. But in fact this is purely a rhetorical tactic, since Clement, paradoxically, is removing Euripides' authority by rewriting his work.[82] Euripides retains his status as a classic author, but he has been appropriated and assimilated into the Christian tradition. He is treated as a convert, just as Clement hopes to convert his own readers. In effect, the authority now belongs to Clement himself – or to the Word of God, as now belatedly revealed in the Euripidean text.

Conclusions

The material discussed in this chapter covers a wide geographical range and a period of over six centuries, but one consistent thread running through it is the centrality of Euripides. Wherever Greek literature was taught, Euripides featured prominently on the syllabus; only Homer was more intensively studied.

Other consistent threads have also emerged. We have identified several distinct but overlapping ways in which Euripides' works functioned within ancient education – as aids to basic literacy, as sources of edifying maxims to be memorized, as examples of classic literature, as objects embodying artistic excellence, as case studies for the formation of good taste, as cultural capital, as repositories of truth (of one sort or another) and as authoritative or quasi-scriptural texts. At the same time, there is little interest in the plays as literature or drama. When these teachers quote Euripidean verses to their pupils, they seldom refer to their original function in the mouths of characters within the distant world of tragedy. How these verses function in the here and now is more important.

What stands out above all is that these Euripidean lessons invariably involve quotations rather than whole plays. Presumably there were teachers and pupils who read or acted out entire tragedies at school, but if so, they have left almost no traces behind.[83] The evidence exclusively points to the use of extracts. This is worth emphasizing because the extensive range of passages quoted in classrooms *might* have given us a clue to the transmission or survival of texts at different periods within antiquity – if only we could be confident that the quotations were taken from complete texts. Does the fact that schoolteachers in Hellenistic and Roman Egypt were making their pupils learn chunks of *Ino*, *Hypsipyle*, *Aegeus* and *Telephus* indicate that these plays were still extant? Did Clement have access to the full texts of all thirty-one tragedies that he quotes? As we have repeatedly observed, questions of this sort are impossible to answer. But it will be clear by now that the way in which these teachers and their pupils approached Euripides did not depend on the availability of texts. From their point of view, it would not actually have made any difference whether or not the plays survived. They were all just studying fragments.

6

Quotation as Performance

This chapter considers some occasions on which Euripidean verses were recited in Athenian lawcourts and at Greek and Roman symposia. What links these ostensibly dissimilar contexts is the sense that quotation is a form of social performance: it requires an audience. In the act of quotation people put themselves on display before others. Quotation can be a form of self-projection, through which one can express one's own character and individuality, but it can also be a way of articulating shared ideas and shared values. To know Euripides, and to display that knowledge, is to belong to a community.

In certain situations it might be thought that what a quotation *does* is more significant than what it says. Some of the examples that we shall encounter in this chapter seem to correspond to what J. L. Austin (in *How to Do Things with Words*, the foundational text of speech act theory) called 'performative utterances', defined as 'some cases and senses in which to *say* something is to *do* something; or in which *by* saying or *in* saying something we are doing something'.[1] In such cases, the circumstances of utterance need to be considered as carefully as the words themselves. One example of a performative utterance might be the swearing of an oath, where the words themselves are '(merely) the outward and visible sign, for convenience or other record or for information, of an inward and spiritual act'.[2] (Incidentally, it is interesting to note that Austin chose a quotation from Euripides – *Hippolytus* 612 – to illustrate this point.) Other examples might include promises, wagers and legal formulas. Quotations in their original dramatic setting may or may not be 'performative utterances' in themselves, but we are concerned here with how they function in their new quoting context. In some instances, the meaning and content of the quoted verses is relatively unimportant, but what the quotations are doing there, essentially, is making an announcement to the quoter's audience: 'I know Euripides'; 'I am a cultured and educated individual'; 'I belong to a certain class in society'; 'I am a good Athenian citizen of sound views'; 'I have a persuasive case to make'; 'I am a Hellenophile'; 'I can be assumed to share your outlook on life' – or something along similar lines.

Performing Euripides in the lawcourt

Euripides was recurrently treated in antiquity as a rhetorician. One obvious explanation for this is that many of his plays feature set-piece debating scenes (*agones*), in which two characters express opposing viewpoints in a pair of extended speeches, somewhat in the style of a court case.[3] More generally, Euripides' language and thought reflect the development of the art of rhetoric during the late fifth century, and all of his characters, without great concern for realism, speak in an exaggeratedly sophisticated and self-consciously eloquent style.[4] These characteristics were recognized during the poet's own lifetime, but in the fourth century BC and long afterwards Euripidean tragedy was used as a model for professional orators. Anyone seeking to acquire the art of forensic or deliberative speaking would be as likely to study Euripides as any other speechwriter. Practical handbooks of rhetoric drew on Euripides for examples of specific rhetorical techniques or figures of speech. Aristotle in his *Rhetoric*, for instance, used seventeen illustrative quotations of this type,[5] and identified Euripides as a pioneer of the art of using ordinary language in a skilful and persuasive way (*Rhetoric* 3.2, 1404b5). Several centuries later, Quintilian was still recommending Euripides as the most useful poet for those preparing themselves to plead in court, on the grounds of his style, his maxims, his ideas, and his ability to stir the emotions (*Institutio Oratoria* 10.1.68). It is in part the influence of writers such as these that led to the preservation of so many 'useful' quotations (fragments) from lost plays.

Another reason for treating Euripides as a rhetorician is that in a broader sense the theatre can be seen as analogous to other public venues such as the Athenian assembly and lawcourts. These venues have obvious features in common. They all involve some sort of performance. They are attended by an audience of a roughly comparable constitution and size, including Athenian citizens of all social classes. The performers there are aiming to interact or communicate with the audience in similar ways, using rational persuasion and emotional manipulation to help them achieve their ends (which range from pure entertainment to matters of life and death). The social, political and ideological content of these various performances can be shown to overlap significantly. All of these analogies have been extensively discussed in recent scholarship.[6]

One noteworthy parallel is the similarity in performance style between actors and orators. Delivering a speech, in court or on stage, was regarded as a histrionic performance, requiring skills in impersonation, voice production, delivery, gesture and body language. Throughout the fourth century, these two activities developed in parallel. Not only did the orator's training include increased emphasis on *hypokrisis* (delivery or acting), but the dramatic festivals saw an increasing professionalism in the careers of performers such as Callippides, Neoptolemus, Theodorus and other famous acting 'stars'.[7] Aristotle expressed the view that *hypokrisis* was the most important aspect of rhetorical style, and observed that in theatrical festivals and political contests alike, those who use their voice properly nearly always win (*Rhetoric* 3.1403b26-33). So it is no surprise to learn that one of the most prominent fourth-century orators, Aeschines, also worked as a tragic actor. His rival Demosthenes repeatedly criticized him for this reason, mocking his vocal excesses and his 'third-rate' acting.[8] But perhaps his motives included envy, since we are told that Demosthenes tried to improve his own oratory by taking lessons from the tragic actor Satyrus. According to Plutarch (*Demosthenes* 7), the orator complained to Satyrus that nobody paid attention when he was speaking:

'ἀληθῆ λέγεις, ὦ Δημόσθενες,' φάναι τὸν Σάτυρον, 'ἀλλ' ἐγὼ τὸ αἴτιον ἰάσομαι ταχέως, ἄν μοι τῶν Εὐριπίδου τινὰ ῥήσεων ἢ Σοφοκλέους ἐθελήσῃς εἰπεῖν ἀπὸ στόματος.' εἰπόντος δὲ τοῦ Δημοσθένους μεταλαβόντα τὸν Σάτυρον οὕτω πλάσαι καὶ διεξελθεῖν ἐν ἤθει πρέποντι καὶ διαθέσει τὴν αὐτὴν ῥῆσιν ὥσθ' ὅλως ἑτέραν τῶι Δημοσθένει φανῆναι. πεισθέντα δ' ὅσον ἐκ τῆς ὑποκρίσεως τῶι λόγωι κόσμου καὶ χάριτος πρόσεστι, μικρὸν ἡγήσασθαι καὶ τὸ μηδὲν εἶναι τὴν ἄσκησιν ἀμελοῦντι τῆς προφορᾶς καὶ διαθέσεως τῶν λεγομένων.

'You are right, Demosthenes', said Satyrus, 'but I shall quickly remedy the cause of your problem, if you care to recite from memory some speech or other from Euripides or Sophocles.' Demosthenes duly recited a monologue, whereupon Satyrus, taking up the same speech after him, gave it such a definite shape and delivered it with such suitable feeling and disposition that it seemed to Demosthenes to be an altogether different speech. Having been persuaded how reliant oratory is upon acting style for its attractive and pleasing qualities, he came to realize that it was of almost no use for someone to practise declaiming if he neglected the delivery and disposition of the words spoken.

Even if its factual status has been questioned,[9] this anecdote confirms the importance of *hypokrisis* and the similarity between different types of performance. It also suggests that it was normal for a young orator to have memorized long extracts from tragedy and to be able to quote them on cue.

When fourth-century orators quote Euripidean extracts in the course of their speeches they are (in most cases) not reading them out but *acting* them out. Quotation in court can be seen as an occasion, albeit a limited and temporary one, for the public reperformance of tragedy. For a brief moment, the performance space is reconfigured, the scene seems to shift from the everyday setting of the court to the far-off world of myth, and the speaker temporarily assumes the role of the tragic character in order to bring the words to life. Thus the voice of the orator, the voice of the character and the voice of the author merge into one. Delivering quotations in this way not only makes them stand out with unusual emphasis; it also implies that the content is personally endorsed by the orator, and that the orator is assuming some of the inherited authority of a classic author. But the acting-out of extracts is also a way of appealing to the goodwill of the audience. No doubt many of the jurors or voters were tragedy fans, who will have appreciated these efforts to entertain them. In this way the orator improves his chances of winning his case.

Some of our sources imply that the quotation of poetry in lawcourt speeches was a widespread practice, as one might expect.[10] But the extant works of Greek oratory contain only a handful of quoted passages.[11] This is probably due to accidents of survival: the majority of our speeches are the work of Demosthenes, who (as we shall see) disapproved of the practice. Nevertheless, the few specimens that we have, from speeches delivered by Aeschines, Demosthenes and Lycurgus during the period 346–330, are full of interest. Lycurgus' re-enactment of Praxithea's monologue from Euripides' *Erechtheus* (F360) in his *Against Leocrates* is a particularly striking case, not only because he performs this monologue in its entirety (fifty-five lines) but because he treats it as a straightforward statement of Athenian civic ideology, oversimplifying its meaning and turning it into political propaganda.[12] We also possess a couple of revealing speeches delivered three or four years apart by bitter rivals – Aeschines 1 (*Against Timarchus*) and Demosthenes 19 (*On the False Embassy*). This pair of speeches have many points of contact, but from our perspective they are valuable because they incorporate a debate on the uses and abuses of quotation in a legal setting.

In *Against Timarchus*, Aeschines is prosecuting Timarchus for having squandered his father's estate and earned money as a prostitute, an activity which could be penalized by disenfranchisement. At one point (1.141), Aeschines says that Timarchus' defence (which is now lost) involved the quotation of passages from Homer's *Iliad* and other poetry to show that homosexuality had always been a normal part of Greek culture:

Ἐπειδὴ δὲ Ἀχιλλέως καὶ Πατρόκλου μέμνησθε καὶ Ὁμήρου καὶ ἑτέρων ποιητῶν, ὡς τῶν μὲν δικαστῶν ἀνηκόων παιδείας ὄντων, ὑμεῖς δὲ εὐσχήμονές τινες καὶ περιφρονοῦντες ἱστορίᾳ τὸν δῆμον, ἵν' εἰδῆτε ὅτε καὶ ἡμεῖς τι ἤδη ἠκούσαμεν καὶ ἐμάθομεν, λέξομέν τι καὶ περὶ τούτων. ἐπειδὴ γὰρ ἐπιχειροῦσι φιλοσόφων ἀνδρῶν μεμνῆσθαι καὶ καταφεύγειν ἐπὶ τοὺς εἰρημένους ἐν τῷ μέτρῳ λόγους, θεωρήσατε ἀποβλέψαντες, ὦ ἄνδρες Ἀθηναῖοι, εἰς τοὺς ὁμολογουμένως ἀγαθοὺς καὶ χρηστοὺς ποιητάς, ὅσον κεχωρίσθαι ἐνόμισαν τοὺς σώφρονας καὶ τῶν ὁμοίων ἐρῶντας, καὶ τοὺς ἀκρατεῖς ὧν οὐ χρὴ καὶ τοὺς ὑβριστάς.

Since you mention Achilles and Patroclus, and Homer and other poets – as if the men of the jury were completely lacking in culture, while you are high-class people who despise the educational attainments of the public – we shall say something on this topic too, so that you will understand that we too have acquired a little knowledge and learning. They are attempting to cite wise men, and to take refuge in words spoken in verse; but look, Athenians! Examine the works of those who by common agreement are good and useful poets, and see what a gulf they perceived between chaste men, who love people of like character, and wanton and outrageous men, who love what they should not.

Aeschines goes on to cite other Homeric passages, establishing the point that Homer never depicted Achilles and Patroclus' relationship as sexual.[13] It is significant that on each occasion Aeschines instructs the court clerk (*grammateus*) to read out the Homeric passage in question, in exactly the same way that this official would read out laws, decrees or witness statements wherever relevant. This draws our attention to the fact that both speakers in this case are using poetic quotations as authoritative documents, equivalent in their function to other categories of evidence. Indeed, Aeschines sorely needs such evidence here, for (as he earlier admitted) no *viva voce* witness statements are available (1.119-24).[14] But using quotations in this way was an accepted practice. Aristotle (*Rhetoric* 1.15, 1375b-1376a) treats quotations as witnesses or proofs, and he classes poets among 'well-known men whose critical opinions are familiar to everyone' (λέγω δὲ παλαιοὺς μὲν τούς τε ποιητὰς καὶ ὅσων ἄλλων γνωρίμων εἰσὶ κρίσεις φανεραί). It is implied that only classic authors such as Homer or Euripides are entitled to be used in this manner. But Aeschines' own deployment of quotations is also openly competitive, in that he is trying to refute the passages cited by Timarchus (whatever they may have been), just as an investigator might ferret out discrepancies between the accounts of two witnesses. Evidently his aim was to uncover inconsistent lines within Homer's works, or to juxtapose Homer with another poet to reveal contradictions between them (the same techniques that would later be employed by Plutarch, for different purposes, in *How the Young Man Should Study Poetry*).[15]

The most interesting feature of this passage is the fact that it does not simply use quotations but also openly comments on the use of quotations, drawing a contrast between good and bad practice. It discusses the relationship between literary quotations and the jurors' level of education, acknowledging that different people respond to quotations in different ways. As in so many other quoting contexts, one inevitably wonders how many people recognized the quotations or fully understood their function. Here in the courtroom, this question takes on a new significance. Aeschines recognizes that quotations can help an advocate to win or lose a case. Yet it is hard to judge his own stance or the precise nuance of his argument. By saying that his opponents 'take refuge' in poetry, is he implying that this is a desperate or misguided strategy, or that they have selected the wrong quotations, or simply that their case is a hopeless one? Is he implying that quoting poetry is invariably an elitist move, likely to alienate a sizeable proportion of the jury? Is he implying that Timarchus and his speechwriter have underestimated the jurors, by quoting verses that they already know well or by insulting their intelligence with clumsy exegesis? It is hard to decide. But when Aeschines uses the phrase 'We too' (καὶ ἡμεῖς), he is obviously ingratiating himself with the audience by pretending to be on exactly the same level as them.[16] He is trying to please everybody at once. All this ambiguity is therefore part of a rhetorical strategy, allowing him to have it both ways. It means that he can simultaneously use quotations himself and imply that other people are somehow misguided when they do so.

Euripides is the next 'good and useful poet' cited by Aeschines in the following portion of his speech (1.151-3):

ὁ τοίνυν οὐδενὸς ἧττον σοφὸς τῶν ποιητῶν Εὐριπίδης, ἕν τι τῶν καλλίστων ὑπολαμβάνων εἶναι τὸ σωφρόνως ἐρᾶν, ἐν εὐχῆς μέρει τὸν ἔρωτα ποιούμενος λέγει που·

ὁ δ' εἰς τὸ σῶφρον ἐπ' ἀρετήν τ' ἄγων ἔρως
ζηλωτὸς ἀνθρώποισιν, ὧν εἴην ἐγώ.

πάλιν τοίνυν ὁ αὐτὸς ἐν τῷ Φοίνικι ἀποφαίνεται, ὑπὲρ τῆς γεγενημένης αὐτῷ πρὸς τὸν πατέρα διαβολῆς ἀπολογούμενος, καὶ ἀπεθίζων τοὺς ἀνθρώπους μὴ ἐξ ὑποψίας μηδ' ἐκ διαβολῆς, ἀλλ' ἐκ τοῦ βίου, τὰς κρίσεις ποιεῖσθαι·

ἤδη δὲ πολλῶν ᾑρέθην λόγων κριτής,
καὶ πόλλ' ἁμιλληθέντα μαρτύρων ὕπο
τἀναντί' ἔγνων συμφορᾶς μιᾶς πέρι.
κἀγὼ μὲν οὕτω, χὤστις ἔστ' ἀνὴρ σοφός,
λογίζομαι τἀληθές, εἰς ἀνδρὸς φύσιν
σκοπῶν δίαιτάν θ', ἥντιν' ἐμπορεύεται.
ὅστις δ' ὁμιλῶν ἥδεται κακοῖς ἀνήρ,

οὐ πώποτ' ἠρώτησα, γιγνώσκων ὅτι
τοιοῦτός ἐσθ' οἵοισπερ ἥδεται ξυνών.
σκέψασθε δέ, ὦ ἄνδρες Ἀθηναῖοι, τὰς γνώμας ἃς ἀποφαίνεται ὁ ποιητής.

Well, then – there is no poet wiser than Euripides, and he says that chaste love is one of the finest things. Somewhere or other he includes love in a prayer:

The kind of love that leads towards chastity and virtue

is enviable among mortals – I pray that I might have such love! [*Stheneboea* F661.24-5]

And again the same poet, in *Phoenix* [F812], expresses his opinion thus, in a defence speech against false accusations brought by the father, trying to accustom people to form judgements based not on suspicion or slander but on life:

In the past I was chosen as a judge in many disputes,

and I came to understand that witnesses made many

contradictory and opposing statements about the same issue.

But I myself, together with every wise man,

reckon that this is the truth, by examining a man's nature

and lifestyle and the way he deals with others.

But I have never questioned anyone who takes pleasure

in associating with base men. I realize that such a person

is just like those with whom he consorts.

My fellow Athenians, consider the opinions which the poet expresses …

These two Euripidean quotations function in a different way from the Homeric quotations that precede. In the first place, Euripides is said to be wiser than Homer or any other poet. This is partly a way of saying that his meaning coincides more conveniently with the speaker's own argument, but the explicit claim that Euripides represents a more authoritative figure than even Homer is unusual. This claim may seem controversial, but it makes perfect sense in relation to the great surge in Euripidophilia at Athens during the mid- to late fourth century.[17] Aeschines can be seen as deliberately playing to an audience of tragedy fans, and Euripides is being hyped above Homer because he represents the people's favourite. The audience will have been even more delighted with the dramatized re-enactment that follows. The major difference between the Homeric and the Euripidean citations is that Aeschines does not ask the court official to read the Euripidean extracts; he acts them out himself. While in some ways this may seem to diminish their status as official evidence, it means that Aeschines can use all the histrionic skills at his disposal to give the words more force and impact. The first extract, consisting of a mere two verses, offers the actor little scope, but the second extract gives more opportunity for Aeschines to get into character.

A further difference between these Euripidean lines and the earlier quotations is that their voice and focalizing perspective is more fluid. The first quotation, part of the opening monologue from *Stheneboea*, is not identified. By saying vaguely that it is found 'somewhere or other', Aeschines may be maintaining his crowd-pleasing posture of not being as intimidatingly well read as Timarchus; or perhaps he found the verses in an anthology and is genuinely uncertain where they come from. Either way, the identity of the original speaker, Bellerophon, is concealed, and the words come across as the voice of Euripides speaking to us directly. In contrast, the second quotation is explicitly said to come from *Phoenix*, and some reference is made to the plot and the dramatic context (in which Phoenix, falsely accused of rape by his father Amyntor's concubine, was forced to defend himself). But still Aeschines does not identify the speaker; nor has anybody else managed to do so (Phoenix himself is ruled out because he is too young).[18] Even though Aeschines proceeds to act out the part of this character himself by dramatically reciting the lines, he nonetheless maintains that the opinions being expressed are those of the playwright. At the same time, by ventriloquizing these sentiments, he gives us to understand that he endorses them completely. Furthermore, he invites the jurors themselves to identify with the author/speaker, arguing that Euripides as an experienced judge of human affairs is exactly parallel to their own status as jurors (1.153). He concludes by urging them to follow 'the reasoning of Euripides' when passing judgment on Timarchus (οὐκοῦν δίκαιον καὶ περὶ Τιμάρχου τοῖς αὐτοῖς ὑμᾶς Εὐριπίδῃ χρήσασθαι λογισμοῖς, 1.154). Thus the quotation from *Phoenix* is functioning simultaneously here as the voice of the original speaker, the voice of Aeschines as advocate-actor, the wisdom of Euripides, the voice of popular morality (echoed by all right-thinking Athenians but not by Timarchus and his kind), and a legal principle on which the outcome of the case may depend. The fact that it originally came from some sort of *agon* scene – where it would have represented one side of an unresolved debate, not an unquestioned statement of principle – is entirely ignored. Similarly, Aeschines conveniently glosses over the dramatic circumstances in which both these utterances were first heard. Since the plots of both *Stheneboea* and *Phoenix* revolved around an older woman's advances towards a young man, they might seem odd choices to illustrate an argument about the ethics of same-sex relationships.

When Demosthenes hits back at Aeschines, in *On the False Assembly*, he specifically attacks his rival for 'collecting iambics' (ἰαμβεῖα ... συλλέξας) instead of producing real-life witnesses or convincing arguments (19.243-5). He sarcastically quotes back some of the same passage from *Phoenix*, showing that

Aeschines' recitation of these verses made a vivid impression on him. He also suggests that Aeschines chose this play to quote because of personal ambition, because he had always wanted to perform in *Phoenix* in the theatre but never got an opportunity to do so (19.246). Elaborating on the theme of Aeschines' acting career, Demosthenes ironically suggests that the role of Creon in Sophocles' *Antigone* would have suited him better (19.246-7):

ἐν ᾗ πεποιημέν' ἰαμβεῖα καλῶς καὶ συμφερόντως ὑμῖν πολλάκις αὐτὸς εἰρηκὼς καὶ ἀκριβῶς ἐξεπιστάμενος παρέλιπεν. ἴστε γὰρ δήπου τοῦθ', ὅτι ἐν ἅπασι τοῖς δράμασι τοῖς τραγικοῖς ἐξαίρετόν ἐστιν ὥσπερ γέρας τοῖς τριταγωνισταῖς τὸ τοὺς τυράννους καὶ τοὺς τὰ σκῆπτρ' ἔχοντας εἰσιέναι. ταῦτα τοίνυν ἐν τῷ δράματι τούτῳ σκέψασθ' ὁ Κρέων Αἰσχίνης οἷα λέγων πεποίηται τῷ ποιητῇ, ἃ οὔτε πρὸς αὐτὸν οὗτος ὑπὲρ τῆς πρεσβείας διελέχθη οὔτε πρὸς τοὺς δικαστὰς εἶπεν. λέγε.

That play contains some iambics that are composed in a fine and fitting fashion; but even though he has often recited them and knows them thoroughly by heart, he left those verses out of his speech. For naturally you are aware that in all tragic plays the tritagonists have the lucky privilege of acting the parts of tyrants and coming on stage with sceptre in hand. Well, then, you shall consider those verses from *Antigone* composed by the poet for Creon-Aeschines, the ones that he did not quote in connection with the embassy and did not recite to the jury. Read them out!

Note the repeated use of ἰαμβεῖα ('iambics') as a disparaging way of referring to quotations from drama, and the fact that Demosthenes pointedly instructs the clerk of court to read out the Sophoclean verses so that he can avoid doing so himself. (It is tempting to imagine the clerk reading the passage in an exaggeratedly dry, deadpan manner, but this is not necessary in order to appreciate the significance of the contrast.) There follows a quotation of *Antigone* 175-90, which we are invited to interpret as evidence of the 'tyrannical' character of Aeschines. It emerges that, in effect, Demosthenes is *parodying* Aeschines' own deployment of quotations here. More specifically, he is criticizing his tendentious choice of extracts, he is questioning the tendency of orators to identify with the sentiments expressed by others and he is poking fun at the assumption that a passage relating to a specific tragic character can be used as evidence for the moral disposition of a completely different real-life person.

Here and throughout the whole speech, Demosthenes makes a special effort to emphasize the *un*theatricality of his own rhetoric, in stark contrast to the exaggerated histrionics of Aeschines (19.23, 206, 208, 209, 216-17). What we have here is 'a purposeful battle of texts', as Nancy Worman puts it in her illuminating discussion of the two speeches.[19] Demosthenes is not only attacking Aeschines' case and his presentation of Timarchus' character but is also offering a critique of his whole approach, courtroom behaviour and general principles. It could scarcely be made any plainer that, in Demosthenes' view, tragic quotations are out of place in a lawcourt. They prove nothing. At worst, they distort the issues at stake; at best, they distract from the truth. Conspicuously, the only occasions on which Demosthenes includes tragic quotations in his own speeches are here and in *On the Crown* (18.267): in each case, he is contemptuously *requoting* verses previously recited by Aeschines.[20] But of course Demosthenes, despite his professed disdain for histrionic displays, is nonetheless performing a role; it is just a different sort of role. Like Aeschines and all of the other orators, he wants to win his case by persuading his audience that he is in the right. The carefully judged deployment – or rejection – of quotations is just one among many tactics used to achieve this end.

Showing off at the symposium

Our impressions of a typical Greek or Roman symposium – the food and drink consumed, the rituals and customs observed, the nature of the entertainment on offer and the behaviour of the guests – are based on a motley and not wholly representative collection of source-material. Apart from the evidence of archaeology, for the archaic period we have self-reflexive descriptions in lyric poetry, while for later periods we have various accounts of parties and banquets in texts such as Plato's *Symposium*, Xenophon's *Symposium* and *Memorabilia*, Plutarch's *Table-Talk*, Athenaeus' *Deipnosophistae*, Lucian's *Symposium* and Macrobius' *Saturnalia*.[21] The artificiality of these texts needs to be acknowledged: their authors are not exactly offering us a window into real-life symposia, but they are presenting us with stylized literary depictions of social and intellectual life in a variety of different periods and places.[22] Nevertheless, our evidence is remarkably consistent in the ways in which it characterizes the symposium as an institution, and some recurrent trends can be identified. Throughout classical antiquity, the symposium emerges as a self-selecting gathering of the upper classes; as a private performance venue for music and poetry, contrasting with the public festivals; as an occasion for conversation about frivolous topics as well as serious ethical or political concerns; as a space in which male identity was formed or tested; and as a prime arena for competitive behaviour.[23] By the time of the Roman Empire, the symposium also came to symbolize cultural superiority and nostalgic fantasy, as an occasion on which members of the Roman elite were able to 'act out their own position within a wider Greek sympotic community stretching back over many centuries' (as Jason König nicely puts it).[24]

This section takes a look at the most important surviving example of sympotic literature, *Deipnosophistae* ('The Intellectuals at Dinner'), which purports to be an eye-witness account of dinner parties at the house of Larensis, a wealthy Roman bibliophile, during the closing years of the second century AD. This extraordinary work, in fifteen books (not all of which survive in full), was composed by Athenaeus of Naucratis, an Egyptian scholar working in Rome under Larensis' patronage. It is unusual in its degree of self-reflexivity, in that the banquet is not simply the setting for the dialogue but also the main topic of conversation: Larensis and his guests talk almost exclusively about food, drink, entertainment and related matters. For our purposes *Deipnosophistae* is valuable partly because it depicts the act of quotation as a central element in table-talk, and partly because of its own unusual design and structure as a literary text. Although it is conventionally assigned to the genre of sympotic literature, it is a unique work without exact parallel (either in the ancient world or in more recent literature). It is essentially a mélange of quotations from over a thousand other texts, including many tantalizing extracts from lost works of classical and Hellenistic literature.[25] The perfunctory framing narrative of each dinner party is little more than a technical device for the arrangement and presentation of extracts from other works. Athenaeus' work is inherently secondary or parasitic in its conception: it owes its entire existence to quotation. It has been described in recent scholarship as, *inter alia*, a virtual library, a web of Ariadne, a dramatization of the act of reading, a guidebook to classical literature, an edited collection of sources, or the equivalent of an anthology with connecting commentary.[26] For these reasons, *Deipnosophistae* is a crucial document for the study of quotation culture.

Throughout this work, quotation is highlighted as a topic of interest in its own right. Near the beginning (1.4c),[27] we are told that each of Larensis' guests arrived at the party carrying a bag of books as their contribution to the feast. This may imply that whenever anyone quotes from a text they are to be imagined as taking the relevant volume out of their bag and reading aloud. Occasionally Athenaeus does appear to be describing recitation from a book (e.g. 7.277b-c), but more typically he shows his characters quoting from memory, often at impressive length.[28] The ability to quote spontaneously is prized as a sign of culture (*paideia*), and those who can effortlessly call to mind the *mot juste* on any occasion are extravagantly praised (e.g. 3.108e-f, 3.113d-e, 13.610b). By contrast, anyone who cannot rise to the challenge earns scorn – such as the poseur Calliphanes, who memorized just three or four lines from the beginning of a few texts in his effort to gain a reputation as a polymath (1.4c). Even Larensis' cook is so learned that he can spout long passages from comic drama (9.381f); Larensis swaggeringly asserts that it is preferable for cooks to learn such passages by heart than to memorize Socratic dialogues. A frequent party game takes the form of a literary quiz, whereby a character comes up with an obscure word or fact and challenges his fellow guests to identify texts in which this detail can be found. The grammarian Ulpian is especially fond of this game, posing such questions as: 'In whose works does the "fattened goose" appear?' (ὁ δὲ σιτευτὸς χὴν παρὰ τίνι;), or refusing to eat his dinner until someone tells him which authors mention wheat puddings.[29]

In order to shine in such company, the partygoer must possess detailed and often highly specialized literary knowledge. Even if the characters are not envisaged as having a *verbatim* recall of every single text that they recite, it is made clear that they know exactly where the required passage is to be found – and that is the crucial issue at stake. Sometimes, they openly admit that they have taken their quotations from intermediate sources rather than first-hand acquaintance with the texts, or they refer to anthologies or notebooks based on reading done long ago (e.g. 6.263a-b, 8.336d-e, 8.347e-f). Similarly, it does not really matter whether Athenaeus himself has personally read every word of the texts that he cites. As Christian Jacob points out, 'knowing' a text can be equivalent to knowing where to find it, or being able to talk intelligently about its contents.[30] What is impressive about Athenaeus and his characters alike is the comprehensive scope of their knowledge, combining a macro-level coverage of the Greek literary corpus and a micro-level focus on specific details.

Athenaeus repeatedly demonstrates that being able to navigate Greek culture and locate arcane bits of trivia – whether in a bookroll, or on the shelves of a library or in the recesses of one's own memory – is a way of acquiring social status, at the expense of others who lack this skill.[31] It is stated (3.97a-b) that while literary quotation is an expected, even compulsory, activity at elite gatherings such as that of Larensis, it is absent from the symposia of 'low-class and common people' (τῶν φαύλων καὶ ἀγοραίων ἀνθρώπων). Since their lack of *paideia* makes them unable to rely on their own conversation, such people resort to harp-girls and dancers. By contrast, Athenaeus explains, if the guests are educated men from the upper classes (καλοὶ καὶ ἀγαθοὶ ξυμπόται καὶ πεπαιδευμένοι), they are able to entertain themselves using their own intellectual resources, even when they are drunk. It could scarcely be made any clearer that quotation is an inherently competitive activity and a way of acting out one's role in the social hierarchy. Sometimes, these upper-class symposiasts might compete with one another to be seen as the *crème de la crème*, but on the whole their quotation-swapping is calculated to increase solidarity and rapport among the social group. It is above all a source of fun and laughter, not a cause of serious conflict or aggression. These men are using *paideia* to emphasize what they have in common: it is this store of knowledge, not wealth or birth alone, that sets them apart from other sections of society.

Where does Euripides fit into this picture? For Athenaeus and his readers, Euripides represents a classic Greek author, a marker of civilization and a source of authority. He is several times called 'Euripides the wise' (ὁ σοφός, 6.270c) or 'the philosopher of the stage' (ὁ σκηνικὸς φιλόσοφος, 4.158e, 13.561a), epithets which are not Athenaeus' own coinages but reflect the wider tradition of Euripides' reception within antiquity.[32] The playwright is treated not only as a source of quotations but also as the subject of biographical anecdotes (13.557e, 10.424e-f, 13.604e-f). One of the diners reflects an ongoing debate about the relative merits of Euripides and Sophocles, quoting Lynceus' *Letter to the Comedian Posidippus* for the view that Euripides is the better of the two at depicting emotions (14.652c-d). Another diner relates that Alexander the Great himself used to quote Euripides from memory at banquets, referring to the memoirs of Alexander's courtesan Nicoboule as evidence (12.537d-e). All this biographical and critical material is cited directly from Hellenistic scholarship and, once again, reflects a well-established tradition of reception.

Tragedy is quoted much less often than comedy or epic (unsurprisingly, since it seldom mentions food or drink), but it still occupies an important place in Athenaeus' 'virtual library'. The fictionalized partygoers use Euripidean quotations, alongside other types of literary and cultural knowledge, as a source of entertainment and a way of showing off. Not all of these quotations function in exactly the same way. Some are inserted as throwaway tags or quasi-proverbial expressions to add a 'literary' flavour to a speech;[33] some are maxims (though Athenaeus includes surprisingly few 'quotational' verses of this sort, in contrast with other quoting authors);[34] some are used as the basis for a learned joke or pun; some depend for their effect on Euripides' status as a classic; some require a certain level of factual recall or a token engagement with the original source play. Many of them, however, are cited purely for their information content or their use of recherché vocabulary. If a speaker happens to be talking about (as it might be) a certain type of ham, or a traditional sympotic custom, or an unusual drinking vessel, or an arcane detail of sacrificial ritual or the origins of alcoholic drink, they might adduce a passage from Euripides to illustrate the detail under discussion – as for instance, at 9.368d (citing *Sciron* F677 for the word κωλῆνες), 11.504b (citing *Cretan Women* F468 on the circulation of the loving-cup), 11.496 (citing *Eurystheus* F379 for the word σκύφος), 8.362f (citing *Medea* 193 for the word εἰλαπίναι), 9.409a-b (citing *Heracles* 929 for the word χερνίψ), 2.40b (citing *Bacchae* 772-4 concerning Dionysus' gift of wine to mortals) and so on. But they might equally use some other text from the vast body of Greek literature to illustrate such phenomena.

Euripides is not the only authority cited – far from it. Nor is there any sense that his works are different in kind from any of the other texts quoted for their factual content. No concession is made to the fact that Euripides' works are tragedies: they are treated as repositories of information, or as books on a shelf, rather than works of drama. For Athenaeus' diners, there is no functional distinction between (say) Euripides' *Medea*, Nicander's *On Beekeeping*, Nicophon's *Sirens*, Semus' *History of Delos* or Mnesitheus' *On Edible Substances*. These and other works cited have the same status, as members of the capacious category of 'classic literature of the past', without differentiation according to genre. Athenaeus conveys almost no sense of the original shape, purpose, meaning, tone, speaker or dramatic context of any of the Euripidean passages that he quotes. Since his own interests are thematically restricted, his quotations cannot be seen as truly representative or typical of the works from which they come. Indeed, if Athenaeus' quotations (or 'fragments') were all that remained to us of the lost tragedies of Euripides, we might well come away with the misleading impression that these plays were all about eating and drinking.

Athenaeus and his partygoers know perfectly well, of course, that tragedy is not much concerned with culinary or domestic matters. This is precisely why it is funny to pretend that it is, by quoting atypical snippets and making it seem as if they reflect the main themes of tragic drama, or by taking ordinary lines and transforming their meaning into something different. This is the same technique that the Greek comedians use when parodying Euripides – fixating on banal details, obtruding everyday realism into the rarefied and sombre world of tragedy, and jarringly juxtaposing 'high' and 'low' elements.[35] A good example of the technique is seen in 1.4a-b where Athenaeus is describing the wit and sophistication of Charmus, a host of dinner parties in Syracuse long ago:

Κλέαρχός φησι Χάρμον τὸν Συρακούσιον εὐτρεπίσθαι στιχίδια καὶ παροιμίας εἰς ἕκαστον τῶν ἐν τοῖς δείπνοις παρατιθεμένων. εἰς μὲν τὸν ἰχθύν·

ἥκω λιπὼν Αἰγαῖον ἁλμυρὸν βάθος,
εἰς δὲ τοὺς κήρυκας·
 χαίρετε, κήρυκες, Διὸς ἄγγελοι,
εἰς δὲ τὴν χορδήν·
 ἑλικτὰ κοὐδὲν ὑγιές,
εἰς δὲ τὴν ὠνθυλευμένην τευθίδα·
 σοφὴ σοφὴ σύ,
εἰς δὲ τὸ ἐν τοῖς ἑψητοῖς ὡραῖον·
 οὐκ ἀπ' ἐμοῦ σκεδάσεις ὄχλον;
εἰς δὲ τὴν ἀποδεδαρμένην ἔγχελυν·
 οὐ προκαλυπτομένα βοστρυχώδεα.

Clearchus reports that Charmus of Syracuse rehearsed appropriate verses and aphorisms to go with each of the dishes served at his banquets. To go with the fish course:
 'I have come, leaving the salty depth of the Aegean.' [Euripides, *Women of Troy* 1]
With the trumpet-shells:
 'Greetings, heralds, messengers of Zeus!' [Homer, *Iliad* 1.334]
With the sausage:
 'twisted and altogether unhealthy'. [Euripides, *Andromache* 448]
With the stuffed squid:
 'Thou art clever, clever!' [Euripides, *Andromache* 245]
For the boiled seasonal fish:
 'Scatter the crowd from my presence!' [*Cypria* F16 Bernabé]
For the flayed eel:
 'not concealing myself with tresses'. [Euripides, *Phoenician Women* 1485]

These quotations from Euripides and epic poetry are being used *as if* they literally referred to the dishes on Charmus' table, but the joke lies in the fact that they obviously do not. Poseidon's opening line from *Women of Troy*, terrifying in its original setting, becomes merely silly if we imagine a fish speaking it; Andromache was criticizing Spartan deviousness, not sausages; Hermione was not thinking of squid but threatening to kill her 'clever' love rival Andromache; this supposed description of an eel was part of an agonized outburst from Antigone, comparing herself to a maenad – and so on. Whether or not we recall the specific source of each quotation, we are meant to be struck by the ludicrous incongruity of these serious verses in a frivolous setting. Charmus is depicted as knowing his texts so well that he can use a carefully calculated irrelevance as the basis for selecting verses. His choice of lines also shows a lively appreciation of wordplay and puns: for example, in turning the metaphor 'twisted' into a literal description, or exploiting the fact that κῆρυξ can refer to either a herald or a trumpet-shell fish. This is precisely the sort of parodic verbal humour and irony that one might find in Aristophanes.

Note that this account of Charmus' dinner parties is directly attributed to a work by Clearchus [= F90 Wehrli], a Peripatetic scholar of the fourth or early third century BC. This is significant not just because it reveals something of Athenaeus' use of source material, but chiefly because it reveals that there was already a flourishing tradition of sympotic quotation, and a scholarly interest in table-talk as a literary genre, centuries before Athenaeus came along. Over the course of fifteen books, Athenaeus cites several previous works devoted to this topic, such as Chamaeleon's *On Pleasure,* Theophrastus' *On Inebriation,* Aristodemus' *Amusing Memoirs,* Lynceus' *Memorable Sayings* and similar books by Timachidas of Rhodes, Numenius of Heracleia and others (all now lost). Many works of this type existed in the Hellenistic period: at 6.244b it is reported that Callimachus' *Pinakes,* an annotated catalogue of the books in the Library of Alexandria arranged by category, had a whole section listing 'authors of descriptions of dinner-parties' (δεῖπνα ὅσοι ἔγραψαν). No doubt much of the content of *Deipnosophistae,* including its use of Euripidean quotations and related anecdotes, derives from literature of this sort.

Euripides was clearly being quoted at fashionable parties from an early period, even during his own lifetime. Although Charmus' banquets cannot be pinned down to a precise date, we know from other sources that Euripides' plays were popular in Syracuse during the 410s BC, so a fifth-century setting cannot be ruled out.[36] The evidence of Aristophanes' *Clouds* is more secure. This comedy, originally performed in 423 BC, features a scene (1353-72) in which a young man (Pheidippides) and his father (Strepsiades) argue about the best sort of poetry to perform at an Athenian symposium. Strepsiades likes to hear Simonides, accompanied by the lyre, but Pheidippides rejects this choice as *passé,* preferring to recite part of a speech from Euripides' *Aeolus.* The performance of tragic extracts must have already been a familiar sympotic practice in order for the comedian to poke fun at it in this way. Another relevant source by a contemporary of Euripides is *Epidemiai* ('Excursions'), a fragmentary work by the tragedian and polymath Ion of Chios. This text, parts of which are preserved by Athenaeus, seems to have been a mixture of autobiography and local history, recounting anecdotes about famous men encountered by Ion during his travels round Greece.[37] In one important fragment of *Epidemiai* [*FGrHist* 392 F6], quoted by Athenaeus at 13.603f-604e, Ion describes the time when he met Sophocles at a dinner party on Chios. Sophocles takes a fancy to the slave who pours his wine, making him blush, and flirtatiously conjures up an apt quotation from a tragedy by Phrynichus:

> ἔτι πολὺ μᾶλλον ἐρυθριάσαντος τοῦ παιδὸς εἶπε πρὸς τὸν συγκατακείμενον· Ὡς καλῶς Φρύνιχος ἐποίησεν εἴπας λάμπει δ' ἐπὶ πορφυρέαις παρῆισι φῶς ἔρωτος.
>
> When the slave boy blushed all the more deeply, Sophocles said to the man sharing his couch: 'Phrynichus put it so well when he said: "the light of love shines brightly on his crimson cheeks" [Phrynichus F3].'

Sophocles' fellow guest praises his cleverness but ventures to contradict him, saying that Phrynichus chose the wrong colour for the boy's cheeks; Sophocles laughs and responds by quoting a description of a girl's 'crimson' mouth from Simonides (*PMG* 585). This fragment from *Epidemiai* gives us a rare and valuable eye-witness account of a fifth-century symposium. Although Ion does not mention Euripides, he vividly depicts a social and intellectual milieu with which he would have been familiar. This is a world in which sophisticated partygoers – including tragedians – sit around the table and display their *paideia* by spouting quotations at one another for fun. To all intents and purposes, it looks the same as the world evoked by Athenaeus centuries later.

Back at Larensis' dinner table (12.530d) Athenaeus also conjures up the spirit of the Hellenistic symposium, citing Aristotle as the source of a joke based on a quotation from *Hippolytus*. Even if the anecdote is apocryphal, we are meant to accept that this is the sort of good-natured banter that philosophers exchange when they are off duty:

> Ἀριστοτέλης Ξενοκράτην τὸν Χαλκηδόνιον σκώπτων ὅτι οὐρῶν οὐ προσῆγε τὴν χεῖρα τῶι αἰδοίωι ἔλεγεν· χεῖρες μὲν ἁγναί, φρὴν δ' ἔχει μίασμά τι.
>
> Aristotle made fun of Xenocrates of Chalcedon because he would not touch his private parts when he was urinating, saying: 'My mind is polluted, but my hands are pure'. [*Hippolytus* 317]

Like the Euripidean lines quoted by Charmus (1.4a), this verse receives a parodic, quasi-Aristophanic treatment. Even though not a word has been altered, the elevated tone of the original is made to seem undignified and ridiculous by the suggestion of a scatological double meaning. What makes the joke funnier is that the line was originally spoken by the distraught Phaedra in answer to the Nurse's question: 'Are your hands clean of blood, my child?' (*Hippolytus* 316, ἁγνὰς μέν, ὦ παῖ, χεῖρας αἵματος φορεῖς;). Aristotle, who would certainly have known this, can be seen as deliberately exploiting the mismatch between the tragic and the sympotic situations. But neither he nor Athenaeus identifies the source of the quotation. Just like 'invisible' quotations in comedy,[38] this joke is obviously designed for a target audience of bookish symposiasts and fellow-intellectuals. Those who recognized the quotation would be rewarded by getting the full effect of the joke. But even if some people at the party failed to identify the source, they would still appreciate the incongruity between solemn and humorous contexts and realize that the tragic line had nothing to do with lavatorial etiquette.

Many other Euripidean quotations in *Deipnosophistae* are unidentified because the symposiast or reader is being challenged to recognize them for himself. In general, though not invariably, one can distinguish between quotations of the 'informative' type, illustrating a factual point (which are normally cited with their author and source reference, thus proving the quoter's scholarly *bona fides*), and 'entertaining' quotations (which tend to be unattributed, as a way of testing the audience's knowledge and powers of recall). Sometimes, quotations from more than one source are invisibly run together to provide an additional challenge – as in the following scene (14.640a-b), in which 'second tables' (i.e. after-dinner snacks) are being served to Larensis' guests:

ἔφη τις τῶν παρόντων·
  αἱ δεύτεραί πως φροντίδες σοφώτεραι·
  τί γὰρ ποθεῖ τράπεζα; τῶι δ' οὐ βρίθεται;
  πλήρης μὲν ὄψων ποντίων, πάρεισι δὲ
  μόσχων τέρειναι σάρκες χηνεία τε δαὶς
  καὶ πεπτὰ καὶ κροτητὰ τῆς ξουθοπτέρου
  πελανῶι μελίσσης ἀφθόνως δεδευμένα,
φησὶν ὁ Εὐριπίδης ἐν Κρήσσαις.

One of the guests said:
'Second thoughts are wiser, I suppose' –
'For what is missing from the table? It is laden; what does it lack? It is full of cooked seafood, and here too are tender cuts of meat from veal, and a feast of goose, and cakes and biscuits, liberally soaked in honey from the fluttering-winged bee',
as Euripides says in *Cretan Women*. [F467]

The mention of 'second tables' leads naturally enough to the line about 'second thoughts' via a process of thought association. But no indication is given that there are two separate quotations here. The second, less famous one is clearly labelled with author and title, either by the speaker or by Athenaeus himself: the fact that speech marks are never used in ancient texts makes it impossible to say who supplied the reference. By contrast, the first one (from *Hippolytus* 436) is invisibly introduced. Perhaps the speaker is deliberately trying to amuse or baffle his listeners by stitching together a patchwork or cento of lines from different plays; or perhaps the two excerpts are functioning in quite distinct ways. Could it be that the *Hippolytus* quotation had become so familiar as an independent maxim (or proverbial expression, or cliché) that it no longer fully counted as a 'quotation' as such?

Another unidentified verse is quoted in an anecdote (5.186d) concerning the philosopher Zeno, who finds himself dining alongside a glutton:

> ὁ δὲ Ζήνων ἐπεί τις τῶν παρόντων ὀψοφάγων ἀπέσυρεν ἅμα τῶι παρατεθῆναι τὸ ἐπάνω τοῦ ἰχθύος, στρέψας καὶ αὐτὸς τὸν ἰχθὺν ἀπέσυρεν ἐπιλέγων· Ἰνὼ δὲ τἀπὶ θάτερ᾽ ἐξειργάζετο.

> When a gluttonous guest tore off the entire upper fillet from a fish as soon as it was served, Zeno flipped it over and tore off the other fillet for himself. As he did so, he said: '...and Ino finished the job on the other side'. [*Bacchae* 1129]

Since *Bacchae* was consistently one of Euripides' most popular plays throughout antiquity, perhaps the quotation is thought to be too well known to require identification. But even if anyone failed to spot that it came from a horrific description of the killing and dismembering of Pentheus by the maenads, Zeno's redeployment of the line is funny because of its clash of 'high' and 'low' registers (like the other humorous examples discussed above) and because the original line so obviously did not refer to filleting fish. Athenaeus evidently thought highly of this witticism – so much so that he included it almost word for word in another book (8.344a), this time with Bion rather than Zeno named as the witty quoter. This inconsistency may seem puzzling, but it reflects the complex nature of Athenaeus' source material and the fact that 'biographical' anecdotes of this sort have a tendency to attach themselves interchangeably to different characters. (See Chapter 7, pp. 159–60.) The factual accuracy of the anecdote is less important than its value as a figurative representation of a social milieu and a characteristic way of looking at the world. Whether or not we take this story literally, it illustrates the sort of repartee that *any* learned person might deliver at a party.

Questions of historical accuracy or realism recur whenever we contemplate the world evoked by *Deipnosophistae*. On the face of it, this compendious work is a true account of the interactions of a specific social group in a specific time and place; it also preserves accounts of countless other social interactions from all over the ancient world. As we have seen, many of these Euripidean examples are quotations within quotations: they appear in extracts from earlier works cited by Larensis' guests rather than in the main framing narrative. Thus we are being presented with snippets of conversations at gatherings ranging across several centuries, in locations as diverse as Athens, Rome, Syracuse, Chios, Babylon and Macedon. It seems that wherever Hellenic culture existed, Euripides was being quoted.

And yet, as already noted, Athenaeus' text is an artificial literary concoction. His world might better be described as a bibliocosm rather than an authentic representation of any real-life setting. We may be tempted to detect a certain paradox in the fact that *Deipnosophistae* simultaneously evokes the symposium *and* the library, combining a sense of fun and playfulness with sober scholarship and dry-as-dust pedantry. Athenaeus has obviously dreamt up these imaginary parties while sitting in the library, surrounded by books – for how else could he have written this enormous work, with its thousands of quotations? But it would be wrong to think of Athenaeus' Roman library as an antisocial space (like a modern university library with its forbidding signs reminding readers that 'Silence is requested'). Ancient libraries were lively settings for human interaction, equipped with social areas, colonnades and communal dining facilities; they encouraged scholarly conversation as well as reading.[39] Perhaps the symposium and the library in antiquity were not so dissimilar as we might assume.

Conclusions

The lawcourt and the symposium, despite obvious differences, can be seen as parallel social environments. In both settings quotations are recurrently associated with performance and display. They function as a way of communicating with an audience, though what the quoters want to communicate is often something about themselves – or, at any rate, it is something very different from the surface meaning of the verses quoted. As we have seen repeatedly, the symbolic significance of a quotation can be just as important as its literal meaning. Far removed from their original settings in tragic drama, these Euripidean verses have been filtered, desensitized, reimagined and redeployed.

In the mouths of advocates or partygoers alike, these verses have a number of distinct but interrelated functions – as evidence or proof to back up an argument; as inherited knowledge shared by all who are present; as flashes of ancient wisdom; as statements of ethical or ideological values; as tools in persuasion; as pawns to be played in the competitive game between rival advocates; as a way of scoring points; as markers of social or intellectual status; or as a source of entertainment. In these settings, quoting Euripides can be an inherently combative act, or it can bring people together; it can have deadly serious consequences, or it can be entirely frivolous and silly.

7

Quotations and Life

In contrast to modern-day critics, who tend to have a more nuanced conception of authorial voice and persona, the majority of Greek and Roman readers routinely treated verses of poetry (not just tragedy) as equivalent to 'personal testaments' from the poet.[1] This chapter begins by discussing the ways in which Euripidean quotations were treated autobiographically – that is, as direct evidence for the poet's life. The principal text under discussion in the first part of the chapter is Satyrus' *Life of Euripides*: this involves some consideration of the wider context of Hellenistic scholarship, including the development of the genre of biography, the significance of the anecdotal tradition in relation to quotation, and the combination of literary criticism and biography in the works of Satyrus and other contemporary scholars. But quotations might also be linked to lives other than that of the poet himself. I go on to examine the use of Euripidean quotations in biographies of other people, with reference to Diogenes Laertius' *Lives of the Philosophers*. In the last part of the chapter the focus shifts to other sorts of connections between Euripidean tragedy and everyday life, with a focus on Cicero's private correspondence and the *Meditations* of Marcus Aurelius. All of these case studies, from very different periods and contexts, illustrate the malleability of quotations and the curious ways in which tragedy can apparently become woven into the fabric of a person's life.

Quotations as autobiography

One of the earliest biographies of Euripides – which also happens to be one of the first surviving examples of biographical writing from the Greek world – was composed by the Hellenistic scholar Satyrus of Callatis, probably during the late third century BC. Satyrus is an obscure figure: he has been linked to the Alexandrian scholarly tradition as well as the Peripatetic school at Athens, but little can be said for certain about his life, background or intellectual affiliations.[2]

His major literary project consisted of a series of *Lives* of philosophers, writers, politicians and kings. At some point these existed in a collected edition of several books, the sixth of which contained *Lives of Aeschylus, Sophocles and Euripides*.[3] Soon after the classical period Satyrus' works all became lost, but happily the *Life of Euripides* resurfaced, in a lacunose but partially intelligible state, in a second-century AD papyrus book first published in 1912.[4] The rediscovery of this text occasioned some disappointment because it does not actually reveal anything new about Euripides' life. Nevertheless, it is of great interest and importance: it adds to our understanding of the early development of biography as a literary genre, it gives us a valuable glimpse of Euripides' reception in the Hellenistic period, and (most importantly for our purposes) it is full of quotations, deployed in a strikingly bold way.

One of the most remarkable features of Satyrus' book is that it does not adopt the format that we might expect of a biography, *viz.* a third-person narrative of the subject's life, recounted from beginning to end in chronological order. Instead, it consists of a dialogue between characters who discuss themes and tendencies in Euripides' life and work, interweaving quotations from the plays with explanatory comments. We lack the opening and concluding sections, which makes it difficult to discern the overall structure of the dialogue. The first surviving portions (frs 1-8) are concerned with the poet's style, diction and use of rhetoric. Subsequent sections deal with poetic inspiration (fr. 9, fr. 16.I); character (frs 10-11); the influence of Anaxagoras (fr. 37.I-III); Euripides' opinions about the gods (fr. 38.I); the relationship between Euripides and Socrates (fr. 38.II-39.II); Euripides' supposed criticisms of the Athenian public (fr. 39.III-V); the relationship between parents and children (fr. 39.VI); the influence of Euripides on New Comedy (fr. 39.VII); Euripides' misanthropy (fr. 39.IX); his unpopularity, especially among Athenian women (fr. 39.X-XVII); his eventual departure from Athens to join the court of Archelaus in Macedon (fr. 39.XVII-XIX); his halitosis (fr. 39.XX); his death (fr.39.XXI); and his friendship with the lyric poet Timotheus (fr. 39.XXII).

The characters who take part in this dialogue can be seen as approximate parallels to the type of figure encountered in sympotic literature. They are depicted as cultured, literate people with a wide knowledge of tragedy, who are easily able to quote and discuss passages from memory, to make unexpected connections between disparate passages and topics, or to disagree about matters of interpretation. In their erudition and powers of recall, as well as their tendency to leap abruptly from one subject to another, they may seem to be direct ancestors of Athenaeus' Deipnosophists.[5] The lacunose state of the text makes it impossible to discern exactly who these characters are, but recent scholars agree that there are either two or three of them: an unidentifiable principal speaker ('Character A'), a secondary character named Diodora or Diodorus and perhaps a third named Eucleia.[6] It is impossible to say whether these speakers are meant to represent real-life historical figures; Stefan Schorn's suggestion that 'Character A' is a teacher discussing Euripides with his pupils is attractive but unprovable.[7] It is also impossible to tell where or when the dialogue is imagined as having taken place, but clearly its notional date must be much closer to Satyrus' period than Euripides' own. Not only do the characters talk about Euripides' death (406 BC), but they also show awareness of New Comedy and quote from Philemon (whose first Dionysia victory was in 327 BC); and more generally the mood of nostalgic retrospection that pervades the dialogue seems characteristic of Hellenistic harking-back to a fifth-century Athenian golden age.

Even though it is not always clear who is speaking, it is obvious that Satyrus' characters are all discussing specific quotations, not only from Euripides' plays but also from other texts including comedy, philosophy and epic. Their interpretative comments might either precede or follow the passage in question, but in each case the method being applied is the same, and it is essentially deductive.[8] Each separate quotation is treated as a *clue*, from which factual information about Euripides can be extrapolated by a quasi-Sherlockian process of literary detection. It is worth noting that this method depends entirely on eclectic reading habits. That is, it works (or seems to work) only when applied to decontextualized extracts rather than complete plays or continuous scenes of dialogue.

Take, for example, the following three-line quotation (F1007d, from an unidentified tragedy):

κτήσασθ' ἐν ὑ[σ]τέροισιν εὔ[κ]λειαν χρόνοι[ς]
[ἅ]πασαν, ἀντλή[σαν]τες ἡμέρας [πόν]ον
ψ[υ]χαῖς [. . .]

Win for yourselves a total reputation for valour in times to come, once you have drained this day dry of toil in your souls . . .

We do not know the dramatic context or speaker of these lines;[9] nor, apparently, did Character A in Satyrus' dialogue, who treats them as the words of Euripides and deduces a real-life situation in which they might have been spoken. At this point in the dialogue (fr. 39.III-IV), the characters are discussing the political content of Euripides' plays and the poet's supposed attitude to the Athenian public:

(B.) πολλὰ καὶ παρὰ τῶν κωμικῶν ποιητῶν, ὡς ἔοικεν, ἅμα αὐστηρῶς λέγεται καὶ πολιτικῶς.
(A.) πῶς γὰρ οὔ; πάλιν γοῦν ὁ μὲν Εὐριπίδης εὖ μάλα πρὸς ἀλκὴν καὶ εὐψυχίαν παρακαλεῖ τοὺς νέους, ὑποβάλ[λ]ων αὐτοῖς ὁρμὰς Λακωινικὰς καὶ θυμοποιῶν τὸ πλῆθ[ο]ς οὕτως· κτήσασθ' ἐν κτλ.

B. Among the comic poets too, so it seems, there are many words that are expressed in a harsh and political fashion.
A. Of course there are! But at any rate Euripides, for his part, very effectively rouses young men to fortitude and courage, urging Spartan zeal upon them and filling the multitude with boldness of heart, as follows: 'Win for yourselves...' [F1007d, as above].

This is a typical example of the way in which Euripides' verses were routinely treated as his own words. It is assumed that Euripides was personally addressing the young men of Athens at a specific moment in history. The precise time and place is unspecified, but Character A may perhaps be envisaging a military context or a political assembly. A broadly didactic function is implicitly ascribed to tragedy, as so often elsewhere, and it is assumed that the sentiments expressed in F1007d were deliberately designed for the purpose of exhortation or morale-boosting. But Character A's assumptions are misplaced. Even if we concede that tragedy may have didactic aims or indirect relevance to Athenian politics, it is obvious that the quoted words were spoken not by Euripides in fifth-century Athens but by a fictional character within a mythical scenario in the distant past, almost certainly with somewhere other than Athens as the *mise-en-scène*. As Schorn points out, it is also unlikely that Euripides, whose plays elsewhere exhibit a problematic attitude towards the Spartans, would have written approvingly of 'Spartan zeal'.[10]

A further example of the 'deductive method' is provided by this four-line quotation (F911, again from an unidentified tragedy):

χρύσεαι δή μοι πτέρυγες περὶ νώτωι
καὶ τὰ Σειρήνων πτερόεντα πέδιλ' ἁρμόζεται,
βάσομαι δ' ἀν' αἰθέρα πουλὺν ἀερθεὶς
Ζηνὶ προσμείξων.

There are golden wings on my back, and the winged sandals of the Sirens are fitted to my feet! I shall fly aloft, up into the wide expanse of the ether, where I shall encounter Zeus!

These lyric verses are clearly part of a choral ode, and they are similar to several other tragic passages in which choruses in dire straits express colourful escape-fantasies, imagining themselves as flying away like birds, or drifting up into the air like smoke.[11] Nevertheless, Satyrus' characters treat these choral utterances as the words or thoughts of Euripides himself, and they deduce the circumstances in which the words might have been uttered (fr. 39.XVI-XVII). Character A begins by explaining, with reference to a quotation from Aristophanes (F595), that Euripides' reputation among the Athenians was harmed by the comedians' treatment of his work, and he goes on to say that Euripides responded to this mockery by quitting Athens:

(A.) οὗτοι μὲν οὖν, ὅπερ εἶπα, πρὸς τὴν πολλῶν ἐπολιτεύοντο χάριν. ἐκεῖνός γε μὴν καθάπερ διαμαρτυρίαν θέμενος ἀπείπατο τὰς Ἀθήνας.
(B.) ποίαν ταύτην;
(A.) ἐν τῶιδε κατακεχωρισμένην τῶι στασίμωι· χρύσεαι δή μοι κτλ.

A. These people (sc. the comedians), just as I said, conducted themselves with a view to pleasing the public. But Euripides renounced Athens by, as it were, making a formal oath.
B. What do you mean?
A. As it is distinctly expressed in the choral stasimon: 'There are golden wings...'
[F911, as above]

Character A goes on to assert that Euripides' reference to Zeus in F911 is a veiled allusion to Archelaus, king of Macedon (where the poet supposedly settled after he had left Athens). This section provides another clear illustration of the deductive method at work, but at the same time it is likely to strike us as a bizarre interpretation of the original lines.

Choral passages such as F911, which are delivered in the first-person singular, might seem to lend themselves to being treated as the 'personal testaments' of the poet. Commentators have compared the way in which first-person statements in Pindar and other lyric poetry have similarly been treated as poetic autobiography.[12] But although Satyrus does cite other first-personal choral passages too,[13] it is clear that in practice *all* tragic utterances are liable to be treated indiscriminately as 'clues' leading to information about the tragedian. Satyrus' characters quote several passages with a cosmological flavour and use them as proof that he was a follower of Anaxagoras (fr. 37.I), and they detect echoes of Socratic philosophy in other quotations (fr. 38.II-fr. 39.II), in each case eliding the distinction between intellectual influences and personal relationships. The line 'Zeus, whether you are the power of necessity present in nature, or whether you are the mind of mortals' (Ζεὺς εἴτ' ἀνάγκη φύσεως εἴτε νοῦς βροτῶν, *Women of Troy* 886), originally a prayer uttered by Hecuba, is quoted as evidence of Euripides' own uncertainty concerning the distribution of heavenly powers (fr. 37.III), and a further passage (incert. fab. F913) is seemingly taken as an expression of Euripides' personal religious beliefs (fr. 38.I).[14] A maxim about the relationship between parents and children (incert. fab. F1007e+f) is cited in support of the view that Euripides possessed prophetic or visionary abilities (fr. 39.VI). Gnomic quotations extolling the value of hard work and criticizing excessive wealth (incert. fab. F590, F1007a+b) are presented to us as proof of Euripides' own character and morality (fr. 38.II-III). It is implied that Euripides' own views on women are being expressed in a speech from *Melanippe the Wise* (F494.5-16) that is quoted in a section concerning Euripides' alleged conflict with the women of Athens (fr. 39.XI). Via this oblique method of interpretation, it seems that almost any extract from any play by Euripides can be read as a clue to the author's life. All of these quotations are selected, sifted, scrutinized (perhaps not too carefully) and reassembled as fragments of an autobiography.

Extracts from works that were not written by Euripides himself are also quoted as if they could provide corroborative details. As Schorn observes, Satyrus' characters employ quasi-legal terminology in this respect, describing quotations as proofs or witness statements in support of their claims.[15] Passages from Plato's *Phaedrus* and Homer's *Odyssey* (fr. 9, fr. 16.I) are (seemingly) included in support of the idea that Euripides was divinely inspired.[16] An Aristophanic joke about Euripides' tongue (incert. fab. F656) is cited to demonstrate Euripides' rhetorical powers (fr. 8.II). Other jokes from comedy are elevated to the status of facts: Aristophanes is said to be 'summoned as a witness' to the fact that Euripides was an antisocial recluse (κεκλημένος, fr. 39.IX), and Philemon F153 is said to 'testify' to Euripides' influence on New Comedy (μαρτυρεῖ, fr. 39.VII). A whole section about Euripides' relationships with women is based, without acknowledgement, on the plot of Aristophanes' comedy *Thesmophoriazusae*, which is treated, naively, as if it were a straightforward historical account (fr. 39.X-XIV). Once again, all of these quotations are treated solely as factual clues to be exploited in the task of biographical detective-work; little heed is paid to the fact that they come from literary texts with their own agenda.

Apart from the quasi-autobiographical content of Euripidean tragedy itself, Aristophanic comedy appears to be the most significant source of clues. Aristophanes is also cited (fr. 39.IX) as the source of the fundamental interpretative principle apparently underlying the *Life of Euripides* as a whole: 'Just as he makes his characters speak, so he is himself' (οἷα μὲν ποιεῖ λέγειν τοῖός ἐστιν, incert. fab. F694). We can see this principle (i.e. Art = Life) being exploited for humorous effect in a number of comedies, including *Acharnians*, *Thesmophoriazusae* and *Frogs*. However, it is not an exclusively Aristophanic concept; it finds parallels in other fifth-century writing, and in fact it is widespread throughout the whole ancient literary-critical tradition.[17] Thus it is scarcely unexpected to find Satyrus, or any other Greek or Roman reader, making connections of one sort or another between a poet's life and his work.

It is widely recognized that many other Hellenistic scholars and early practitioners of what we now call 'biography' – including Hermippus, Aristoxenus, Antigonus and Chamaeleon – regularly and unsystematically combined literary-critical, exegetical, biographical and historical subject matter in their writings.[18] Apart from Satyrus' *Life of Euripides*, we also find a number of miscellaneous, quasi-biographical Euripidean anecdotes in other Greek and Roman texts,[19] which similarly treat quotations as a basis for understanding the poet's character or for reconstructing specific episodes from his life, however unconvincing or factitious such interpretations may be. It is likely that this well-developed anecdotal tradition ultimately derives from Hellenistic scholarship and can be seen as directly parallel to Satyrus in its methods and materials.[20] In a broader sense, the assumption that literature and life are inextricably intertwined seems to have been entirely typical of Greek and Roman biographical thought, along with a lack of concern for strict factual accuracy.[21] As the later author Plutarch memorably put it, in the preface to his *Life of Alexander* (1.2), biography is a different sort of thing from history, with different standards of truth: 'often a little thing such as a saying or a joke makes a greater revelation of a man's character than battles in which thousands fall, or the greatest armaments, or sieges of cities'. All of this means that even though Satyrus' *Life* may strike modern-day readers as a decidedly odd work, it fits squarely within a recognizable historical and intellectual context. The fact that this *Life* and other comparable scholarly works exist only in a fragmentary state makes it hard to judge how typical or atypical Satyrus really was in his approach to Euripides.

Nevertheless, the remains of the *Life* are substantial enough to allow us to pin down more precisely the sort of relationship that is conceived of as existing between the poet and his poetry. Satyrus' characters use quotation as a way of articulating this relationship in six distinct but intersecting ways. First, it is taken for granted that the verbal style of the poetry reflects the poet's own manner of speaking (fr. 1). Second, it is argued that the *ethos* of Euripides, i.e. his character or ethical outlook, corresponds to that of his fictional characters (fr. 8.II; frs 10-11). Third, it is asserted that Euripides embodied 'greatness' in a general sense, both in his soul and in the overall quality of his poetic oeuvre (fr. 8.II): this formulation looks remarkably like a foreshadowing of Longinus' conception of the sublime.[22] Fourth, Satyrus contrives to create an impression that Euripides was an intransigent citizen by citing controversial or provocative passages from his plays (fr. 37.III; fr. 38. I; fr. 39. II, XI, XVIII). Fifth, it is assumed that opinions expressed by tragic characters are identical to the opinions of the poet (fr. 37.I-III; fr. 38.I-III; fr. 39.II, IV, VI, XI, XIV, XVII). Sixth, and least convincingly, specific details or motifs from tragic plots are imagined as mirroring specific events in the poet's life (fr. 38.IV; fr. 39.I, IV, XVII-XVIII). The question of Satyrus' originality remains open, since all six strands are paralleled in other ancient biographical or critical writings, but it is nonetheless interesting to observe all these different variations on the theme of 'Art = Life' within a single work.

Another respect in which it is hard to assess Satyrus' originality is in his selection of quotations. Did he take them all at first hand from complete texts of the tragedies, thoughtfully plucking out passages that caught his eye, or did he rely on pre-existing collections of extracts? As usual, it is impossible to say.[23] Some of the quotations in the *Life* are found in other works, including essays by Plutarch, the Euripidean scholia, the anonymous later biography known as the 'Life and Ancestry of Euripides' (*Bios Euripidou kai genos*), and works by Clement of Alexandria and Stobaeus: it seems clear that such passages were serially cited and became well established in the anthology tradition.[24] But Satyrus does not always cite these passages in the same form as other authors;[25] and a substantial proportion of the quotations (both Euripidean and non-Euripidean) preserved by Satyrus are not found in any other ancient source.[26] This seems to suggest either that Satyrus had access to a different range of sources from those used by other writers, or that he made more extensive use of these sources when selecting extracts for inclusion. The evidence also suggests that subsequent writers and quotation-collectors did not know Satyrus' *Life*, even if they drew on common source material.

Such source material would almost certainly have included early anthologies of quotations. In addition, Graziano Arrighetti suggests that Satyrus may have drawn on pioneering works of literary scholarship from the earlier Hellenistic period or late fifth century, and that scholarship of this sort will have represented the initial stage in sifting out passages on key themes which later became more firmly established in the gnomological tradition.[27] This scenario is impossible to prove, but we do happen to know of the existence of several relevant-sounding scholarly works which Satyrus might have been able to consult, including *On Euripides* by Philochorus of Athens (*TrGF* 5 T206), *On Euripides and Sophocles* by Douris of Samos (*TrGF* 5 T207), *On the Three Tragedians* and *On the Plots of Euripides' and Sophocles' Plays* by Heraclides of Pontus (*TrGF* 5 T209), and *On Tragedians* by Aristoxenus (*TrGF* 5 T211). One can only imagine the contents of these lost works, but it is plausible that they supplied Satyrus with a ready-made selection of quotations or with models for the method of interweaving biography and literary criticism.

On balance, then, Satyrus' *Life of Euripides*, despite its *prima facie* eccentricity, can be seen as conventional in its outlook and derivative in its content. Nevertheless, this work does have a couple of remarkable features which merit further discussion. The first is its exclusive focus on just a handful of selected quotations (and no other sources of evidence at all). The second is the fact that, rather like Euripides' plays themselves, the *Life* consists of a dramatic dialogue between different characters, which means that Satyrus' own authorial presence is invisible. Let us consider the relationship between these two features and their possible consequences for our interpretation of the text.

As already noted, the 'deductive' or 'autobiographical' method seems to work only for short extracts read out of context, when the speaker and situation in the plot can be ignored; it is self-evidently unsuitable as a way of interpreting whole scenes or plays. This may make it seem unlikely that Satyrus had the complete texts of Euripides' tragedies in front of him as he wrote. But what is truly extraordinary about Satyrus is not his application of the deductive method to Euripides' poetry, a method which is adopted by others, but his apparent lack of knowledge of any 'clues' other than the extracts that he cites. Satyrus' characters treat all these verses as free-standing utterances by Euripides, with scarcely any acknowledgement that they are actually quotations from dramatic works. They give no references for any of the quotations; they do not mention the title of a single play; they show no awareness of the characters or plots of any tragedies; and they seem oblivious to the dates or circumstances of any productions, even when this sort of information would be highly relevant to the biographical narrative that is being constructed (e.g. fr. 37.III; fr. 39.IV, XI, XVII). Of course it must be borne in mind that certain portions of the *Life* are missing, but the complete absence of background detail in what survives is very conspicuous. This lack of detail is hard to explain, given the resources that were available to scholars in Satyrus' lifetime. Complete texts of most plays remained extant and would have been relatively easy to obtain. Even if Satyrus relied on anthologies, it is very likely that such collections would have included source references in the form of play titles. Even if reliable facts about the real-life Euripides were hard to come by in the third century BC, inscriptions concerning festivals and performance records remained on public display, and scholarly works such as Aristotle's *Didaskaliai,* commentaries and hypotheses (and so on) would have been available in libraries. It seems that Satyrus has either failed to consult such external evidence or deliberately excluded it from discussion.

It is easy to criticize Satyrus for defective methodology or simple ignorance. Nevertheless, it is also possible to view his apparent blind spots as part of a deliberate literary strategy. Could it be that the *Life of Euripides* is a more complex and self-aware text than is normally assumed? The answer to this question depends in part on the crucial fact that we are dealing with a text in dialogue form. Because Satyrus' own voice is not explicitly present in the dialogue, as his own readers we are forced into exactly the same position as that in which readers of Euripides inevitably find themselves: we have to attempt to identify Satyrus' opinions or interpret his overall argument by indirect methods. We can, if we wish, apply the interpretative principle 'just as he makes his characters speak, so he is himself', but we are not obliged to do so. Indeed, it might strike us as suspicious that this principle, despite its ostensibly programmatic function, does not occupy a more prominent position within the *Life*. Buried away in the middle of the dialogue, it is not even given as the personal opinion of one of the main characters. Instead, it appears (as it were) within quotation marks, explicitly labelled as a line from an Aristophanic comedy. Perhaps it is being offered up as a proposition to be tested and debated, rather than as a principle that Satyrus himself is straightforwardly endorsing.

Much the same could be said of any of the other opinions expressed in the dialogue. By placing them all in the mouths of his characters, Satyrus could be seen as implicitly distancing himself from their interpretations – which, as we have seen, are often wayward or illogical. In one passage in particular (fr. 39. XVIII), the characters are made to draw our attention to the possibility of misinterpretation. Here the quotation under scrutiny is F911 (the 'golden wings' passage discussed earlier):

(A.) ἢ οὐκ ἀ[κούει]ς ὅτι κα[ὶ τοῦ]τ' ἔσθ[θ' ὅ] φη[σιν] αὐτ[ός;]
(B.) πῶς οὖν;
(A.) [Ζ]ηνὶ συμμείξων ὁρμᾶν λέγω[ν] μεταφορικῶς ἐμφαίνει τὸν μόναρχον, ἀλλὰ καὶ σ[υ]ναύξων τἀνδρὸς τὴν ὑπεροχήν.
(B.) κομψότε[ρ]α φαίνε[ι] μο[ι] λέγειν ἤπε[ρ] ἀληθινώτερα –
(A.) ἅπερ ἔστιν ὡς θέλεις ἐκδέχεσθαι.

A. Do you not understand that it is this that he is saying?
B. What do you mean?

A. When he says 'I shall encounter Zeus in my flight' he is metaphorically referring to the king [Archelaus], and simultaneously increasing that man's prestige.
B. I think that you are speaking ingeniously rather than truthfully.
A. It is possible to understand the lines however you like.

As already noted, Character A's reading of F911 is outré; but the specific meaning of F911 is less important than the general critical principle at stake. This exchange is extremely significant because, unlike the other surviving portions of the dialogue, it openly acknowledges and dramatizes the process of disagreement among readers. Its function is to heighten our awareness that interpretation is not always a straightforward process. Quotations are clues that may lead to more than one valid conclusion, 'ingenious' interpretations are not necessarily the same as the truth, and the way in which individual readers make sense of Euripidean verses is admitted to be more or less arbitrary. Character A's final observation, 'it is possible to understand the lines *however you like*', is surprising because it seems to encapsulate a principle of hermeneutic relativism. In other words, the meaning of all of these quotations is up for grabs. If we are to reconstruct the historical Euripides exclusively on the basis of selected quotations, there may end up being as many Euripideses as there are individual readers.

Even if one chooses to read Satyrus' *Life of Euripides* as an utterly conventional exploration of the 'Art = Life' theme, it still comes across as a valuable example of early Greek biographical writing and a good illustration of the uses to which quotations might be put. But alternatively, one may choose to read it as a more subversive and playful text, which makes its readers work hard by adopting the dialogue format as a source of irony and a way of making it hard to pin down what its author really thinks. I suggest that, rather than simply illustrating the 'deductive method' in action, this *Life* may have been designed to test out the method, to expose its limitations, or to parody or criticize its use by other early biographers such as Chamaeleon. By rehearsing the process of autobiographical interpretation based solely on a handful of Euripidean extracts – as if anthologies of quotations constituted the *only* evidence for the poet's life and career – Satyrus can be seen as implicitly questioning the validity of this method and asking whether it provides an acceptable basis on which to construct a writer's biography. It has to be admitted that not enough survives of Satyrus' *Life* or other proto-biographical works to be confident that this latter reading is the correct one, but there are signs that this is a considerably more interesting text than it might seem.

Euripides in the lives of others

The principle that poetry in some way reflects its own author's life and personality is a perfectly reasonable one, even if the application of this principle in specific cases might often strike us as haphazard. What is more surprising is that ancient biographies of other people also incorporate poetic quotations in such a way as to suggest that there is an intimate connection between the poetry and the life of the subject. The quotations might be related to specific incidents within it, or they might be seen as illuminating some aspect of his character.

The subjects of Diogenes' Laertius' *Lives and Opinions of Eminent Philosophers* illustrate this tendency especially well. Even though these figures differ greatly from one another in their philosophy and approach to life, they all either quote Euripides themselves or behave in ways which make their biographer call his words to mind. It transpires that the tragedian is equally relevant, and his life lessons equally applicable, to Platonist and Cynic, Stoic and Epicurean alike.

Diogenes Laertius compiled his *Lives* at some point after the end of the second century AD, but his work draws heavily on Hellenistic biography and scholarship: it has been characterized as 'a thick stew of names, dates, events, titles, anecdotes, sayings, theories and more'.[28] In his method and approach to biography Diogenes seems to differ very little from Satyrus and his contemporaries. He often explicitly cites writers such as Satyrus, Hermippus, Antigonus and Aristoxenus as his sources.[29] Euripides is not the only poet whose works are quoted – these *Lives* also contain snippets from epic, elegy lyric poetry, hexameter verse, epigrams and comedy – but Euripides is quoted much more often than any other poet, including Homer and the other tragedians. The ten books of Diogenes' collected *Lives* feature twenty-six quotations from Euripidean tragedy, while Sophocles, by comparison, is quoted only three times, and Aeschylus never.[30]

In a few cases, Euripidean quotations are included in the biographies of Euripides' own contemporaries. For instance, in the *Life of Anaxagoras* (2.10) we are invited to read a line from *Phaethon* as evidence that Euripides was one of Anaxagoras' pupils, and in the *Life of Socrates* (2.33, 2.44) passages from *Auge* and *Palamedes* are interpreted as signs indicating Euripides' personal attitude towards Socrates. Both of these cases treat quotations as 'clues' in precisely the same manner as Satyrus, and the specific personal connections that they identify between Euripides and the philosophers are also the same, strongly suggesting that Diogenes and Satyrus both drew on common source material.[31] Euripides himself features as a supporting character in the *Life of Plato* (3.6–7), in which we are told that the poet accompanied the adolescent Plato on an expedition to Egypt. It is said that Euripides was cured of sickness by Egyptian priests who made him drink seawater, whereupon he immediately wrote the line θάλασσα κλύζει πάντα τἀνθρώπων κακά ('the sea washes away all human ills', *Iphigenia among the Taurians* 1193 – words that were spoken in the play by Iphigenia when explaining Greek rituals to the barbarian king Thoas). This anecdote relies on the premise that gnomic generalities in Euripides' plays originated in specific real-life experiences, and here as elsewhere we are encouraged to interpret tragedy as equivalent to autobiography, however far-fetched the alleged connection between art and life may be.

In these fifth-century examples, the Euripidean quotations can plausibly be seen as part of the contemporary backdrop to the life and times of the subjects. But for the most part, Diogenes quotes Euripides in the context of lives that were lived considerably earlier – such as that of Solon (1.56) – or later – up to the third century BC and the life of the Sceptic philosopher Pyrrhon (9.72–3). Chronology and strict contextual relevance are largely unimportant.[32] What matters more is Euripides' status as a source of timeless observations on universal themes.

A typical illustration of Diogenes' method is provided by the *Life of Aristippus*. Here Diogenes portrays Aristippus (founder of the Cyrenaic school of philosophy) as involved in a series of encounters with other people, in the course of which Aristippus demonstrates his character traits and philosophical views via memorable *aperçus* and witty rejoinders to questions or remarks from interlocutors. In one such episode (2.78), Aristippus comes into contact with Dionysius, tyrant of Syracuse:

καί ποτε παρὰ πότον κελεύσαντος Διονυσίου ἕκαστον ἐν πορφυρᾶι ἐσθῆτι ὀρχήσασθαι, τόν μὲν Πλάτωνα μὴ προσέσθαι, εἰπόντα·
  οὐκ ἂν δυναίμην θῆλυν ἐνδῦναι στολήν·
τὸν δ' Ἀρίστιππον λαβόντα καὶ μέλλοντα ὀρχήσασθαι εὐστόχως εἰπεῖν·
  καὶ γὰρ ἐν βακχεύμασιν
  οὖσ' ἥ γε σώφρων οὐ διαφθαρήσεται.

On one occasion, at a symposium, Dionysius ordered each of the guests to dress themselves in purple and dance. Plato declined to do so, saying: 'I could not bring myself to don female clothes' (*Bacchae* 836). But Aristippus put on the dress and, just as he started to dance, uttered the following well-aimed remark: 'A person who is naturally chaste will not be corrupted even amid Bacchic revelry'.
Bacchae 317-18

This revealing anecdote shows the two philosophers quoting Euripides in conflicting ways to justify their own behaviour and moral choices. Both passages, though they express contradictory viewpoints, are taken from the same tragedy

(*Bacchae*), but neither the play nor the author is named. This means that Diogenes' readers are left to identify the source for themselves. Whether or not every reader was capable of doing this, it is clearly implied that both Plato and Aristippus were so familiar with Euripides that they could quote his tragic verses as effortlessly as formulating their own words. Indeed, the speakers give no explicit signal that the quotations *are* quotations, apart from the fact that they are in iambic metre. In this respect, they resemble the majority of others who quote Euripides in the pages of Diogenes' *Lives*. These quotations are almost always 'invisible' ones, in the sense that they are unattributed and seem to arise naturally in the course of ordinary speech and everyday social interactions, without being marked or announced in any obvious way.[33]

At the same time, the use of tragedy here is essentially competitive, resembling the combative 'capping' or 'flyting' seen in other sympotic and literary contexts.[34] One quotation is being used to refute another, and Aristippus' deployment of *Bacchae* 317–18 is figuratively described as 'well aimed' or 'hitting the target' (εὐστόχως), as if this were an archery contest or a duel rather than a conversation at a party. If Aristippus seems to win the contest, it may be implied that this is because he is more familiar with *Bacchae* than Plato, or better able to recall its contents impromptu so as to come up with the *mot juste*. But we can also read the anecdote as a demonstration that Euripides (rather like the Bible) can be quoted as a source of authority in apparent support of almost any point of view, including diametrically opposed positions.

This combination of anecdote plus embedded saying – generally known as a *chreia* – is typical of Diogenes' autobiographical method, though it is widely found in other biographical, historical and rhetorical works.[35] The saying in question tends to be a *bon mot* uttered by the subject of the anecdote himself, though in some cases, as here, it takes the form of a quotation from another source. It is unlikely that Diogenes himself was responsible for linking together the quotation and the anecdote: more probably he inherited the *chreia* wholesale from an earlier scholarly work, such as Sotion's *Successions of Philosophers* or Bion's *Lectures*, both of which are cited by Diogenes in the immediately preceding section of this *Life*. It seems that in many cases the saying and the accompanying anecdote will have been transmitted together as a single unit. In other words, what is being 'quoted' in examples such as this one is not simply the quotation itself but the anecdote as a whole. This is neatly demonstrated by another *chreia* in a later chapter of the same *Life* (2.82), which incorporates a couple of Sophoclean lines, followed by a witty rejoinder from Aristippus, in an anecdote about an argument between Aristippus and Dionysius over the question of whether a tyrant's subjects become his slaves. As in the example above, both interlocutors combatively quote contradictory gnomic verses from the same author to express their ethical outlook.[36] As before, no author or title attribution is supplied, but after recounting this episode Diogenes mentions that his own source was Diocles' work *On the Lives of Philosophers*. He also tells us that this *chreia* was found in different sources, and that 'others' attribute the same incident – including the same quotations – to Plato rather than Aristippus. Plutarch also includes the same pair of quotations in two separate works, but in *How the Young Man Should Study Poetry* (33d) they are credited to Zeno, while in the *Life of Pompey* (78.7) they are credited to Pompey. This information is hugely significant because it shows how a textual unit consisting of anecdote-plus-quotation could be passed down as an indivisible entity. It also shows that the characterizing function of a *chreia*, though in theory illustrative of the unique personality of a named individual, was in fact easily transferable from one person to another.[37] The essential point of the anecdote in this case, which could be summed up as 'speaking truth to power', could potentially apply to many people and situations; it is not inherently tied to any one specific figure.

Elsewhere, stronger connections are made between tragedy and individual characters. For instance, Diogenes tells us of Stoic philosophers who 'continually' (συνεχές) quoted certain Euripidean maxims, suggesting that they had internalized the verses in question to such a degree that they came to represent a personal mantra or credo – such as Zeno, who kept repeating Euripides' description of Capaneus' character (*Suppliant Women* 861-3) as a model of noble behaviour and a lesson for the young (7.22), or Chrysippus, who would quote lines about good versus bad fortune (*Orestes* 540–1) every time he argued with Cleanthes (7.179). Another Stoic, Cleanthes, when asked by someone what sort of lesson he should teach his son, is said to have replied with a quotation from Euripides (*Electra* 140), as if this summed up his own views on education (7.172), while his pupil Chrysippus is said to have quoted Euripides' *Medea* so extensively that one waggish reader referred to the play as 'the *Medea* of Chrysippus' (7.180).

Diogenes' *Life of Crantor* (4.24–7) provides an especially good example of the interweaving of tragedy with personal experiences. According to Diogenes' depiction, Crantor (the early Academic philosopher and commentator on Plato) practically lived and breathed poetry. His whole outlook on life was apparently inspired by the verse that he had read, he wrote poetry as well as philosophical works on topics such as love, and (even more significantly) all of his recorded utterances are either poetic quotations or critical evaluations of poets. Diogenes records that Crantor used to admire Homer and Euripides above all other writers, and that he valued Euripides for having composed tragedy that was emotionally affecting but also written in everyday language (4.26). As an example of this tendency, Diogenes tells us that Crantor used to quote a verse from *Bellerophon*: οἴμοι· τί δ' οἴμοι; θνητά τοι πεπόνθαμεν ('Alas! – but why do I say alas? Our suffering is only human,' F300). As in the cases of Zeno and Chrysippus just mentioned, Diogenes gives the impression that Crantor's citation of *Bellerophon* was not just a witty one-off but a repeated, habitual action that should be seen as typical of his character. No doubt it was the naturalistic quality of Euripidean diction that made it so suitable for being incorporated by Crantor into his day-to-day conversation. But there are signs that the subject matter of Euripidean tragedy was also reflected in Crantor's behaviour.

We are told (4.29–30) that Crantor came into contact with a young student of Theophrastus named Arcesilaus, fell in love with him, and proceeded to re-enact a scenario from Euripides' *Andromeda*:

ὁ δὲ φιλοσοφίας ἤρα, καὶ αὐτοῦ Κράντωρ ἐρωτικῶς διατεθεὶς ἐπύθετο τὰ ἐξ Ἀνδρομέδας Εὐριπίδου προενεγκάμενος·

ὦ παρθέν', εἰ σώσαιμί σ', εἴσει μοι χάριν;

καὶ ὃς τὰ ἐχόμενα·

ἄγου μ', ὦ ξέν', εἴτε δμωΐδ' ἐθέλεις εἴτ' ἄλοχον.

ἐκ τούτου συνήστην ἀλλήλοιν. ἵνα καὶ τὸν Θεόφραστον κνιζόμενόν φασιν εἰπεῖν ὡς εὐφυὴς καὶ εὐεπιχείρητος ἀπεληλυθὼς τῆς διατριβῆς εἴη νεανίσκος.

Arcesilaus loved philosophy; and Crantor, being passionately in love with him, asked him a question, citing the following verse [F129] from Euripides' *Andromeda*: 'Young maiden, if I should rescue you, will you show me your gratitude?' And Arcesilaus quoted the next verse [F129a] in reply: 'Take me with you, stranger, whether it is a servant or a wife that you want.' After this they lived together; and this resulted in the irritation of Theophrastus, who is alleged to have said: 'What a naturally clever and versatile young man has left my school!'

This is (I believe) the only recorded instance of a Euripidean quotation being used successfully as a chat-up line. Its success relied on the fact that Arcesilaus instantaneously recognized the quotation and responded with a counter-quotation, thus demonstrating his knowledge of the play as well as his willingness to accept Crantor's advances. (In fact, Arcesilaus' reply is a slight misquotation or truncation of the original, perhaps suggesting that he – or the author of the anecdote – was quoting the play from memory without checking a text.[38]) Euripides is seen as providing an opportunity for the two men to communicate, by means of a sort of code or private language, the fact that they belong together. These quotations function as a neat, economical way of articulating their common cultural background and shared intellectual interests as well as their romantic compatibility. As James Warren points out, the anecdote also has the secondary functions of presenting the teacher–pupil relationship in eroticized terms and suggesting that the pursuit of philosophy itself may be analogous to sexual desire.[39]

In this anecdote, Euripides is treated less as a tragedian than a writer of erotic verse suitable for quotation by lovers. This is unsurprising in view of the fact that Euripides wrote many plays on erotic themes, and that he was sometimes regarded as one of the most skilful writers at depicting love and other emotions.[40] But it is striking that *Andromeda* in particular is the tragedy chosen for quotation by Crantor and Arcesilaus. This lost play appears to have been one of Euripides' most popular works, to judge by the number of citations and works of art which it inspired. Its plot centred on the hero Perseus' rescue of Andromeda from a sea-monster, and their subsequent marriage.[41] It seems that its impact derived not simply from the love-story itself, but more specifically from the subtlety of its depiction of the psychology of *erôs* and the phenomenon of love at first sight: the play is famous for containing the first attested example of the phrase 'fall in love' (εἰς ἔρωτα πίπτουσιν, F138).[42] This extraordinary tragedy is mentioned in other contexts in which it is said to have aroused powerful psychological reactions in its audiences. Aristophanes, for instance, depicts one of its characters as being affected by an overwhelming erotic passion (πόθος) as a direct result of reading *Andromeda* (*Frogs* 52–4). Lucian also records a bizarre incident in which the entire population of Abdera became deranged after watching a performance of the play and went around the city reciting memorable extracts, apparently under the delusion that they were characters or actors in it (*On the Writing of History* 1). Lucian tells us that the Abderites kept quoting portions of speeches by Perseus, including σὺ δ' ὦ θεῶν τύραννε κἀνθρώπων Ἔρως ('O Eros, tyrant of gods and humans alike', F136.1). Such contextual details may colour the way in which we read Diogenes' anecdote. Perhaps we are to conclude that Euripides' play does not simply reflect or illustrate the philosophers' characters but has had a definitive, formative influence on their behaviour.

In effect, these men are not just quoting from the play but actively reliving the events of its plot in real life, with Crantor in the role of Perseus, Arcesilaus as Andromeda and Theophrastus as the monster. It may be that they, like the Abderites, were all so powerfully under the spell of *Andromeda* that they could not help behaving as they did. If this is so, the *Life of Crantor* provides us with a much more peculiar instance of life imitating art than Diogenes' neutral narrative style might suggest. What we are seeing here is a fantasy scenario in which real-life biography, tragedy and myth have become curiously intertwined. Whether or not it really took place is impossible to know, but Diogenes invites us to accept that the relationship between Crantor and Arcesilaus, even if it did not develop in precisely the way described, is predicated on their relationship with the work of Euripides. It is also implied that knowledge of Euripides' play can help us, as readers, to make sense of these men.

It may be, of course, that every one of these anecdotes is completely fictional. There is no very strong reason to think that any of the supposed incidents in Diogenes' *Lives* actually happened. But even if all the stories are fantasies or fabrications, they are not meant to strike us as inherently implausible. Quite the opposite: they are presented to us as illuminating or representative accounts of the personalities involved, and we are obviously meant to see these Euripidean phrases as the sort of thing that Diogenes' subjects *might* have said in certain circumstances. The quotations are treated as an intrinsic element in the story of each life. They are presented to us as not only typical of these men's behaviour and outlook, but also as summing up their essential character even more appositely than their own words could have done.

Euripides in everyday life

Ancient biographies contain much that is invented or distorted: they intermingle fact and fiction in what can strike modern readers as an arbitrary fashion, and they often seem to value a sort of symbolic or rhetorical meaning above literal truth. Other types of evidence for the real lives of people in antiquity present similar challenges. We are almost always dealing with stylized literary texts, deliberately designed with an audience in mind, rather than direct, unprocessed records of everyday words and actions. But we can discern glimpses of real lives in certain types of more intimate or private writing that have happened to survive, such as an author's personal correspondence or notebooks. Despite their appearance of ordinariness and spontaneity, such documents have been edited and transmitted to us as literature: this means that they cannot be treated as entirely unvarnished accounts of reality. Nevertheless, they were not designed primarily with a view to publication, and they can, if handled with caution, bring us a little closer than other sorts of text to the daily experiences and inner lives of their writers.

For example, Cicero's correspondence with his family and friends, although it has obviously been carefully shaped and curated for subsequent publication,[43] conveys a vivid sense of his personality and conversational style. The large number of letters that Cicero wrote to Atticus, Quintus and others cover many topics, but literary quotations are scattered abundantly throughout these letters, irrespective of the main subject under discussion. Predictably, Latin literature is quoted much more often than Greek, but there are well over a hundred Greek quotations in the corpus, among which the two best represented authors by far are Homer and Euripides. Cicero's letters show that Greek tragedy remained familiar to educated Roman citizens during the first century BC. It is clear that Euripides' work has come to form part of the mental furniture of Cicero and his correspondents, so thoroughly absorbed into their language and thought processes that it can be cited or called to mind in almost any context.

One common function of Euripidean tragedy in the letters, as so often elsewhere, is as a source of universal wisdom in the form of maxims. Cicero refers to the 'true precepts of Euripides' (*vera praecepta* Εὐριπίδου, *Ad Familiares* 13.15) and frequently quotes gnomic verses. In one letter in particular (*Ad Familiares* 16.8), Cicero seems to treat Euripidean tragedy exclusively as a repository of *testimonia* ('testaments' or 'factual statements'), an exaggeration which nonetheless highlights an important point about the way in which the tragedian's work was used by its Roman readers. In this document, written around 49 BC, Cicero expresses concern about his friend Tiro's health and the dangers of undertaking a long journey in winter:

> Vix in ipsis tectis et oppidis frigus infirma valetudine vitatur, nedum in mari et via sit facile abesse ab iniuria temporis. ψῦχος δὲ λεπτῶι χρωτὶ πολεμιώτατον, inquit Euripides. cui tu quantum credas nescio; ego certe singulos eius versus singula testimonia puto.

> If one is in poor health, it's hard enough to avoid the cold when indoors or in town, but it's much less easy still to avoid inclement weather when travelling by sea or road. As Euripides says, 'Cold is the worst enemy to delicate skin' [incert. fab. F906]. I don't know how far you trust him, but I certainly consider every single one of his verses to be a testament to the truth.

This example is typical, not just in the way in which it treats Euripides as a wise companion and guide to life, but in the way in which it incorporates the quotation naturally into the epistolary rhetoric. If the words on the page are seen as the embodiment of a social relationship or the equivalent of a real-life conversation, Euripides can be seen as just another participant alongside Cicero himself. He seems to function here not as a remote literary figure from Greek antiquity so much as a living presence, an extra voice taking part in the conversation and supporting Cicero in offering friendly guidance to Tiro. Unlike many gnomic quotations, which encapsulate lofty philosophical truisms or ethical precepts, this particular example seems to consist simply of practical advice about the importance of wrapping up warm. Did it have greater depth or resonance in its original context? Perhaps so; but the fact that the quoted saying was originally a line in a tragedy is forgotten or ignored. The words are attributed to Euripides, but there is no mention of their original speaker or the title of the play. This information is irrelevant to Cicero's purposes, and we may question whether he knew it anyway.[44] Perhaps Cicero was quoting from a play that was so well known to him and Tiro as not to require identification, or perhaps the line was in circulation as a free-floating proverb. It is impossible to say what Cicero's source may have been, but at any rate this Euripidean fragment does not seem to have been widely quoted or anthologized. No other source preserves the verse, and it remains unidentified.

Tellingly, Euripides is almost never named by Cicero when quoting from his plays. Except in the two examples above, both of which cite Euripides as an authoritative source of wisdom, all Euripidean quotations appear anonymously and without any explicit form of reference or citational frame.[45] Usually they take the form of a short phrase that is incorporated seamlessly into Cicero's sentence structure, so as to seem almost indistinguishable from Cicero's own words and thought processes. For example:

> si vero etiam Carfulenus, ἄνω ποταμῶν (*Ad Atticum* 15.4.1)
>
> If Carfulenus too is really joining in, **wonders will never cease** (literally 'rivers are flowing uphill' – from *Medea* 410).
>
> aequo essem animo; nunc vero αἰσχρὸν σιωπᾶν (*Ad Atticum* 6.8.5)
>
> I should be facing the situation with equanimity; but as it is, **it is a disgrace to keep silent** (from *Philoctetes* F769)
>
> οὐ ταὐτὸν εἶδος. credebam esse facile ... (*Ad Atticum* 13.11.1)
>
> **Things look different now**; I thought that it was easy, but ... (from *Ion* 585)

Of course the fact that the quotations appear in Greek necessarily marks them out as different from the surrounding Latin text. This sort of bilingual 'code-switching', seen relatively frequently in the letters of Cicero, Pliny, Seneca and others, is a much studied aspect of Roman epistolography. It has been described as part of the idiolect of an educated elite in Roman society, a marker of 'in-group solidarity' and 'membership-only, in-group communication', a way of establishing or maintaining intimate relationships between correspondents, a means of highlighting central themes and topics for discussion, a device for heightening emotion or a source of humour.[46] As J. N. Adams argues:

> This is the sort of game which takes place between two members of a self-conscious cultural élite. If there is an intimacy here, it is the intimacy of a shared cultural background and not merely of mutual affection, and at issue as well is membership of an in-group. Such disputants are conscious of their common Greek education and keen to use literary allusion which draws upon that education. This is a highly artificial form of intimacy or solidarity.[47]

Artificial it may be, but it could also be described as entirely natural, in the sense that it is part of Cicero's ingrained behaviour and his habitual mode of communication with like-minded friends. Cicero's inclusion of Euripidean quotations is striking precisely because it seems to be a normal feature of everyday discourse. The specific content, meaning and dramatic context of these extracts are irrelevant in their new setting. All of these Euripidean snippets have become utterly detached from the plays in which they appeared, and they function in the letters as preformed linguistic units (that is, as autonomous phrases, proverbs, universal truisms, clichés, or colourful ways of expressing a commonplace) rather than literary quotations as such. Perhaps Cicero can be seen as playing some sort of intertextual game with the recipients of these letters by inviting them to recall the sources of the quotations, but it seems to me that these phrases are included simply because they form part of the normal vocabulary of a well-educated person. Any 'quotation marks' here are so underemphasized as to be almost imperceptible. No sense is given that the quotations mark a shift of register to a more solemn or elevated level (such as we might encounter in, say, the comedians' use of tragic quotations or paratragic language). The voice that speaks the words may sound Greek, but it is still Cicero's own voice that we are hearing rather than that of Euripides or his characters.

A very different but in some ways comparable text, dating from more than two centuries after Cicero's death, is the so-called *Meditations* of Marcus Aurelius. This hard-to-classify work resembles some sort of journal or commonplace book. It is unusual not only in its literary form but also in the fact that its author was Emperor of Rome (161–80 AD) as well as a student of Stoic philosophy. Marcus seems to have assembled the book's contents over a period of several years, during periods of free time snatched from his other activities. The inclusion of retrospective autobiographical material in Book 1, together with the fact that Marcus sometimes alludes to his old age (e.g. 2.2, 2.6, 5.31, 10.15), indicates that the book was composed towards the end of the author's life and represents the distillation of a lifetime's experience and thought. The contents of the *Meditations* are very miscellaneous, including personal memories, anecdotes, ethical reflections and philosophical *pensées*. Though Marcus was Roman, he writes in Greek and quotes only Greek authors. His own thoughts are interspersed with quotations and paraphrases from other writers – mainly philosophers (Epictetus, Democritus, Empedocles, Heraclitus, Plato, Diogenes and others) but also the dramatists Aristophanes and Euripides. All of these heterogeneous 'meditations' are arranged in chapters (if that is the right word) of unequal length, without any easily discernible order or structure linking them together.[48]

In terms of its form, content and genre this work is without parallel within the ancient world. Richard Rutherford, whose monograph on the *Meditations* is a penetrating discussion of its literary texture as well as its ethical content, cites more recent works such as Pascal's *Pensées* or Larochefoucauld's *Maximes* as loose analogies for the deployment of the soundbite or fragment as a vehicle for philosophical reflection, but he observes that these works differ from the *Meditations* in their structure and in the fact that they were designed for a wide external readership.[49] It is generally accepted – on the basis of features such as its apparently arbitrary organization, its absence of references, and its cryptic allusions or half-references to people and events known only to the author – that Marcus' book was not written for public consumption but intended as a private document for its author's own use.[50] The work has been described by critics as 'memoranda', 'working notes towards a more formal literary composition', 'self-address', 'therapy', 'a (philosophical) autobiography', 'a critical (self-) evaluation of inner life', 'spiritual exercises' or 'Marcus talking to himself'.[51] *Meditations* was not the author's own title; nor was 'To Himself' (εἰς ἑαυτόν), the heading found in the earliest printed edition (based on a now lost manuscript). It seems unlikely that Marcus gave the work a title, though in one chapter (3.14) he refers to his 'little notebooks' (ὑπομνημάτια) or 'the deeds of ancient Greeks and Romans and extracts from their writings, which you stored away for your old age' (τὰς τῶν ἀρχαίων Ῥωμαίων καὶ Ἑλλήνων πράξεις τὰς ἐκ τῶν συγγραμμάτων ἐκλογάς, ἃς εἰς τὸ γῆρας σαυτῶι ἀπετίθεσο).

Most of the quotations from other authors – including Euripides – are introduced without any form of label or announcement. They are simply inserted into the text side by side with Marcus' own reflections, as if they had the same status within the work and occupied the same position in his mind. In this respect, Marcus can be seen as comparable to Cicero: both writers essentially treat these quotations as extensions of their own thoughts. This is seen, for instance, in 7.30–51, chapters which consist of a long series of quotations and paraphrases without any prefatory explanation or accompanying discussion. In this section are included extracts from Plato, Democritus, Epicurus and Antisthenes, a couple of unidentified hexameter fragments and some of Marcus' own ideas, interspersed with six gnomic quotations from Euripides:

(7.38) τοῖς πράγμασιν γὰρ οὐχὶ θυμοῦσθαι χρεών·
μέλει γὰρ αὐτοῖς οὐδέν

There is no point in being angry at what befalls us,
for they do not care a jot. [*Bellerophon* F287.1-2]

(7.40) βίον θερίζειν, ὥστε κάρπιμον στάχυν,
καὶ τὸν μὲν εἶναι, τὸν δὲ μή

We must harvest our life like a ripe ear of corn;
one man must live, another must die. [*Hypsipyle* F757.94-5]

(7.41) εἰ δ' ἠμελήθην ἐκ θεῶν καὶ παῖδ' ἐμώ,
ἔχει λόγον καὶ τοῦτο

If my twin sons and I were neglected by the gods,
even this can be explained. [*Antiope* F208.1-2]

(7.42) τὸ γὰρ εὖ μετ' ἐμοῦ
καὶ τὸ δίκαιον

Good fortune will go with me, and justice will be my ally. [incert. fab. F918.4-5]

(7.50) καὶ τὰ μὲν ἐκ γῆς φύντ' εἰς γαῖαν,
τὰ δ' ἀπ' αἰθερίου βλαστόντα γονῆς
εἰς οὐράνιον πόλον ἦλθε πάλιν

That which was born from the earth returns to the earth, and that which had its origin in ethereal seed returns to the expanse of heaven. [*Chrysippus* F839.9-11]

(7.51) σίτοισι καὶ ποτοῖσι καὶ μαγεύμασι
παρεκτρέποντες ὀχετόν, ὥστε μὴ θανεῖν

[I despise] people who strive to turn aside the tide of death by means of food and drink and incantations. [*Suppliant Women* 1110-11]

There is no obvious thematic link between these passages. They are simply edifying sentiments, of a sort that naturally lend themselves to being copied out, stored up, memorized and treated as sources of moral guidance or consolation – and that is apparently the only thing they have in common. The way in which

Marcus presents the quotations here makes them resemble part of an anthology, and it seems almost certain that he is reproducing this selection of verses, ready-made, from some earlier collection. All the passages here are repeatedly quoted by many other ancient writers, including Stobaeus and Clement of Alexandria.[52] An especially telling aspect of Marcus' mode of citation is that in every case he gives an abbreviated form of an extract which appears in a longer version in these other sources; but, conversely, he never adds any words that these sources do not include.

It cannot be claimed that Euripides is of especial importance to Marcus. As usual, he is the best represented tragedian, but in general the *Meditations* do not make much use of poetry; philosophical prose is far more common. Nevertheless, what is significant is not the frequency of Euripides' appearances but the manner in which he is quoted – that is, the fact that Euripides' words seem to have been completely assimilated into Marcus' own cognitive processes. These quotations are never explicitly identified as Euripidean. Indeed, they are almost never acknowledged to be quotations at all: they are simply incorporated into the mass of material in the book. Their content and their ethical applicability to Marcus' own situation are evidently more important than their authorship or source. The fact that they were once uttered by mythical characters in specific situations has been forgotten. For Marcus, they represent timeless distillations of wisdom, companions and guides in daily life, suitable for inclusion in a Stoic self-help book but potentially relevant as sources of inspiration to many others of different persuasions (as shown by the subsequent reception history of the *Meditations* in later periods and cultures).[53]

Even though Marcus' book lacks any programmatic authorial statements or other outward-facing material addressed to readers, it does contain a few self-reflexive comments on the reading process, including some valuable discussion of the way in which quotations can enter a person's mind and shape their character. Apart from the passage about 'little notebooks' (3.14, quoted above), which provides an insight into Marcus' eclectic reading habits, there is an extended meditation on the uses of tragedy (11.6):

πρῶτον αἱ τραγωιδίαι παρήχθησαν ὑπομνηστικαὶ τῶν συμβαινόντων καὶ ὅτι ταῦτα οὕτω πέφυκε γίνεσθαι καὶ ὅτι, οἷς ἐπὶ τῆς σκηνῆς ψυχαγωγεῖσθε, τούτοις μὴ ἄχθεσθε ἐπὶ τῆς μείζονος σκηνῆς. ὁρᾶται γάρ, ὅτι οὕτω δεῖ ταῦτα περαίνεσθαι καὶ ὅτι φέρουσιν αὐτ' καὶ οἱ κεκραγότες Ἰὼ Κιθαιρών. καὶ λέγεται δέ τινα ὑπὸ τῶν τὰ δράματα ποιούντων χρησίμως, οἷόν ἐστιν ἐκεῖνο μάλιστα·
    εἰ δ' ἠμελήθην ἐκ θεῶν καὶ παῖδ' ἐμώ,
    ἔχει λόγον καὶ τοῦτο

καὶ πάλιν·
   τοῖς πράγμασιν γὰρ οὐχὶ θυμοῦσθαι
καὶ·
   βίον θερίζειν ὥστε κάρπιμον στάχυν
καὶ ὅσα τοιαῦτα.

Tragedies were originally produced as reminders of real-life events, to show us that such things naturally happen, and to encourage us not to experience distress when the sort of things that beguile us in the theatre occur in the greater theatre of our life. This is because we can see that these things must be endured, just as the characters who cry out: 'O, Cithaeron!' [Sophocles, *Oedipus Tyrannus* 1391] must endure them too. Furthermore, the works of the playwrights contain some useful sayings, such as the following examples in particular:
   'If my twin sons and I were neglected by the gods, even this can be explained'
                                       [Euripides, *Antiope* F208.1–2]
and again:
   'There is no point in being angry at what befalls us'
                                       [Euripides, *Bellerophon* F287.1]
and:
   'We must harvest our life like a ripe ear of corn'
                                       [Euripides, *Hypsipyle* F757.94]
   – and how many more there are of the same sort!

This is (by the standards of ancient criticism) a conventional description of the social function of tragedy, which is treated as a representation of the world around us and as a source of didactic wisdom; the conceit that life itself is a theatre ('All the world's a stage …') is also encountered elsewhere.[54] The key point is that tragedy is a source of 'useful sayings' of a sort that can be excerpted and reapplied to real-life situations. For Marcus, these sayings are 'useful' not in the sense that they can help you to win your case in court, or get on in society, or impress your fellow symposiasts by your erudition, but specifically because they can help you to cope with life's challenges and bear what happens with equanimity.[55]

Two of the three Euripidean examples included in 11.6 are identical to verses quoted in earlier chapters of the *Meditations* (7.38, 7.41). This may imply, once again, that Marcus was drawing on anthologies rather than first-hand acquaintance with the plays, but more importantly it shows that he continually called the same verses to mind for repeated use. In this respect, we can compare another passage in which Marcus is discussing the process of ethical self-improvement (5.16). Here he writes that the reinforcement of ideas through frequent repetition is a valuable method of mental training:

οἷα ἂν πολλάκις φαντασθῆις, τοιαύτη σοι ἔσται ἡ διάνοια· βάπτεται γὰρ ὑπὸ τῶν φαντασιῶν ἡ ψυχή. βάπτε οὖν αὐτὴν τῆι συνεχείαι τῶν τοιούτων φαντασιῶν.

Your mind will take on the character of whatever you think about frequently, for the soul is dyed by these thoughts. Dye your soul, therefore, with a continuous repetition of thoughts such as these.

As John Sellars acutely observes, this self-analytical passage has important implications for an understanding of Marcus' philosophical outlook as well as an understanding of the compositional principles underlying the *Meditations* as a document.[56] Even though this text has often been criticized for its chaotic structure, redundancy or careless duplication of material, it could well be that the repetition of fundamental ideas is entirely deliberate. We could see it as reflecting the fact that Marcus was already thinking about the same lines over and over again before he wrote them down; or perhaps it was a mnemonic strategy intended to embed these ideas more deeply in his mind. Elsewhere in the text Marcus also dwells on the importance of memorization, recollection and repetition in connection with important precepts and axioms.[57] It has been observed that 'always remember' is one of his favourite phrases (occurring more than forty times throughout the work).[58] Note that the key word used by Marcus in the passage above is *phantasiai* (which may be translated as 'thoughts', 'ideas', mental 'impressions' or similar).[59] Even though in 5.16 Marcus is not explicitly talking about literature, what he says here can easily be applied to quotations. It seems clear that Euripidean quotations can be treated alongside other types of *phantasiai*, and that Marcus sees his soul as being 'dyed' in these ideas. If we follow Marcus' argument to its conclusion, it seems that Euripides' thoughts have become virtually indistinguishable from Marcus' own. Through this process of cognitive 'dyeing' it is possible for a person to be quoting Euripides and living out his precepts without even consciously realizing that they are doing so.

It will be clear that reading Marcus Aurelius' work is an unusually intimate experience. The *Meditations* (or whatever we wish to call it) comes nearer than any other ancient text to giving us a direct window into an individual's private thoughts. It also represents an aspect of quotation culture quite different from any of the other material under discussion in this book. Unlike many of those who made use of quotations in the ancient world, Marcus is not displaying his knowledge to anybody else. Quotation is not necessarily to be understood as a performative act; it need not take place within a social situation; it need not constitute a form of communication or the acting-out of a role; it can be understood in cognitive terms as an entirely introspective process.

Conclusions

Literary scholars and students in the twenty-first century are regularly called upon to defend their subject against charges of 'irrelevance'. To anyone in the ancient world this would have seemed an odd state of affairs. It seems to have been universally accepted during antiquity that literature is relevant to life. The authors discussed in this chapter may seem to represent a rather motley selection (indeed, they were chosen partly for that reason). They were all writing in different times and places and for very different purposes. They do not all treat quotations in the same way, nor do they perceive exactly the same sort of relevance in the words that they quote. But what they all have in common is the conviction that literature and life are intimately bound up with one another. They also share the assumption that Euripidean drama not only reflects its author's personal experience but expresses profound truths about the human condition more generally. For Satyrus, Diogenes, Cicero and Marcus – and for many others as well – quoting Euripides is an activity with an inherently ethical and personal dimension. Euripides is certainly not unique in this respect, but the fact that so many connections were traced between his plays and the lives of people in the real world is a sign of the richness and resonance of his work; it also testifies to his continual popularity and his centrality within Greek and Roman education.

All the writers discussed in this chapter are using quotations to demonstrate that Euripides has had a profoundly formative influence on his readers, affecting their spoken discourse, their thoughts, their actions, their personality or their entire worldview. Euripides' tragedies – or parts of them – have been committed to memory; their valuable lessons have been learnt; their ethical content has been thoroughly absorbed; uttering lines and phrases from these plays has come to seem like a normal feature of everyday conversation, or even a habitual component of a person's inner dialogue and thought processes. We are thus encouraged to think that those who come into contact with Euripides do not just *read* his words but even, in a sense, *live* them.

Notes

Chapter 1

1. *Blackwood's Edinburgh Magazine* (June 1875), 722.
2. Maxwell and Rumbold (2018) suggest many points of comparison and contrast.
3. This section incorporates a revised version of Wright (2016b), reproduced by kind permission of Johns Hopkins University Press.
4. Cf. Morson (2011), 92: 'a line interpreted as an independent work differs fundamentally from the same line interpreted as part of some larger work'.
5. Plett (1991), Derrida (1988), Eco (2004), Said (1975), Barthes (1973) and Sternberg (1982).
6. Cf. Hunter (2009) for a similar approach.
7. F662-671: Kannicht (*TrGF* 5, pp. 652-6) gives details of quoting sources.
8. See Compagnon (1979), esp. 36-7 on 'le travail de la citation'; cf. Garber (2003) and Morson (2011).
9. See Dover (2000) and Mastronarde (2009) on the 'fragments' of surviving texts.
10. *P.Oxy.* 2455 (Kannicht T iia).
11. So Goldhill (1991), 216; Sommerstein (1996), 263-5.
12. For further discussion, see Chapter 4, pp. 75-80.
13. See Sommerstein (1996), 263-5.
14. Cf. *Stheneboea* F663, lines which became so famous that they were hardly ever quoted in full: see, e.g., Aristophanes, *Wasps* 1074; Plato, *Symposium* 196e; Aristides, *Oration* 26.3.
15. *Stheneboea* F663 and F665 are parodied by Aristophanes' *Wasps* of 422 BC, i.e. 423 is the earliest possible date. Collard, Cropp and Lee (1995), 83, estimate a date of c. 431-425. The metrical evidence for fragmentary plays is unreliable but suggests a date earlier than 420: see Cropp and Fick (1985), 22, 70.
16. Collard, Cropp and Lee (1995), 79-97.
17. See Chapter 4, pp. 80-8. Several scenes in fifth-century comedy are based on the same premise: e.g. Aristophanes, *Frogs* 1050-88; *Thesmophoriazusae* 177-8, 193-201, 383-456.
18. A similar attitude is implied by Diphilus, *Synoris* F74; cf. Menander, *Epitrepontes* 1123-6.
19. The lines immediately before 407 are mutilated or missing, making it impossible to tell exactly what preceded the quotation: see Gomme and Sandbach (1973), 96.

20 The other lines quoted include Chaeremon, *Achilles Thersitoktonos* F2; Aeschylus, *Niobe* F154.15-16; Carcinus II F5a; Euripides, *Orestes* 1-2; Chaeremon F42 (or Euripides F944a). See Ireland (2010), 101; cf. Cusset (2003), 144–58.
21 Evidence for the social spread of literacy in classical Greece is poor, but a few literary sources mention literate slaves: e.g. Plato, *Theaetetus* 143b-c (a reference to slaves working in the public archives); cf. [Aristotle] *Athenian Constitution* 47.5, Demosthenes 29.11, 33.17, 45.72. Theophilus F1, dating from a similar period to Menander, assumes that literate slaves were exceptional. See Thomas (1992), 143–4.
22 Discussed further in Chapter 4. For different views about the 'competence' (i.e. literary knowledge) of classical theatre audiences, see Mastromarco (2006), Revermann (2006) and Wright (2012).
23 Aristotle, *Rhetoric* 2.21.2-4, 1394b-1395a, cf. 2.21.11-15, 1395b. See also Aristotle F13 Rose for the view that maxims and proverbs are the property of ordinary people.
24 Several scholars treat *gnomai* or proverbs as a genre in a formal sense: e.g. Russo (1997) and Martin (2009). Quotations are also seen as a distinct genre by Morson (2011).
25 See Hunter and Russell (2011), 11–16.
26 Helmbold and O'Neil (1959) and Russell (1972), 26–47.
27 Lardinois (2006).
28 Xenophon, *Memorabilia* 1.2.56: ἔφη δ' αὐτὸν ὁ κατήγορος καὶ τῶν ἐνδοξοτάτων ποιητῶν ἐκλεγόμενον τὰ πονηρότατα καὶ τούτοις μαρτυρίοις χρώμενον διδάσκειν τοὺς συνόντας κακούργους τε εἶναι καὶ τυραννικούς. For μαρτύρια in the sense of 'testimony' or 'proof' (LSJ I), cf. Herodotus 8.55, 8.120; Thucydides 1.33, etc.
29 LSJ s.v. ἀνειλίσσω I. 1, 2; cf. Plato, *Philebus* 15e.
30 See Jenny (1982), 44, on 'linear' versus 'non-linear' reading; cf. Compagnon (1979), 64, on reading as 'fragmentation' and Konstan (2011), 21–2, on the variety of ancient reading practices.
31 Hunter (2014), 7. On unity in the ancient literary-critical tradition, by contrast, see Heath (1989).
32 Plato, *Laws* 7.811a; Lycurgus, *Against Leocrates* 92; Isocrates, *To Demonicus* 51-2 (cf. *To Nicocles* 43-4 on selected *gnomai* from poetry as a source of education); Plutarch, *Moralia Moralia* 79c-d; Lucian, *Fisherman* 6; Aulus Gellius, *Attic Nights praef.* 1. Other relevant passages include Plato, *Protagoras* 338e, *Phaedrus* 228b2, 267a-b, *Laws* 811a-b; Aristotle, *Rhetoric* 2.21.2-4, 1394b-1395a, *Topics* 105b; Aeschines, *Against Ctesiphon* 135; Seneca, *Epistle* 33. Many similar passages are cited and discussed by Barns (1950); cf. Konstan (2011).
33 Stages in the development of the anthology from antiquity to the modern day are discussed by Barns (1950); Regier (2010), 46–96; Morson (2011), 23–36.
34 See Konstan (2011). On Euripides' place within the gnomological tradition cf. Pernigotti (2003), Most (2003).

35 Aristophanes, *Frogs* 1114 (βιβλίον τ' ἔχων ἕκαστος μανθάνει τὰ δεξιά): see Havelock (1982), 288–9, cf. 302–3 on *Frogs* 1199-1323 ('one detects an increasing tendency to view language as though it were broken up into bits and pieces'). Other passages which have been read as references to collections of excerpts include *Acharnians* 398-400 and *Wasps* 725-6, 1259-60; performances of excerpts or highlights are apparently alluded to at *Clouds* 1354-76, *Knights* 529-30, *Daitales* F234, *Gerytades* F161.

36 E.g. Aristophanes, *Thesmophoriazusae* 177-8 (Euripides, *Aeolus* F28), 411-13 (Euripides, *Phoenix* F804); *Wasps* 1071-4 (Euripides, *Stheneboea* F663). Cf. Wright (2012), 143–56, on Aristophanes' use of quotations.

37 Cratinus F342: the translation is taken from LSJ (Suppl. 1996). The same fragment contains the words ὑπολεπτολόγος ('pedantic') and εὐριπιδαριστοφανίζων ('Euripidaristophanist'), which may or may not refer to the same individual. On the interpretation of this fragment see Bakola (2010), 24–9. For similar language, cf. γνωμοτυπικός ('clever at coining maxims', LSJ III.3), Aristophanes, *Knights* 1379; γνωμοτύπος ('maxim-coining' or 'sententious'), Aristophanes, *Clouds* 952, *Frogs* 877, Aristotle, *Rhetoric* 1395a7; γνωμολογίαι ('collections of maxims'), Plutarch, *Cato Major* 2.

38 Bowie (2012).

39 Sider (2007).

40 Hunter (2014), esp. 4–33, 75–86, comparing the Hesiodic *Precepts of Chiron* (F283-5 M-W) and the fragments of Phocylides; Canevaro (2015), 8–28.

41 Xenophon, *Memorabilia* 4.2.1: καταμαθὼν γὰρ Εὐθύδημον τὸν καλὸν γράμματα πολλὰ συνειλεγμένον ποιητῶν τε καὶ σοφιστῶν τῶν εὐδοκιμωτάτων. Socrates mentions these γράμματα later in the same passage (4.2.8-10), describing them as θησαυροὺς . . . σοφίας (9) but questioning what sort of 'wisdom' Euthydemus will acquire from his collection. On 'home-made books', see Pinto (2013), who links this passage with Alcidamas, *On Those Who Write Speeches* 4.

42 Hippias DK86 B6 (Clement of Alexandria, *Stromateis* 6.15); the *Synagoge* is also named and cited by Athenaeus, *Deipnosophistae* 13.609a (=DK86 B4).

43 For speculation on the content of the *Synagoge*, see Patzer (1986), 33–42.

44 Carrara (2009), 100–13, 120–9, 182–95; see also the *Leuven Database of Ancient Books* 1030, 1034, 1041, 1054, 1057.

45 Antiphanes F111 (Athenaeus, *Deipnosophistae* 4.134b): ὁ τὰ κεφάλαια συγγράφων Εὐριπίδηι. Cf. Menander, *Shield* 414 γνωμολογεῖν ('collect maxims').

46 As in Plato, *Laws* 7.811a (quoted above); cf. Phocylides T i Gerber (*Suda* IV.754.19 Adler).

47 LSJ II.2. The word can mean 'main points' (e.g. Pindar, *Pythian* 4.116; Isocrates 3.62, 5.154) or 'summaries' (e.g. Demosthenes 19.315; Plato, *Timaeus* 26c; Aristotle, *Metaphysics* 1042a4).

48 *Athenaeum Fragment* 24 (1798) = Schlegel (1991), 21: 'Viele Werke der Alten sind Fragmente geworden. Viele Werke der Neueren sind es gleich bei der Entstehung.'
49 Morson (2011), 37–8, 81–5, 96–7; cf. Garber (2003), 16, on the 'ventriloquism' of quotations.
50 Some of these characteristics are explored by Friis Johansen (1959), Lardinois (2006), Martin (2009) and Russo (1997).
51 Woodward (2001), Tronzo (2009) and Harbison (2015) discuss artistic and literary fragments and their enthusiasts from a variety of angles.
52 See Heath (1989) for the background to classical conceptions of unity.
53 Adorno (1997), 175–99, esp. 176; cf. Adorno (1951), 24–5 ('Das Ganze ist das Unwahre,' a much quoted aphorism formulated in contrast to Hegel's dictum 'Das Wahre ist das Ganze').
54 Barthes (1973), (1975), 92–5, (1977); cf. Bayard (2007), discussed in Chapter 3.
55 Iser (1978), esp. 1–18, 108–18, 195–7.
56 Barthes (1977), 142–8.
57 The only other known examples of such a technique are Euripides, *Heracleidae* 1-5; *Orestes* 1-3, *Aeolus* F13a, *Phoenix* F803a and Sophocles, *Trachiniae* 1-5.
58 Race (1992), 17–18, adducing as examples Sappho F16, Alcaeus F42, Pindar, *Olympian* 1.1-7, 11.1-15, *Pythian* 5.1-4, *Isthmian* 3.1-3, Bacchylides 14.1-20.
59 Segal (1992), 92–3. Cf. Erbse (1984) on formal and conventional aspects of Euripidean prologues.
60 Genette (1997), 269.
61 Ibid., 158.
62 See Kenyon (1951), 1–37, Turner (1987) and Casson (2001), 17–30, on the evidence for early Greek books.
63 As noted by Vitruvius, *On Architecture* 6 pref. 3. Stobaeus Book 4 ('On the Instability of Human Fortune') records dozens of nearly synonymous *gnomai*; cf. Collard, Cropp and Lee (1995), 92, for other passages from fifth-century literature, including Herodotus 1.32.4-5 (who attributes the sentiment to Solon); Euripides, *Suppliant Women* 170, *Alexandros* F45, *Auge* F273, etc.

Chapter 2

1 Dio Chrysostom 18.7, 35.17a; Quintilian, *Institutio* 10.1.68; Valerius Maximus 3.7 ext. 1a. Cf. *TrGF* 5.1, T196-7.
2 Σ *Phoenissae* 388, Σ *Hecuba* 603, Theon, *Progymnasmata* 1.149, etc.
3 Noted by Kannicht (1997), 68–71; Most (2003). The remains of other tragedians, including Agathon and Chaeremon, suggest a similar penchant for epigrammatic or gnomic formulations, though it is impossible to know how prominent the surviving

quotations/fragments were within the original plays: see Wright (2016a), 73-7, 123-7. For comparison and contrast see Cuny (2007) on Sophoclean maxims.

4   Examples of rhymes and jingles include *Alcestis* 782-5, *Andromache* 269-72, 764-5, *Bacchae* 655, *Hecuba* 377-8, 902-4, *Hippolytus* 427-8, *Medea* 408-9, *Suppliant Women* 269-70, 746-9, 951-3. On rhyming verse in tragedy see Rutherford (2012), 62, 114. Cf. Most (2003), 146, on the phraseology of Euripidean *gnomai*.

5   Schlegel, *Athenaeum Fragment* 206 (1798) = Schlegel (1991), 197: 'Ein Fragment muss gleich einem kleinen Kunstwerke von der umgebende Welt ganz abgesondert und in sich selbst vollendet sein wie ein Igel.' On fragmentariness in relation to unity and completeness/incompleteness, cf. Cascardi (2014), 171-6.

6   On the development of quotation marks and related conventions in modern print culture, see Compagnon (1979), 40-1; Garber (2003), 7-32.

7   Brombert (1980) has insights into the '*phrase de réveil*' in narrative fiction which can also be applied to ancient drama. On beginnings in classical and modern literature more generally see, e.g., Said (1975); on tragic prologues, see Erbse (1984).

8   E.g. Aristophanes, *Frogs* 1099-1247, *Thesmophoriazusae* 849-928, *Aeolosikon* F1, *Gerytades* F156.1-2; Menander, *Shield* 407-24; Nicostratus F29; Eriphus F1.

9   Brombert (1980) explores the *incipit* as, *inter alia*, an 'indicator of literary genre' and 'signal of referentiality'.

10 Ancient authors quote the opening lines of seventeen lost plays: *Aeolus, Andromeda, Antigone, Archelaus*, Auge, Melanippe Sophe*, Meleager*, Oedipus, Peliades, Stheneboea, Sciron, Scyrioi, Telephus, Hypsipyle, Phoenix, Phrixus I, Phrixus II* (* denotes a problematic or disputed case: see Kannicht, *TrGF* 5 on each of the works in question).

11 Meccariello (2021) discusses ancient scholars' use of the *incipit* or *arche* (not exclusively from drama) as a form of reference.

12 Wright (2019), 270-1; Erbse (1984), 1-19.

13 Euripides, *Heracleidae* 1-5, *Orestes* 1-3, *Aeolus* F13a, *Phoenix* F803a; Sophocles, *Trachiniae* 1-5. Kannicht (*TrGF* 5.1, p. 438) also suggests that the gnomic F391 may have been the opening of *Thyestes* (on the basis of its similarity to *Stheneboea* F661).

14 Wilkins (1993), 46, compares *Archelaus* F262 (πάλαι σκοποῦμεν).

15 Stobaeus 3.10.1; Theodorus Metochites, *Miscellanea* 85.

16 So Friis Johansen (1959), 75-6.

17 E.g. allusions to *kainotes* ('novelty') or other innovations at *Orestes* 126-31, 239, 790, 875, 977-8, 1503, 1520-2, 1591-2. See Torrance (2013), 45-57.

18 Dio Chrysostom 4.8.2, Lucian, *Zeus Tragedian* 1, Stobaeus 4.34.48, *Suda* A 3819 Adler, Cicero, *Tusculan Disputations* 4.63 (in Latin translation) and others: see Biehl (1975), 108.

19 On Euripidean closure in general, see Dunn (1996).

20 See Barrett (1964), 417-18 (on *Hippolytus* 1462-6); cf. Kannicht (1969), II.438-40 (on *Helen* 1688-92).

21 *Hecuba* 1295. Battezzato (2018), 256, points out that some other tragedies end on 'a thematically crucial word' (though not a *gnome*): e.g. *Cyclops* 709, *Suppliant Women* 1234; Aeschylus, *Persians* 1077, *Choephoroe* 1076, *Prometheus Bound* 1093; Sophocles, *Trachiniae* 1278.
22 Dunn (1996), 17–18. Gibert (2019), 352–3, also judges the lines irrelevant.
23 Various editors delete all or parts of the final scene as interpolated: see Mastronarde (1994), 642–3.
24 Cf. Friis Johansen (1959), 151–9, on 'conclusive reflections'.
25 Cf. (perhaps) the last words of characters destined to die shortly: e.g. *Heracleidae* 574-99, *Hecuba* 546-52, *Iphigenia at Aulis* 1552-61.
26 Cf. Friis Johansen (1959), 155 n. 17: 'It appears that there is no preference for attributing the reflection to "attractive" characters.' It is theoretically possible that maxims spoken by divine characters carry more weight, e.g.: *Hippolytus* 1339-41 (Artemis), *Bacchae* 641 (Dionysus), *Rhesus* 980-2 (the Muse), *Women of Troy* 95-7 (Poseidon).
27 The conclusion reached by Friis Johansen (1959); cf. Most (2003), 150.
28 *Andromache* 319-20, *Bacchae* 201-3, 265-6, 1251-2, *Electra* 367, *Heracleidae* 297-303, *Hecuba* 863-7, 1187-94, 1195, *Helen* 711-15, *Hippolytus* 486-7, *Ion* 585-6, 1512-17, *Orestes* 640-1, 1155-7, *Phoenician Women* 452-3, 469-72, 499-502, 528-30, *Rhesus* 510-11, *Suppliant Women* 195-218.
29 *Alcestis* 669-72, 800-2, *Andromache* 100-2, 177-8, 185, 269-72, 636-41, 745-6, 985-6, *Bacchae* 260-2, 641, 773-4, 1325-6, *Electra* 522-3, *Heracleidae* 458-60, 593-6, 890-1, 939-40, *Hecuba* 227-8, 293-5, 375-8, 844-5, 1177-82, *Helen* 752-7, 851-4, 951-3, 1678-9, *Hippolytus* 423-6, *Iphigenia at Aulis* 366-75, 502-3, 1249-52, *Ion* 373-80, 388-400, 440-51, 673-5, *Medea* 264-6, 516-19, 573-5, 1224-30, *Orestes* 70, 715-16, 1175-6, *Phoenician Women* 524-5, 954-9, *Rhesus* 980-2, *Suppliant Women* 40-1, 269-70, 331, 506-10, 726-30, 855-6, *Women of Troy* 1203-6, 1248-5, *Hypsipyle* F757.80-1 (879-80).
30 *Bacchae* 1150-2, *Electra* 80-1, 426-31, *Helen* 1617-18, *Suppliant Women* 1108-13, *Women of Troy* 95-7.
31 *Helen* 1640-1, *Ion* 1311-19, *Orestes* 454-5, 727-8, *Suppliant Women* 953-4.
32 *Andromache* 764-5, 1007-8, *Bacchae* 1150-2, *Hecuba* 627-8, 902-4, *Heracles* 101-6, 633-6, 732-3, *Hippolytus* 120, *Iphigenia at Aulis* 160-2, 749-50, *Ion* 1045-7, *Iphigenia among the Taurians* 122, 380-91, *Medea* 123-5, 408-9, *Orestes* 314-15, 805-6, *Phoenician Women* 198-201, *Suppliant Women* 775-7, 953-4.
33 *Andromache* 181-2, 184-5, 642-4, *Bacchae* 376-7, *Electra* 236-7, *Heracleidae* 179-80, *Hecuba* 846-9, *Helen* 698-9, 758-60, *Iphigenia at Aulis* 917-18, *Ion* 381-3, *Orestes* 542-3, 605-6, *Phoenician Women* 526-7, *Rhesus* 316-17, *Suppliant Women* 250-1.
34 At beginning: *Hippolytus* 668-9, *Medea* 629-31, *Rhesus* 206, *Suppliant Women* 372-3, *Cresphontes* F453.15. At end: *Iphigenia at Aulis* 596-7, 1090-7, *Ion* 508-9, *Phoenician Women* 689.

35 *Andromache* 465-70, 471-7, 478-85, 766-75, 776-87, *Bacchae* 386-401, 417-31, 877-81 (= 897-901), *Heracles* 772-80, *Heracleidae* 608-17, *Iphigenia at Aulis* 543-57, 558-72, incert. fab. F897, F898.
36 Friis Johansen (1959), 34–5. Cf. Cuny (2007) on Sophocles.
37 This section contains material from Wright (2016c), reproduced by permission of the editors of *GRBS*.
38 LSJ *s.v.* φεῦ (I) and (II). Cf. Collard (1991) on *Hecuba* 1238: 'the exclamation φεῦ expresses any vehement emotion, from grief to delight'. Other nuances have been detected, e.g. commiseration or sarcasm: see Kamerbeek (1974) on Sophocles, *Electra* 1021.
39 Apart from tragedy, see Aristophanes, *Acharnians* 457, *Birds* 162, *Lysistrata* 198, 312, *Clouds* 41, *Wealth* 362, *Frogs* 141, *Wasps* 309-10 (some of which may be paratragic); cf. Bacchylides, *Dithyramb* 3.119; Xenophon, *Cyropaedia* 3.1.39, *Agesilaus* 7.5; Plato, *Phaedrus* 263d5, 273c7, *Hippias Major* 287b4.
40 Allen and Italie (1954), 644.
41 Sophocles, *Ajax* 1266, *Tympanistai* F636 (cf. *Oedipus Tyrannus* 316); Euripides, *Alcestis* 727, *Andromache* 183, *Electra* 367, *Hecuba* 864, 956, 1238, *Hippolytus* 431 (cf. 925), *Ion* 1312, *Medea* 330, *Orestes* 1155, *Suppliant Women* 463, *Aeolus* F25, *Alcmeon* F80, *Antiope* F211, 218, *Danae* F329, *Dictys* F333, *Ino* F401, *Theseus* F439, *Meleager* F536, *Polyidus* F645b, *Scyrioi* F684, *Temenidai* F739, *Philoctetes* F800, incert. fab. F961, F1034; Critias, *Tennes* F21 *TrGF* (= Euripides F695 Nauck); Apollonides F1. This usage is noted, without discussion, by Denniston (1939) on Euripides, *Electra* 367; cf. Lee (1997) on *Ion* 1312.
42 Other cases where gnomic content *and* strong emotion seem to combine after φεῦ include *Alcestis* 727 and *Ion* 1312; but most instances (cited in n. 41) are more ambivalent.
43 Biehl (1975), in his commentary on this line, interprets φεῦ as 'Ausdruck der Rührung, zugleich Einleitung zu allgemeinen Reflexion'; but he does not specify (and I cannot decide) what *sort* of feeling is being conveyed.
44 Cf. *Andromache* 182-5, where a gnomic couplet from the Chorus is followed immediately by another *gnome* from Andromache (introduced by φεῦ φεῦ, which acts as a means of separating the two unrelated maxims). For strings of consecutive maxims, cf. *Phoenician Women* 390-407 and *Erechtheus* F362: see pp. 50–2.
45 See Rutherford (2012), 368–81, on the apparent banality of many tragic *gnomai* on these topics.
46 Cf. Sophocles, *Trachiniae* 1-3; Euripides, *Hecuba* 294-5, *Helen* 513-14, *Medea* 964-5, *Danae* F321, *Melanippe Sophe* F508; see also pp. 48–50.
47 Romero-Trillo (2013).
48 Norrick (2009), 888: 'many primary interjections function in the participation and information frameworks of discourse, *rather than marking emotional involvement*' (my italics).

49 The sole exception in dialogue is Sophocles, *Philoctetes* 234 (non-gnomic). In lyric passages φεῦ normally appears at the beginning of a verse or period (contrast, e.g., Aeschylus, *Eumenides* 781, 841, 874; Sophocles, *Trachiniae* 987; Euripides, *Hippolytus* 365, *Iphigenia among the Taurians* 651, *Phoenician Women* 246), though colometry is often uncertain.

50 Tragic papyri occasionally feature marginalia indicating notable passages: see *P.Oxy.* 2452 fr. 3; Turner (1987), 56 and Figure 27; cf. Turner (1968), 116–17 on the symbols χ and χρ (for χρῆσις) to denote 'useful' passages suitable for quotation. Highlighting and marginal symbols, e.g. γνώ (for γνώμη, γνωμικόν or γνωμικῶς), ὡρ(αῖον) and ση(μείωσαι), are used in Byzantine manuscripts to draw attention to notable passages: see Zuntz (1965), 133; Turyn (1943), 123. Cf. also Hunter (1951) on the marking of *sententiae* in Elizabethan and later printed books, and Petersen (2018) on 'printed marks of sententiousness' in the margins of the first edition of Shakespeare's *Lucrece* (1594).

51 The metaphor of *ciseaux et pot à colle* comes from Compagnon (1979), 17–37.

52 Culler (2015), 8: the phenomenon is defined as 'addressing the audience of readers by addressing or pretending to address someone or something else'.

53 *Electra* 339-47 (Zeus), 503-13 (old men), *Hecuba* 1187-94 (Agamemnon), *Heracleidae* 740 (Iolaus), *Hippolytus* 616-69 (Zeus), *Ion* 440-51 (Phoebus), *Medea* 516-19 (Zeus), *Phoenician Women* 84-7 (Zeus), *Suppliant Women* 134-6 (Zeus), 549 (men), 744-9 (men), *Aeolus* F28 (Macareus and Canace?), *Alexandros* F48 (Priam), F62 (Hecabe), *Alcmeon in Corinth* F75 (Amphilochus), *Antiope* F206 (Amphion), *Danae* F316 (Eurydice), *Dictys* F337 (an old man), *Thyestes* F396 (Atreus?), *Ino* F415 (Themisto?), *Hippolytus Veiled* F430 (Theseus), *Palamedes* F580 (Agamemnon), *Peliades* F603 (one of Pelias' daughters), *Chrysippus* F843 (Laius?), incert. fab. F928b (Zeus).

54 *Andromache* 319-20 (ὦ δόξα δόξα), *Ion* 1512-17 (ὦ . . . τύχη), *Suppliant Women* 1108-13 (ὦ δυσπάλαιστον γῆρας), *Andromeda* F136 (ὦ θεῶν τύραννε κἀνθρώπων Ἔρως), *Danae* F324 (ὦ χρυσέ), *Ino* F400 (ὦ θνητὰ πράγματα), *Hippolytus Veiled* F436 (ὦ πότνι' Αἰδώς), *Phoenix* F803a (ὦ πλοῦθ'), incert. fab. F916 (ὦ πολύμοχθος βιοτὴ θνητοῖς); cf. the gnomic lyric fragment *Cresphontes* F453.15 (Εἰρήνα).

55 The lines were anthologized by Stobaeus (2.31.8) and Orion (*Florilegium Euripideum* 18).

56 Cf. Friis Johansen (1959), 83: 'The pathos itself has a general moral object; the charge is directed against the whole world-order, and Hippolytus is only one instance of a universal calamity.'

57 E.g. Aristotle, *Rhetoric* 1395a2-7.

58 *Aeolus* F28, *Antiope* F206, *Archelaus* F233, 254, *Bellerophon* F291, *Melanippe* (*Sophe* or *Desmotis*) F504, *Peliades* F603, *Peleus* F619.

59 The indicative verb 'you see . . .' (singular or plural) is used in an analogous way to introduce *gnomai* at *Ino* F420 (ὁρᾶις) and *Philoctetes* F794 (ὁρᾶτε). Cf. characters

Notes to pp. 44–52   181

who use the verb παραινῶ ('I give [this] advice') when introducing gnomai: *Danae* F317, *Hippolytus Veiled* F440.

60 E.g. Stobaeus 3.13.7, 4.22.115, 4.22.180; Plutarch, *Moralia* 107b-c. Stobaeus 4.51.13 and Orion *Florilegium Euripideum* 8.4 (quoting *Alcestis* 782-4) are exceptions.

61 For discussion of this strand in Euripidean criticism see Friis Johansen (1959), 173-4, Scodel (1999-2000). Cf. Rutherford (2012), 365-6, on 'relevance' as a criterion in textual criticism where excision of gnomic lines is at stake.

62 The imperative λεύσσετε at *Phoenician Women* 1758, addressed primarily to the citizens of Thebes (ὦ πάτρας κλεινῆς πολῖται), may have a similar function in introducing a general reflection on the outcome of the plot; cf. *Andromache* 957-8 for a maxim about the importance of listening to advice.

63 Parker (2007), 208, pronounces this run of *four* rhyming lines unique (but supplies some partial parallels).

64 See n. 4 above; cf. Rutherford (2012), 55, 62, 114, on rhyme as a device for character portrayal.

65 The phrase comes from Heath (1987), 159-60, who discusses 'commonplaces of tragic wisdom, recurrent motifs drawn from that way of thinking about the world that is characteristic of tragedy'. Most (2003), 149, describes the speaker as 'il portavoce di una saggezza popolare anonima'.

66 Morson (2011), 96-7.

67 E.g. *Andromache* 182, *Helen* 715, *Heracles* 102, *Ion* 1329, *Women of Troy* 1051, *Alexandros* F59, *Alcmene* F93, *Archelaus* F237.1, *Bellerophon* F290, *Philoctetes* F798, *Phrixus* (*I* or *II*) F823, incert. fab. F945, F1012. Cf. Moles (2001), 206-7, 219, on uses of ἀεί by Thucydides to imply that his *History* is a 'timeless project' or 'a text for any context'.

68 Cf. *Andromache* 418, *Heracleidae* 863-6, *Medea* 1224, *Suppliant Women* 744, 949.

69 On this and other formulas of transition in monologues, see Friis Johansen (1959), 54-101.

70 E.g. *Heracleidae* 596, *Hippolytus* 262, *Andromeda* F151, *Antiope* F222, *Licymnius* F474; cf. *Ion* 508-9, *Antigone* F167, *Archelaus* F253.

71 Cf. *Aeolus* F25 and *Dictys* F333 (quoted at pp. 39-40).

72 E.g. Agathon *TrGF* 1.39 F5, F6, F8, F9, F11, F19; Philemon F28, F75, F97, F119, F148 K-A. For discussion, see Wright (2016a), 73-7.

73 Aristotle, *Rhetoric* 2.1395a9-11.

74 See Collard, Cropp and Lee (1995), 148-94, and Sonnino (2010).

75 F352, F353, F354, F355, F356, F358, F359, F360, F360a, F364, F365. On the political use of quotations from *Erechtheus*, see Hanink (2014), 70-87, and Volonaki (2017).

76 Xenophon, *Memorabilia* 1.6.14, quoted and discussed in Chapter 1, pp. 17-18. Cf. Plato, *Philebus* 15e.

77 Stobaeus (3.3.18) quotes 1-34 as a single passage but also quotes individual *gnomai* from the passage separately at 4.31.97 (11-13), 4.31.25 (14-17), 3.14.3 (18-20), 4.50.3

(21-3), 3.17.6 (24-7). Plutarch quotes 18-20 (*Moralia* 63a) and 29-31 (*Moralia* 337f) separately. Other snippets from the *Erechtheus* 'anthology' are quoted separately by anthologists and paroemiographers: see *TrGF* 5, pp. 402-5.

Chapter 3

1 Bayard (2007), 56.
2 Ibid., esp. 46, 82, 150.
3 Ibid., 82.
4 The problem is addressed, with reference to Euripides and other tragedians, by, e.g., Pearson (1917), I.xlvi–xci, Zuntz (1965), 255–7, Collard (1975), I.39–41, and Collard (2007), 69–92.
5 Stobaeus 4.36.2-4 (*Orestes* 229-36 lemmatized as distinct quotations rather than a single passage); Stobaeus 4.19.1-2 (*Helen* 726-33 treated in a similar way). *Erechtheus* F362 is quoted either consecutively or as separate sections by different quoters (see *TrGF* 5, pp. 402–5); cf. *Antiope* F200, F208, *Bellerophon* F285, 286b, *Phrixus* II F819, etc.
6 See *TrGF* 5, pp. 214–18, 465–74, 548–53, 866–76.
7 Σ Aristophanes, *Birds* 1242 = Euripides, *Licymnius* T*iia. Three separate branches of scholia are represented in the manuscripts: see *TrGF* 5, p. 519.
8 Σ *Hippolytus* 58 = *Alexandros* Tv.
9 [Dionysius of Halicarnassus] *Rhetoric* 9.11 = *Melanippe Sophe* Tiia and F485.
10 Tzetzes, *On Tragedy* (in *Anecdota Parisiana* I.19-20 Cramer) = *Alcmeon in Corinth* F74.
11 Dio Chrysostom, *Orations* 52 and 59 = *Philoctetes* Tiiib, iiiv, F789b-d.
12 Philo, *Quod Omnis Probus Liber Sit* 98-104 = *Syleus* Tiiib; F687-91.
13 *Temenidae* or *Temenus* F727e (= F1083 Nauck); on attribution, see Harder (1985), 278–9 and Kannicht, *TrGF* 5, p. 719. On Strabo's use of quotations, cf. Bianchi (2020).
14 Helmbold and O'Neil (1959); Russell (1972), 26–47. Di Gregorio (1976) argues, on the basis of the number of tragic quotations in Plutarch's work and the range of titles cited, that Plutarch had a vast first-hand knowledge of the genre.
15 See Di Gregorio (1976), 158–64.
16 Plutarch, *Moralia* 756b (= *Melanippe Sophe* F480, F481), 19d-e (= *Ixion* Tiii Kannicht).
17 On the working methods of scholiasts, see Nünlist (2009).
18 Σ *Medea* 663 = *Peliades* F602 (the same scholion also includes *Peliades* F601).
19 E.g. Σ *Frogs* 1182, 1186, 1391 (identifying/quoting *Antigone* F157, F158, F170); Σ *Thesmophoriazusae* 1065, 1069, 1098 (identifying/quoting *Andromeda* F114, F124); Σ *Peace* 126a (identifying/quoting *Stheneboea* F669); Σ *Frogs* 1238 (quoting an alternative opening line to *Meleager* [F515] which is different from the line quoted in *Frogs* itself [F516]). Many other examples are cited by Rau (1967).

20 Σ *Acharnians* 471-2 = *Aeolus* F568. On Symmachus (probably first century AD), see Dunbar (1995), 38, 40–1; Dickey (2007), 29.
21 See Dickey (2015), 505–8, and Mastronarde (2017), 9–26.
22 Mastronarde (2017), 26.
23 Plato, *Gorgias* 484d6-506b4 (*Antiope* F182b, F184-8): see Kannicht, *TrGF* 5, pp. 284–90.
24 Σ *Gorgias* 484e and 485e; Olympiodorus, *On Plato's Gorgias* 34.4 (*Antiope* *F187a Kannicht); Longinus, *On the Sublime* 40.4 (*Antiope* F221).
25 Cicero, *De Finibus* 1.2.4 (*Antiope* Tviia).
26 Morson (2011), 79–80, distinguishes between 'quotations' (in the sense of 'short literary works' possessing 'quotationality') and 'extracts' (in the sense of 'verbal citations').
27 [Aristotle], *Rhetoric to Alexander* 18.1433b13-15. On textual difficulties in this passage, see Kannicht, *TrGF* 5, pp. 841–2.
28 Aeschines 1.152, followed by Demosthenes 19.245-6, Diodorus 12.14.1 and other rhetorical and gnomological texts: see Kannicht, *TrGF* 5, pp. 851–2. See further pp. 124–6, on the uses of Euripides in rhetorical training.
29 *Stheneboea* F661 = Ioannes Logothetes, *On Hermogenes, Means of Rhetorical Effectiveness* 30 (separate portions of the speech are quoted by other authors: see *TrGF* 5, pp. 649–51); *Melanippe Sophe* F481 = Ioannes Logothetes, *On Hermogenes, Means of Rhetorical Effectiveness* 28 (separate portions are quoted by other authors: see *TrGF* 5, pp. 530–1); *Bellerophon* F285 = Stobaeus 4.33.16; *Bellerophon* F286 = [Justin] *On Monarchy* 5.6; *Erechtheus* F360 = Lycurgus, *Against Leocrates* 100; *Erechtheus* F362 = Stobaeus 3.3.18 (see my earlier discussion, pp. 50–2); incert. fab. F 898 = Athenaeus, *Deipnosophistae* 13.599f; incert. fab. F912 = Clement of Alexandria, *Stromateis* 5.11.70.3; incert. fab. F1063 = Stobaeus 4.23.26a. Cf. (perhaps) *Peirithous* F1 and *Sisyphus* F19, sometimes attributed to Euripides but more plausibly assigned to Critias: see Wright (2016a), 50–8.
30 See, e.g., Carrara (2009), 100–3, with reference to P.Hamb. 118-19, a third-century BC anthology of prologue speeches.
31 E.g. Aristophanes, *Clouds* 1370-3 mentions sympotic recitation of a speech from *Aeolus* (= *Aeolus* Tiva); cf. Menander, *Epitrepontes* 1122-6, where someone offers to recite 'a whole speech from *Auge*', and Plutarch, *Demosthenes* 7, where the young Demosthenes is said to be able to recite Euripidean and Sophoclean speeches from memory.
32 For a partial plot summary, see P.Oxy. 2457 (*Aeolus* Tii); cf. Wright (2019), 144–6.
33 *Aeolus* F13a = incert. fab. F947 Nauck (Orion, *Florilegium Euripideum* 3, p. 55 Schneidewin). Orion's anthology is itself fragmentary: see Haffner (2001); Dickey (2007), 99–100.
34 P.Oxy. 2457 = *Aeolus* Tii.

35 See Meccariello (2021).
36 *Archelaus* F228 (cf. Aristophanes, *Frogs* 1206-8), *Meleager* F515, F516, *Melanippe Sophe* F480, F481. See Kannicht, *TrGF* 5, p. 315.
37 Bianchi (2020).
38 See Kannicht, *TrGF* 5, pp. 163–4, for references.
39 Cf. Avery (1968) on the afterlife of another 'notorious' Euripidean line (*Hippolytus* 612).
40 Stobaeus 3.5.36, citing Serenus, an Athenian grammarian of uncertain date and the author of Ἀπομνημονεύματα ('Memorable Deeds and Sayings'): cf. *Suda* Σ 249. The manuscripts of Stobaeus offer different readings, naming Euripides' interlocutor as either Plato or Diogenes: see Kannicht, *TrGF* 5, p. 165.
41 Plutarch, *How the Young Man Should Study Poetry* 33c; cf. Hunter and Russell (2011), 187. See further discussion of Plutarch in Chapter 5, pp. 98–103.
42 Rosen (2006); cf. Chapter 4, pp. 73–5.
43 *Clouds* 1370-3 (with Σ). But perhaps the reference to *Aeolus* was inserted only in the later (revised) version of *Clouds* that survives.
44 Collard and Cropp (2008), II.709–10, collect many references.
45 Athenaeus, *Deipnosophistae* 4.159c; Plutarch, *How the Young Man Should Study Poetry* 34d; Sextus Empiricus *Against the Grammarians* 271; Gregory of Nazianzus, *Carmina Moralia* 10.
46 Plutarch, *Moralia* 25c, 369b, 474a. Cf. Theophrastus, *Metaphysics* 18 for part of verse 4.
47 Plutarch, *Moralia* 285b, 786a, 1094f; Stobaeus 4.50.71. On the textual problem, see Kannicht, *TrGF* 5, p. 167.
48 For comparable examples of elliptical 'half-quotation', cf. *Stheneboea* F663 alongside the citing sources listed by Kannicht (*TrGF* 5, pp. 650–1).
49 Plutarch, *Moralia* 98d, 959c; cf. Stobaeus 4.13.4, Arsenius 13.36 (*CPG* 2.334.17).
50 Cf. Chapter 4, pp. 76–80, on 'visible' *versus* 'invisible' quotations in comedy.
51 See pp. 41–4.
52 On these problems see Kannicht, *TrGF* 5, p. 172: it is possible that the second of the two verses quoted is a separate *comic* fragment (see *PCG* VII, p. 317).
53 See Kannicht (1969), I.83–93, for a survey of all citations (or 'fragments') of *Helen*; cf. Collard (1975), I.39–41, on *Suppliant Women* and Mastronarde (2009) on *Phoenician Women*.

Chapter 4

1 Kristeva (1980), 66.
2 See Rau (1967), Silk (2000), Wright (2012), 141–72, Wright (2013) and Farmer (2017).

3 Cratinus F342 (Εὐριπιδαριστοφανίζων): see Bakola (2010), 24–9.
4 Silk (2000), 49–97.
5 On this process of 'classicization', see Rosen (2006). Even as early as 405 BC, Aristophanes' *Frogs* has been seen as according quasi-canonical status to Euripides: see Hunter (2009), 10–52.
6 See Farmer (2017), 41–5, on these comedies of 'tragic fandom'.
7 On tragic reperformances see Lamari (2017); 'old drama' was a category at the City Dionysia from 386 BC (*IG* II².2318.1009-11).
8 [Plutarch], *Lives of the Ten Orators* 841f. For discussion of this decree and its consequences, see Hanink (2014), 62–103.
9 *Orestes* 279 is quoted by several comedians because the line was delivered oddly by the actor Hegelochus at the play's premiere in 408 BC: see Aristophanes, *Frogs* 302-4 (with Σ), Sannyrion F8, Strattis F1 and F63. Cf. Farmer (2017), 30–3, for illuminating discussion.
10 For differing views of the composition and theatrical 'competence' of Greek audiences at different dates, see Gomme and Sandbach (1973), 22, Revermann (2006), Mastromarco (2006), Roselli (2011), 1–15, and Wright (2012).
11 A point emphasized by Bennett (1997), 1–20, 91; cf. Roselli (2011), esp. 1–15, with reference to fifth-century Athenian audiences.
12 On Athenian literacy and books, see Yunis (2003), esp. 189–212; cf. Missiou (2011).
13 *Peace* 58-161 (incorporating *Aeolus* F17, F18, *Stheneboea* F669): see Rau (1967), 89–97. For a similar mixture of 'visible' and 'invisible' in other parodic scenes, cf. Rau (1967) 185–212; see also Wright (2012), 100–2, on embedded quotations and allusions in *Frogs*.
14 Strattis, *Phoenician Women* F46 (Euripides, *Hypsipyle* F752): see Orth (2009), 208.
15 Eubulus, *Medea* F64 (Euripides, *Orestes* 37). Hunter (1983), 150, suggests that the lines also allude to the *Medea* of Morsimus or Melanthius.
16 Aristophanes, *Frogs* 855-67; Alexis, *Eisoikizomenos* F63.7: Arnott (1996), 191–2, suggests that Alexis' parody was inspired by a recent production of *Telephus* or that the quotation had become proverbial.
17 Cf. Hunter (1983), 91: 'it is very unlikely that a large number of the audience remembered (or were expected to remember) the original context'.
18 On poets and parody in Eupolis, see Storey (2003), 327–33.
19 Longinus, *On the Sublime* 16.3. See Telò (2007), 257–61; Halliwell (2022), 262.
20 Storey (2003), 329.
21 For detailed discussion and reconstruction, see ibid., 142–69, and the commentaries of Telò (2007) and Olson (2017), all of which differ substantially from one another.
22 Text and translation from Storey (2011), II.110–11.
23 *Frogs* 1077-82, 1478; cf. Euripides, *Polyidus* F638 and *Phrixus* F833 for similar paradoxes. See Kannicht, *TrGF* 5, pp. 627, 873–4.

24 Tragedy and comedy do differ from one another in their handling of the iambic metre, which sometimes makes it easier to identify quotations or paratragic formulations: see West (1982), 88–90.
25 See Wright (2012) and (2013).
26 See Biles and Olson (2015), 395; cf. also *Knights* 999-1000 (chests full of oracles), *Birds* 959-91 (collections of oracles in a homemade commonplace book).
27 See Wright (2012), 151–6.
28 See pp. 9–11.
29 The lines were preserved in full by Stobaeus 3.30.1 and in part by Sextus Empiricus, *Against the Experts* 6.35. On the characters and plot of *Antiope*, see Collard, Cropp and Gibert (2004), 259–329.
30 See Orth (2009).
31 The lines are preserved by Athenaeus (*Deipnosophistae* 4.160b), along with the speaker's name. See Orth (2009), 208, Farmer (2017), 91–2.
32 See Morson (2011), 147–50, on quotations misattributed to quotable figures (e.g. Oscar Wilde, Sherlock Holmes, Winston Churchill), and cf. 155: 'the ascription of an author may be an intrinsic part of a quotation'. Kannicht accepts the line as genuine (= incert. fab. F894, *TrGF* 5, p. 906) but discusses the possibility that δειπνεῖν ('dines') may be a comic substitution of an original tragic verb such as φεύγειν ('flees'). Cf. Diphilus, *Parasite* F60 (based on Euripides incert. fab. F915) for a similar example of a comic alteration of a tragic line; cf. also Eriphus F1 for the phrase οὐ κακῶς ἔχον to denote an apparently approving but essentially ironic attitude towards a tragic *gnome*.
33 For a list of Euripidean *gnomai* transmitted among the *Menandrou monostichoi*, see Kannicht, *TrGF* 5, p. 1063.
34 Aristotle, *Rhetoric* 1371a28, Plato, *Laws* 797d. On the reception of *Orestes* within antiquity, see Luschnig (2015), 239–41.

Chapter 5

1 See Marrou (1956), 153–5, 163–4; Cribiore (1996), 44–9; Cribiore (2001a), 178–80, 185–99.
2 Morgan (1998), 65–70, 115–17.
3 Cribiore (2001a), 179.
4 Plato, *Protagoras* 325a-326c, *Statesman* 277e2-278c1; Xenophon, *Symposium* 4.2, 4.27; Isocrates, *Antidosis* 296-7, *Panathenaicus* 18; Herodas, *Mimiamb* 3.1-41; Quintilian 1.1.15-16, 1.1.24-37, 1.9.3, 5.14.31, 10.1.16-20; Seneca, *Epistle* 94.51; Clement of Alexandria, *Stromateis* 5.8.48-9. Discussion in Marrou (1956), 153–64, Morgan (1998), 19–72, Cribiore (2001a), 1–180.
5 Cribiore (1996): see especially the catalogue of school exercises, pp. 173–287.

6   Morgan (1998), 115-16 and tables 22-3.
7   Cribiore (1996), cat. nos 130, 241, 270, 282, 303, 379. Cf. Cribiore (2001b) on the reception of *Phoenician Women* in antiquity.
8   Cribiore (1996), cat. nos 129, 182, 234, 236, 240, 242, 244, 246, 277, 304, 379.
9   Guéraud and Jouguet (1938) = Cribiore (1996) 269 (cat. no. 379). See also Carrara (2009), 127-9.
10 For a photograph and transcription see Guéraud and Jouguet (1938), plates III-IV.
11 For references, see Mastronarde (1994), 298-300; Kannicht, *TrGF* 5, pp. 453-4.
12 The view of Guéraud and Jouguet (1938), xviii.
13 For discussion of the textual difficulties in Stobaeus and other sources, see Kannicht, *TrGF* 5, pp. 453-4.
14 See Pfeiffer (1968), 99-104.
15 Diogenes Laertius 5.81. On *chreiai*, see also Chapter 7, pp. 158-9.
16 See Carrara (2009), 8-10, 120-6, 182-209, 588.
17 E.g. Guéraud and Jouguet (1938), xx-xxi, Morgan (1998), 120-51, and Cribiore (2001a), 178-9.
18 Marrou (1956), 153.
19 Note, however, that Plutarch (*Moralia* 14e) mentions works used in the education of the very young, including Aesop's *Fables*, *Tales from the Poets*, Heraclides' *Abaris* and Ariston's *Lycon*; cf. Cicero, *De Natura Deorum* 1.34, Diogenes Laertius 5.65.
20 See e.g. Cribiore (1996), cat. nos 241, 244, 246, 282.
21 E.g. Helmbold and O'Neil (1959); Russell (1972), 26-8, 46-9; Di Gregorio (1976); Bowie (2008).
22 The estimate of Hunter and Russell (2011), 1-2.
23 See Halliwell (2002), 296-302, on Plutarch's essay as a response to Plato.
24 Shown by Di Gregorio (1976), 156-8, 173-4; Hunter (2009), 175-98.
25 See discussion and the references in Hunter and Russell (2011), 11-12.
26 Plutarch refers to his notebooks (*hypomnemata*) at *Moralia* 464f; cf. Chapter 1, pp. 12-13.
27 For the use of βασανίζειν ('interrogate') in connection with literary criticism, see *Frogs* 802, 1121; cf. Wright (2012), 165. On Aristophanes' influence on the literary-critical tradition, see Hunter (2009).
28 Plutarch is not unique in this method: see parallels cited by Hunter and Russell (2011), 115-16.
29 The inference of Hunter and Russell (ibid.), 116. For opposing *gnomai* in consecutive verses of stichomythia, cf. *Phoenician Women* 388-98.
30 Each line of F254 is quoted separately by Justin, *On Monarchy* 5.6 and Plutarch *Moralia* 1049e (= Chrysippus F1125 von Arnim); Stobaeus (4.31.59) quotes the second line of F1069.
31 Pfeiffer (1968), 71, 94, 110.

32 Konstan (2004).
33 See Porter (2016).
34 Cf. *On the Sublime* 2.3; see Halliwell (2022), xxviii, 99.
35 *On the Sublime* 1.2, 9.6, 9.10, 9.15, 12.4, 12.5, 17.1, 25, 26.2, 26.3, 29.2, 30.1, 33.4, 35.4, 39.1, 39.2.
36 See Halliwell (2022), x–xix, with reference to previous discussions.
37 Halliwell (ibid.), 455–6, supplies a list.
38 Halliwell (ibid.) identifies signs of Longinus' quoting from memory, or from his own notes, at 3.2, 32.5, 43.1, but suggests that 'composite' quotations from Homer (e.g. 9.6, 9.8) may come via anthologies; Usher (2007) argues that these verses are not gleaned from intermediate sources but conflated by Longinus himself on the basis of thematic correspondences.
39 Note the frequent use of words for 'wonder' or 'amazement' (θαυμάζειν, ἔκπληξις, ἔκστασις): 1.4, 7.1, 30.1, 35.4, 36.1, etc.
40 'One of the oldest critical procedures in antiquity': Hunter and Russell (2011), 85–6, with many supporting references.
41 Higbie (2017), esp. 52–4, 77, 238–9.
42 See Too (2010), 192–7.
43 Bourdieu (1977), 89.
44 Ibid. (1993), 1–34, and (1996), 113–40. Cf. Whitmarsh (2001), 57–71, for a reading of Longinus' work as 'a means of constructing and reifying idealized identities'.
45 Bourdieu (1984), 6.
46 Hunter (2009), 129; Halliwell (2022), xxvi–xxxii.
47 The key passage is *On the Sublime* 33.1, concerning 'scrupulous discrimination or considered judgement' (Halliwell's translation of ἐπικρίσεως ἐξ ἅπαντος). Cf. 1.2, 6, 7.4, 12.5, 14.2, 36.1, 44.9, with Halliwell (2022), xxviii–ix, 125–6. Even the claim that judgement can be taught at all is competitive (2.1-3), since Longinus is arguing against critics who deny this.
48 Most (1990), 52.
49 Halliwell (2022), 237–8, supplying many references. Plutarch quoted the same scene six times: see Helmbold and O'Neil (1959), 31.
50 Cf. Plato, *Ion* 533e-534e for the idea that bad poets can produce good work on occasion.
51 Kannicht tentatively assigns it to *Alexandros* (F*62f), but in Nauck's edition it appears as incert. fab. F935.
52 Only at 3.2, 15.7, 23.3.
53 Plutarch (*Moralia* 405e, 622c, 762b) clearly treats the verses as proverbial. Cf. Aristophanes, *Wasps* 1074 (with Σ), Plato, *Symposium* 196e2-3, Stobaeus 4.20.36 and other quoting authors cited by Kannicht, *TrGF* 5, pp. 652–3.
54 See Kannicht (*TrGF* 5, pp. 652–3) for textual discussion.

55 Russell (1964), 174.
56 See Morson (2011), 37–68, on 'former quotations'.
57 Halliwell (2022), 452.
58 So ibid., 452–3.
59 Kannicht (*TrGF* 5, p. 335) does not include the verse among the fragments of *Auge*. Cf. Chapter 7, pp. 156–62, on Diogenes' biographical anecdotes and quotations.
60 Some editors (following Wilamowitz) delete *Electra* 373-9; but see Page (1934), 74–5, and Denniston (1939), xlii–xliii, 94–5, who point out that the verses appear in a third-century BC papyrus (*P. Hibeh*).
61 Denniston (1939), 94, compares Sophocles, *Oedipus Tyrannus* 979.
62 See Chadwick (1966), Zeegers-Vander Vorst (1972) and Morlet (2020).
63 Neymeyr (1989), 45–93; Oborn (2005), 5–23.
64 On affinities between *Stromateis* and the miscellany genre, see Heath (2020); cf. Neymeyr (1989), 79–81.
65 See the index in Stählin (1936), with modifications by van den Hoek (1996): Homer accounts for 38 per cent of poetic references and Euripides 18 per cent.
66 Zeegers-Vander Vorst (1972), 36; Morlet (2020), 351–5.
67 Cf. *Stromateis* 1.33.6, 6.89.2. For the same metaphor, see, e.g., Plutarch, *Moralia* 41e-f, 79c; Isocrates, *To Demonicus* 51; Lucian, *Fisherman* 6; Seneca, *Epistle* 83 and other passages cited by Barns (1950), 132–4. Heath (2020), 177–82, suggests that the bee/meadow image in *Stromateis* may additionally recall Euripides, *Hippolytus* 73-4.
68 Chadwick (1966) presents Clement as an urbane and genuinely knowledgeable reader; Zeegers-Vander Vorst (1972) identifies several clusters of quotations common to Clement and other quoting authors; Friesen (2015) shows that not only Clement's quotations but his interpretations of those quotations are sometimes taken from earlier sources; Morlet (2020), 358–65, argues for heavy reliance on anthologies by Clement and other Christian writers; van den Hoek (1996) is judiciously open-minded; Heath (2020), 69–72, argues for a mixture between first-hand and second-hand citation.
69 On Clement's source referencing habits, see van den Hoek (1996), 231 with nn. 67–8.
70 On trends in interpretation, see Michelini (1987), 11–27, and Lefkowitz (2015).
71 See Collard, Cropp and Gibert (2004), 310. Cf. *Helen* 16-21 for scepticism towards the myth that Zeus assumed the form of a swan to rape Leda.
72 Euripides, *Oedipus* F545, F*545a (incert. fab. F909 Nauck), F546. On text and attribution, see Kannicht, *TrGF* 5, pp. 57–8.
73 F545 and F546 are quoted by Stobaeus (4.22.85, 4.22.187). Cf. Zeegers-Vander Vorst (1972), 270, on other passages apparently taken by Clement from secondary sources.
74 See Zeegers-Vander Vorst (1972), 280–2, and Riedweg (1987), 148–58.
75 Riedweg (1987), 158–61, cf. 133–7. Massa (2020) similarly interprets this use of *Bacchae* as an example of 'cultural transfer'.

190 Notes to pp. 120–6

76 Ogden (2001), 269–70, comparing Aeschylus, *Persians* 607-15.
77 Compagnon (1979).
78 Cf. Sternberg (1982), 109, on quotation as 'perspectival montage'.
79 Cf. Morson (2011), 96–7, for the idea that many quotations have a 'shadowy second speaker'.
80 The epithet was used by others apart from Clement, e.g. Athenaeus (*Deipnosophistae* 4, 158e; 13, 561a), Vitruvius (*De Architectura* 8 pr. 1), Diogenes Laertius (7.180), etc.: see Euripides T166a-169, Kannicht (*TrGF* 5, pp. 122–3).
81 Plett (1991), 322–4.
82 This is seen acutely by Karanasiou (2016).
83 The only example I have found is Libanius, *Epistle* 1066.2, which seems to refer to students acting or reading tragedies (he does not specify whose) in his school in fourth-century AD Antioch.

Chapter 6

1 Austin (1962), 12.
2 Ibid., 9.
3 Dubischar (2001) is the most up-to-date treatment.
4 On Euripidean rhetoric see Mastronarde (2010), 204–75; cf. Rutherford (2012), 52–5, on style.
5 Aristotle, *Rhetoric* 1.11, 1370b4 (*Andromeda* F133); 1.11, 1371a20 (*Orestes* 234); 1.11.1371b31 (*Antiope* F184); 2.23, 1394b2-6 (*Stheneboea* F661, *Medea* 296-7, *Hecuba* 858, *Women of Troy* 1051); 2.22, 1395b (*Hippolytus* 989); 2.23, 1397a17 (*Thyestes* F396); 2.23, 1400b29 (*Women of Troy* 990); 3.2, 1405a29 (*Telephus* F705); 3.6, 1407b4-5 (*Iphigenia among the Taurians* 727); 3.9, 1409b8 (*Meleager* F515); 3.11, 1411b2 (*Iphigenia at Aulis* 80); 3.14, 1415b10 (*Iphigenia among the Taurians* 1162); 3.15, 1416a8 (*Hippolytus* 612); 3.16, 1417a13 (*Oeneus* F558); cf. *Rhetoric to Alexander* 18, 1433b11 (*Philoctetes* F797).
6 Ober and Strauss (1990); Hall (2006), 353–92; Serafim (2017).
7 See evidence collected in Csapo and Slater (1994), 231–8; cf. Csapo (2010).
8 Demosthenes 18.139, 18.242, 18.267, 19.23, 206, 208, 209, 243-5.
9 Hall (2006), 369–70. A similar story is told in [Plutarch] *Lives of the Ten Orators* 844-5.
10 Aristotle, *Rhetoric* 1.1375b13-1376a2; Demosthenes 19.245-6; Hermogenes, *On Types of Style* 2.338, 2.389-90, 2.403.
11 Petrovic (2013), table 8.1; cf. Perlman (1964) and Wilson (1996).
12 Illuminatingly discussed by Wilson (1996), 313–14; Hanink (2014), 25–59; Volonaki (2017).

13 Aeschines 1.144 (*Iliad* 18.324-9), 1.148-9 (*Iliad* 18.333-5, 23.77, 18.95).
14 See Perlman (1964), 167.
15 See Chapter 5, pp. 101-3.
16 Cf. Ober and Strauss (1990), 252-3, citing Demosthenes 19.247 as parallel.
17 See Chapter 4, pp. 73-5.
18 See Kannicht, *TrGF* 5, pp. 851-2; cf. Collard and Cropp (2008), VIII.417, with 405-7 on the play's plot more generally. Kannicht (following Meineke) marks a lacuna after line 6, indicating that Aeschines has truncated or altered the quotation to make it suit his argument better.
19 Worman (2008), 247-55 (quotation from 253); cf. Easterling (1999), 159-61.
20 Demosthenes 18.267 quotes Euripides, *Hecuba* 1 and accuses Aeschines of 'mangling' it (ἐλυμαίνου): see Serafim (2017), 83-4.
21 The modern bibliography is vast. Especially important works include Braund and Wilkins (2000), König (2012) and Jacob (2013).
22 A point emphasized by König (2012), 20-3, Hobden (2013), 197.
23 See Hobden (2013).
24 König (2012), 97, cf. ibid. (2008) 86-7.
25 Olson (2012), 219-360; cf. Jacob (2000).
26 Too (2000); Jacob (2000), (2004) and (2013); Wilkins (2008); Paulas (2012), 405.
27 The start of *Deipnosophistae* (up to 3.74a) survives only in the form of an epitome.
28 Cf. Too (2000), 120, on memory as 'entry requirement for the elite symposium' in fifth-century Greece (citing Xenophon, *Symposium* 3.5-6); also Jacob (2004) 171 on 'la performance mnémotechnique' and Jacob (2013), 240-59 on Athenaeus' thematization of memory and mnemonics.
29 *Deipnosophistae* 9.384a; cf. 3.127a-b, 6.270c-d, 9.396a. Cf. pp. 75-80 on quotation-spotting 'quizzes' in comedy.
30 Jacob (2013), 247.
31 The metaphor of Athenaeus *qua* 'navigator' is taken from Wilkins (2008).
32 The same epithets are used elsewhere: see Kannicht, *TrGF* 5, pp. 122-3 (T166a-169). Cf. pp. 119-21 on Clement of Alexandria).
33 *Deipnosophistae* 2.38f, 3.97a, 4.158e-f, 10.421f-422a, 12.546b, 13.608f, 14.641c, 15.665a, 15.677b.
34 *Deipnosophistae* 2.36e, 6.270c, 13.600d, 14.640a, 14.641c, 15.677b.
35 See, e.g., Wright (2012), 156-64. Cf. Chapter 4, pp. 76-80.
36 Plutarch, *Nicias* 29; Satyrus, *Life of Euripides* (*P.Oxy.* 1176) fr. 39.XIX. On tragedy in fifth-century Sicily see Bosher (2021), 9-10, 147-9, 193-4.
37 See Pelling (2008).
38 See pp. 76-7.
39 See Too (2010), 215-43.

Chapter 7

1 Mayer (2003).
2 Momigliano (1993), 80-1; Schorn (2004), 5-15; Hägg (2012), 82-3.
3 Schorn (2004), T3 (a-f), pp. 79-80.
4 *P.Oxy.* 1176. Schorn (2004), F6, pp. 86-113, is the fullest and most reliable modern edition, which I cite here.
5 Cf. Hägg (2012), 78: 'What we overhear sounds like the polite conversation between interested members of a literary salon.' See pp. 133-5 on Athenaeus.
6 Arrighetti (1964), 34, 133-4 (two speakers?), Schorn (2004), 31-5 (three speakers?), Hägg (2012), 78 (three speakers?).
7 Schorn (2004), 32.
8 The 'deductive method' (in Satyrus and other biographers) is identified and analysed by Arrighetti (1987), 145; Momigliano (1993), 80-1, describes this as 'a good Peripatetic method' (cf. the Aristotelian *Problems*).
9 Collard and Cropp (2008), II.571, and Schorn (2004), 247, note similarly patriotic-sounding passages elsewhere, e.g. *Andromeda* F134, *Archelaus* F233, F236-7, F240, *Licymnius* F474.
10 Schorn (2004) 246. Cf. Hall (2018) on Sparta as a contrast or foil to Athenian self-definition in Euripides' plays.
11 E.g. Aeschylus, *Suppliant Women* 777-8; Sophocles, *Oedipus at Colonus* 1081; Euripides, *Hippolytus* 732-5, *Andromache* 861-4. See Padel (1974).
12 Schorn (2004), 221-2; cf. Lefkowitz (1991). Schorn (p. 235) also cites the claim of Pollux (*Onomasticon* 4.111 = *Danae* Tiii) that Euripides' *Danae* featured a parabasis as in comedy; cf. Σ *Alcestis* 962 for a similar claim.
13 Fr. 37.III (Euripides F912); fr. 38.II (Euripides F960); fr. 38.III (Euripides F1007a+b).
14 There is some ambiguity concerning where the quotation begins: Schorn (2004) 94 prints a text of F913 slightly different from *TrGF* (see Schorn's commentary, pp. 216-20).
15 Schorn (2004), 265-6. Cf. pp. 126-30 on Aeschines' use of Euripidean quotations.
16 Lacunae make it impossible to be certain how these quotations are being deployed: see Arrighetti (1964), 105, and Schorn (2004), 192-5.
17 See Wright (2012), 123-5; cf. Arrighetti (1987), 149-55, and Hägg (2012), 10-21, on fifth-century scholars – e.g. Ion of Chios, Stesimbrotus of Thasos and Theagenes of Rhegium – who combined biographical and literary-critical interests.
18 Arrighetti (1987), 141-58, and (1993); Momigliano (1993), 8-22, 69-84; Hägg (2012), 1-95; De Temmermann (2020), 1-13.
19 See 'Testimonia vitae atque artis' in Kannicht, *TrGF* 5, pp. 45-145. Of particular relevance are T46 (Seneca, *Epistle* 115.15), T98 (Aristotle, *Rhetoric* 1416a28-35), T112 (Plutarch, *Moralia* 604d).
20 Arrighetti (1993), 234-5; cf. Kivilo (2010) and Lefkowitz (2012), 87-103.

21 Hanink and Fletcher (2016), 3–4, use the description 'potent biographical fiction' to characterize ancient *Lives* of writers and artists; cf. De Temmermann (2020), 5–6 on 'creative and meaningful' *versus* 'factual' approaches to biography.
22 'Furthermore, he was also great in his soul, just as in his poetry', [ἔτι δ]ὲ καὶ τὴν [ψυ]χὴν μέγας [ἦν] σχεδὸν [ὡς] ἐν τοῖς [ποιή]μασιν (fr. 8.II): see Arrighetti (1964), 104–5, Schorn (2004), 187–90. Cf. Longinus, *On the Sublime* 9.2 for the definition of sublimity as 'the echo of a noble mind' (ὕψος μεγαλοφροσύνης ἀπήχημα) and *ibid.* 7.2-3, 11.2, 30.1, 35.2 on sublimity in relation to the soul (ψύχη) of the writer or reader. See Halliwell (2022), 152.
23 See Chapter 3. Cf. Arrighetti (1964), 27–9, and Schorn (2004), 37–46.
24 For citation of *Women of Troy* 886 cf. Plutarch, *Moralia* 381b, 1007c, 1026b, Clement of Alexandria, *Protrepticus* 2.25.3 and other sources cited by Schorn (2004), 215 n. 291; for F911 cf. Clement of Alexandria, *Stromateis* 4.26.172.1; for F912 cf. Σ *Orestes* 982, Clement of Alexandria, *Stromateis* 5.11.70.3; for F960 cf. Plutarch, *Moralia* 36c; for *Melanippe Sophe* F494 cf. *Genos kai Bios* (Euripides T1 *TrGF*), P.Berlin 9772, Athenaeus 14.613d, Stobaeus 4.22.78, Eusebius, *Preparation for the Gospel* 10.3.19.
25 F913 is cited in a more extensive form by Satyrus (fr. 38.I) than by Clement of Alexandria, *Stromateis* 5.14.137.2; different portions of F960 are cited by Satyrus (fr. 38.II) and Plutarch (*Moralia* 36c).
26 F1007a+b, F1007c, F1007d, F1007e+f, F**1007h, as well as Aristophanes F656, Philemon F153, com. adesp. F1025.
27 Arrighetti (1964), 107–8.
28 White (2020), 251.
29 E.g. Diogenes Laertius 1.33, 1.42, 1.107, 2.12, 2.55, 3.9, 4.17, 8.58. On Diogenes' sources and scholarly methods, see Warren (2007) and White (2020). Hägg (2012), 305–18, discusses Diogenes as a 'transmitter' of Hellenistic scholarship.
30 Euripidean quotations appear at Diogenes Laertius 1.56, 2.10, 2.33, 2.44, 2.78 (twice), 3.6–7, 3.63, 4.26, 4.29–30, 4.34–5, 4.51, 5.3, 6.36, 6.55, 6.98, 6.104 (paraphrase), 7.22, 7.60, 7.172, 7.179, 7.180, 7.182, 9.60, 9.72, 9.73. Cf. 2.82, 4.35, 10.137 (Sophocles), and 4.25, 6.95, 7.67, 9.12 for other, unidentified tragic quotations.
31 Cf. Satyrus, *Life of Euripides* (F6 Schorn), fr. 37.I–III (Anaxagoras), fr. 38.II–fr.39.III (Socrates).
32 But not entirely unimportant: e.g. Diogenes (2.44) sensibly points out that *Palamedes* F588 cannot be a response to Socrates' death, as some claim, since Philochorus records that Euripides predeceased Socrates.
33 Comparable examples from the *Lives* include 4.34–5 (Arcesilaus/Euripides F976), 4.51 (Bion/*Hipp.* 424), 5.3 (Aristotle/*Philoctetes* F796), 6.36 (Xeniades/*Medea* 410), 6.55 (Diogenes of Sinope/*Phoen.* 40), 6.98 (Hipparchia/*Bacchae* 1236), 7.182 (Chrysippus/*Orestes* 253–4), 9.60 (Anaxarchus/*Orestes* 271). Cf. my discussion of 'visible' versus 'invisible' quotations, pp. 76–7.

34 See Collins (2004). Cf. Regier (2010), 39, on 'weaponized' quotations. See also Diogenes Laertius 4.34–5 for another similar example of competitive quotation.
35 See Hägg (2012), 310–13; cf. Gow (1965), 12–15. Diogenes cites among his sources several works with the title *Chreiai* (e.g. 2.85, 7.163).
36 Sophocles F873. See Radt, *TrGF* 4, pp. 586–7; Hunter and Russell (2011), 188.
37 Cf. Morson (2011), 129–32, who observes that one speaker can displace another one as the acknowledged author of a quotation: 'famous lines change authors, perhaps frequently if they survive long enough'.
38 See Kannicht, *TrGF* 5, p. 248. The Euripidean original, preserved by Herodian, *On Figures* 45, is ἄγου δέ μ', ὦ ξεῖν', εἴτε πρόσπολον θέλεις | εἴτ' ἄλοχον εἴτε δμωΐδ' ('Take me with you, stranger, whether it is an attendant or a wife or a servant that you want'). Cf. Diogenes of Sinope's misquotation/paraphrase of *Antiope* F200 in the *Life of Menedemus* (Diogenes Laertius 6.104).
39 Warren (2007), 144–5.
40 Longinus, *On the Sublime* 15.3, Plutarch, *Moralia* 748e–71e.
41 Collard, Cropp and Gibert (2004), 133–68, present the fragments and testimonia with commentary.
42 See Gibert (1999–2000).
43 Hutchinson (1998), 1–24.
44 Horsfall (1979) questions the extent to which Cicero and his contemporaries were familiar with complete texts of Greek literature (as opposed to selected snippets).
45 Cicero's quotations from Euripides in the letters: *Ad Atticum* 2.25.1 (*Andromache* 448, *Phoenician Women* 393), 6.8.5 (*Philoctetes* F769), 6.18.1 (F918), 7.3.5 (*Women of Troy* 455), 7.11.1 (*Phoenician Women* 506), 7.13.4 (F973), 8.8.2 (F918), 9.2a.2 (F958), 13.11.1 (*Ion* 565), 15.1.3 (*Andromache* 448), 15.4.1 (*Medea* 410); *Ad Familiares* 13.15.2 (F905), 16.8.2 (F906); *Ad Quintum fratrem* 2.14.4 (*Suppliant Women* 119), 3.1.18 (*Hippolytus* 436).
46 Adams (2003), 297–416; Elder and Mullen (2019), 1–23.
47 Adams (2003), 312 (with primary reference to Cicero, *Ad Atticum* 13.42 but with wider application).
48 See, most recently, Gourinat (2012).
49 Rutherford (1989b), x–xi.
50 Brunt (1974), 2–5; Rutherford (1989a), 8–13; Ceporina (2012), 45–7.
51 Dickson (2009), 102–3; Hays (2003), lvi, xxxvii; Männlein-Robert (2012); Hadot (1998); Rutherford (1989a), 14–21.
52 See Kannicht, *TrGF* 5, pp. 299, 357, 776–7, 880–1, 924.
53 Kraye (2000).
54 For the theatre as a metaphor for life, cf. *Meditations* 3.8, 9.29, 12.36; Epictetus, *Handbook* 17; Palladas, *Palatine Anthology* 10.73; Shakespeare, *As You Like It* II.7, etc. See also Rutherford (1989a), 231–2.

55 Cf. *Meditations* 3.13, where Marcus describes *dogmata* ('precepts') as analogous to medicines to be kept close at hand in case of illness.
56 Sellars (2012), 458–60, comparing Seneca, *Letter* 2.2-4, Epictetus, *Discourses* 3.21.1–4, *Handbook* 46 on the importance of repetition in reading or teaching.
57 *Meditations* 4.32, 7.75, 9.6; cf. Rutherford (1989a), 34–5.
58 Brunt (1974), 3 n. 18.
59 Gill (2006), 79, 329.

Bibliography

Adams, J. N. (2003) *Bilingualism and the Latin Language*. Cambridge.
Adorno, T. (1951) *Minima Moralia: Reflexionen aus dem beschädigten Leben*. Frankfurt.
Adorno, T. (1997) 'Towards a theory of the artwork', in *Aesthetic Theory*, tr. R. Hullot-Kentor, 175-99. Minneapolis.
Allen, J. T. and Italie, C. (1954) *A Concordance to Euripides*. Berkeley.
Arnott, W. G. (1996) (ed.) *Alexis: The Fragments*. Cambridge.
Arrighetti, G. (1964) (ed.) *Satiro: Vita di Euripide*. Pisa.
Arrighetti, G. (1987) *Poeti, eruditi e biografi*. Pisa.
Austin, J. L. (1962) *How to Do Things with Words*. Oxford.
Avery, H. C. (1968) 'My tongue swore, but my mind is unsworn', *Transactions of the American Philological Association* 99: 19-35.
Bakola, E. (2010) *Cratinus and the Art of Comedy*. Oxford.
Barns, J. (1950) 'A new gnomologium: with some remarks on gnomic anthologies (I)', *Classical Quarterly* 44: 126-37.
Barrett, W. S. (1964) (ed.) *Euripides:* Hippolytus. Oxford.
Barthes, R. (1973) *Le plaisir du texte*. Paris.
Barthes, R. (1975) *Roland Barthes par Roland Barthes*. Paris.
Barthes, R. (1977) *Image–Music–Text*. London.
Battezzato, L. (2018) (ed.) *Euripides:* Hecuba. Cambridge.
Bayard, P. (2007) *How to Talk about Books You Haven't Read*, tr. F. Prose. London.
Bennett, S. (1997) *Theatre Audiences*, 2nd edn. London.
Bianchi, F. P. (2020) 'Il geografo e il teatro: le citazioni drammatiche nell' opera di Strabone', *Geographica Antiqua* 29: 57-74.
Biehl, W. (1975) (ed.) *Euripides:* Orestes. Leipzig.
Biles, Z. and Olson, S. D. (2015) (eds) *Aristophanes:* Wasps. Oxford.
Bosher, K. (2021) *Greek Drama in Ancient Sicily*. Cambridge.
Bourdieu, P. (1977) *Outline of a Theory of Practice*, tr. R. Nice. Cambridge.
Bourdieu, P. (1984) *Distinction*, tr. R. Nice. Cambridge.
Bourdieu, P. (1993) *The Field of Cultural Production*, tr. R. Johnson. Cambridge.
Bourdieu, P. (1996) *The Rules of Art*, tr. S. Emanuel. Cambridge.
Bowie, E. L. (2008) 'Plutarch's habits of citation: aspects of difference', in A. Nikolaidis (ed.), *The Unity of Plutarch's Work*, 143-57. Berlin and New York.
Bowie, E. L. (2012) 'An early chapter in the history of the *Theognidea*', in X. Riu and J. Pòrtulas (eds), *Approaches to Greek Poetry*, 121-48. Messina.
Braund, D. and Wilkins, J. M. (2000) (eds) *Athenaeus and His World*. Exeter.

Brombert, V. (1980) 'Opening signals in narrative', *New Literary History* 11: 489–502.
Brunt, P. (1974) 'Marcus Aurelius in his *Meditations*', *Journal of Hellenic Studies* 64: 1–20.
Canevaro, G. L. (2015) *Hesiod's* Works and Days: *How to Teach Self-Sufficiency*. Oxford.
Carrara, P. (2009) *Il testo di Euripide nell'antichità*. Messina.
Cascardi, A. (2014) *The Cambridge Introduction to Literature and Philosophy*. Cambridge.
Casson, L. (2001) *Libraries in the Ancient World*. New Haven.
Ceporina, M. (2012) 'The *Meditations*', in van Ackeren (2012), 45–61.
Chadwick, H. (1966) *Early Christian Thought and the Classical Tradition*. Cambridge.
Collard, C. (1975) (ed.) *Euripides:* Supplices. Groningen.
Collard, C. (1991) (ed.) *Euripides:* Hecuba. Warminster.
Collard, C. (2007) *Tragedy, Euripides and Euripideans*. Exeter.
Collard, C. and Cropp, M. (2008) (eds) *Euripides: Fragments*. Cambridge.
Collard, C., Cropp, M. and Gibert, J. (2004) (eds) *Euripides: Fragmentary Plays II*. Oxford.
Collard, C., Cropp, M. and Lee, K. (1995) (eds) *Euripides: Fragmentary Plays I*. Warminster.
Collins, D. (2004) *Master of the Game: Competition and Performance in Greek Poetry*. Cambridge.
Compagnon, A. (1979) *La seconde main, ou la travail de la citation*. Paris.
Cribiore, R. (1996) *Writing, Teachers and Students in Greco-Roman Egypt*. Atlanta.
Cribiore, R. (2001a) *Gymnastics of the Mind: Greek Education in Hellenistic and Roman Egypt*. Princeton.
Cribiore, R. (2001b) 'The grammarian's choice: the popularity of Euripides' *Phoenissae* in Hellenistic and Roman education', in Y. L. Too (ed.), *Education in Greek and Roman Antiquity*, 241–59. Leiden.
Cropp, M. J. and Fick, G. (1985) *Resolutions and Chronology in Euripides*. London.
Csapo, E. (2010) *Actors and Icons of the Ancient Theatre*. Malden.
Csapo, E. and Slater, W. (1994) *The Context of Ancient Drama*. Ann Arbor.
Culler, J. (2015) *Theory of the Lyric*. Cambridge.
Cuny, D. (2007) *Une leçon de vie: les réflexions générales chez Sophocle*. Paris.
Cusset, M. (2003) *Ménandre ou la comédie tragique*. Paris.
De Temmermann, K. (2020) (ed.) *The Oxford Handbook of Ancient Biography*. Oxford.
Denniston, J. D. (1939) (ed.) *Euripides:* Electra. Oxford.
Derrida, J. (1988) 'Signature Event Context', in *Limited Inc.*, tr. S. Weber and J. Mehlman, 1–23. Evanston.
Dickey, E. (2007) *Ancient Greek Scholarship*. Oxford and New York.
Dickey, E. (2015) 'The sources of our knowledge of ancient scholarship', in F. Montanari, F. Matthaios and A. Rengakos (eds), *Brill's Companion to Ancient Greek Scholarship*, 459–514. Leiden.
Dickson, K. (2009) 'Oneself as others: Aurelius and autobiography', *Arethusa* 42: 99–125.

Di Gregorio, L. (1976) 'Plutarco e la tragedia greca', *Prometheus* 2: 151-74.
Dover, K. J. (2000) 'Frogments', in F. D. Harvey and J. M. Wilkins (ed.), *The Rivals of Aristophanes*, xvii-xx. London and Swansea.
Dubischar, M. (2001) *Die Agonszenen bei Euripides*. Stuttgart.
Dunbar, N. (1995) (ed.) *Aristophanes:* Birds. Oxford.
Dunn, F. (1996) *Tragedy's End*. Oxford and New York.
Easterling, P. E. (1999) 'Actors and voices: reading between the lines in Aeschines and Demosthenes', in S. Goldhill and R. Osborne (eds), *Performance Culture and Athenian Democracy*, 154-66. Cambridge.
Eco, U. (2004) *On Literature*. Orlando.
Elder, O. and Mullen, A. (2019) *The Language of Latin Letters*. Cambridge.
Erbse, H. (1984) *Studien zum Prolog der euripideischen Tragödie*. Berlin.
Farmer, M. (2017) *Tragedy on the Comic Stage*. Oxford and New York.
Friesen, C. (2015) *Reading Dionysus*. Tübingen.
Friis Johansen, H. (1959) *General Reflection in Tragic Rhesis*. Munksgaard.
Garber, M. (2003) *Quotation Marks*. London and New York.
Genette, G. (1997) *Paratexts*, tr. J. E. Lewin. Cambridge.
Gibert, J. (1999-2000) 'Falling in love with Euripides (*Andromeda*)', *Illinois Classical Studies* 24-5: 75-91.
Gibert, J. (2019) (ed.) *Euripides:* Ion. Cambridge.
Gill, C. J. (2006) *The Structured Self in Hellenistic and Roman Thought*. Oxford.
Goldhill, S. (1991) *The Poet's Voice*. Cambridge.
Gomme, A. W. and Sandbach, F. H. (1973) *Menander: A Commentary*. Oxford.
Gourinat, J.-B. (2012) 'The form and structure of the *Meditations*', in van Ackeren (2012), 317-32.
Gow, A. (1965) (ed.) *Machon*. Cambridge.
Guéraud, O. and Jouguet, P. (1938) *Un livre d'écolier du IIIe siècle avant J.-C.* Paris.
Hadot, P. (1998) (ed.) *Marc Aurèle: écrits pour lui-même*. Paris.
Haffner, M. (2001) *Das Florilegium des Orion*. Stuttgart.
Hägg, T. (2012) *The Art of Biography in Antiquity*. Cambridge.
Hall, E. M. (2006) *The Theatrical Cast of Athens*. Oxford.
Hall, E. M. (2018) 'Euripides, Sparta and the self-definition of Athens', in P. Cartledge and A. Powell (eds), *The Greek Superpower: Sparta in the Self-Definitions of Athenians*, 115-38. Swansea.
Halliwell, S. (2002) *The Aesthetics of Mimesis*. Princeton.
Halliwell, S. (2011) *Between Ecstasy and Truth*. Oxford.
Halliwell, S. (2022) (ed.) *Pseudo-Longinus: On the Sublime*. Oxford.
Hanink, J. (2014) *Lycurgan Athens and the Making of Classical Tragedy*. Cambridge.
Hanink, J. and Fletcher, R. (2016) (eds) *Creative Lives in Classical Antiquity: Poets, Artists and Biography*. Cambridge.
Harbison, R. (2015) *Ruins and Fragments*. London.
Harder, A. (1985) (ed.) *Euripides: Kresphontes and Archelaus*. Leiden.

Havelock, E. (1982) *The Literate Revolution in Greece and Its Cultural Consequences*. Princeton.
Hays, M. (2003) (tr.) *Marcus Aurelius:* Meditations. London.
Heath, J. M. F. (2020) *Clement of Alexandria and the Shaping of Christian Literary Practice*. Cambridge.
Heath, M. (1987) *The Poetics of Greek Tragedy*. London.
Heath, M. (1989) *Unity in Greek Poetics*. Oxford.
Helmbold, W. and O'Neil, E. (1959) *Plutarch's Quotations*. Baltimore.
Higbie, C. (2017) *Collectors, Scholars and Forgers in the Ancient World*. Oxford.
Hobden, F. (2013) *The Symposion in Ancient Greek Society and Thought*. Cambridge.
Horsfall, N. (1979) '*Doctus sermones utriusque linguae?*' *Echos du monde classique* 23: 79–95.
Hunter, G. K. (1951) 'The marking of *sententiae* in Elizabethan printed plays, poems and romances', *The Library* 5-6: 171–88.
Hunter, R. (1983) (ed.) *Eubulus: The Fragments*. Cambridge.
Hunter, R. (2009) *Critical Moments in Classical Literature*. Cambridge.
Hunter, R. (2014) *Hesiodic Voices*. Cambridge.
Hunter, R. and Russell, D. A. (2011) (eds) *Plutarch: How the Young Man Should Study Poetry*. Cambridge.
Hutchinson, G. (1998) *Cicero's Correspondence*. Oxford.
Ireland, S. (2010) (ed.) *Menander:* The Shield *and* Arbitration. Oxford.
Iser, W. (1978) *The Act of Reading*. Baltimore.
Jacob, C. (2000) 'Athenaeus the librarian', in Braund and Wilkins (2000), 85–110.
Jacob, C. (2004) 'La citation comme performance dans les Deipnosophistes d'Athénée', in C. Darbo-Peschanski (ed.), *La citation dans l'antiquité*, 147–74. Grenoble.
Jacob, C. (2013) *The Web of Athenaeus*, tr. A. Papaconstantinou. Washington.
Jenny, L. (1982) 'The strategy of forms', in T. Todorov (ed.), *French Literary Theory Today*, 34–64. Cambridge.
Kammerbeek, J. C. (1974) (ed.) *Sophocles:* Electra. Leiden.
Kannicht, R. (1969) (ed.) *Euripides:* Helen. Heidelberg.
Kannicht, R. (1997) 'TrGF V Euripides', in G. W. Most (ed.), *Collecting Fragments/Fragmente sammeln*, 67–77. Göttingen.
Karanasiou, A. (2016) 'A Euripidised Clement of Alexandria or a Christianised Euripides?', in E. Cueva and J. Martinez (eds), *Splendide Mendax*, 331–46. Groningen.
Kenyon, F. E. (1951) *Books and Readers in Ancient Greece and Rome*. Oxford.
Kivilo, M. (2010) *Early Greek Poets' Lives: The Shaping of the Tradition*. Leiden.
König, J. P. (2008) 'Sympotic dialogue in the first to fifth centuries CE', in S. Goldhill (ed.), *The End of Dialogue in Antiquity*, 85–113. Cambridge.
König, J. P. (2012) *Saints and Symposiasts*. Cambridge.
Konstan, D. (2004) 'The birth of the reader: Plutarch as a literary critic', *Scholia* 13: 3–27.
Konstan, D. (2011) 'Excerpting as a reading practice', in G. Reydams-Schils (ed.), *Thinking Through Excerpts: Studies on Stobaeus*, 9–22. Turnhout.

Kraye, J. (2000) '"Ethnicorum omnium sanctissimus": Marcus Aurelius and his *Meditations* from Xylander to Diderot', in J. Kraye and M. Stone (eds), *Humanism and Early Modern Philosophy*, 107–34. London.

Kristeva, J. (1980) 'Word, dialogue and novel', in L. Roudiez (ed.), *Desire in Language: A Semiotic Approach to Literature and Art by Julia Kristeva*, tr. T. Gora et al., 64–91. New York.

Lamari, A. (2017) *Reperforming Greek Tragedy*. Berlin and New York.

Lardinois, A. (2006) 'The polysemy of gnomic expressions in Ajax's deception speech', in I. de Jong and A. Rijksbaron (eds), *Sophocles and the Greek Language*, 213–23. Leiden.

Lee, K. (1997) (ed.) *Euripides:* Ion. Warminster.

Lefkowitz, M. (1991) *First-Person Fictions*. Oxford.

Lefkowitz, M. (2012) *The Lives of the Greek Poets*, 2nd edn. Baltimore.

Lefkowitz, M. (2015) *Euripides and the Gods*. Oxford.

Luschnig, C. E. (2015) '*Orestes*', in R. Lauriola and K. Demetriou (eds), *Brill's Companion to the Reception of Euripides*, 238–58. Leiden.

Männlein-Robert, I. (2012) 'The *Meditations* as a (philosophical) autobiography', in van Ackeren (2012), 362–81.

Marrou, H. (1956) *A History of Education in Antiquity*. London.

Martano, A., Matelli, E. and Mirhardy, D. (2012), *Praxiphanes of Mytilene and Chamaeleon of Heraclea: Text, Translation and Discussion*. New York.

Martin, R. (2009) 'Gnomes in poems: wisdom performance on the Athenian stage', in E. Karamalengou and E. Makrygianni (eds), *Antiphilesis: Studies on Classical, Byzantine and Modern Greek Literature and Culture*, 116–27. Stuttgart.

Massa, F. (2020) 'Reading and rewriting Euripides in Clement of Alexandria', in Schramm (2020), 335–49.

Mastromarco, G. (2006) 'La paratragodia, il libro, la memoria', in E. Medda (ed.), *Komoidotragoidia*, 137–91. Pisa.

Mastronarde, D. (1994) (ed.) *Euripides:* Phoenissae. Cambridge.

Mastronarde, D. (2009) 'Euripides' lost *Phoenissae*: the fragments', in J. Cousland and J. Hume (eds), *The Play of Texts and Fragments*, 459–96. Leiden.

Mastronarde, D. (2010) *The Art of Euripides*. Cambridge.

Mastronarde, D. (2017) *Preliminary Studies on the Scholia to Euripides*. Berkeley.

Maxwell, J. and Rumbold, K. (2018) (eds) *Shakespeare and Quotation*. Cambridge.

Mayer, R. (2003) 'Persona problems: the literary persona in antiquity revisited', *Materiali e discussioni per l'analisi dei testi classici* 50: 55–80.

Meccariello, C. (2021) 'Well begun is half done: uses and misuses of incipits in Greek antiquity', in F. Ginelli and F. Lupi (eds), *The Continuity of Classical Literature through Fragmentary Traditions*, 57–78. Berlin and New York.

Michelini, A. N. (1987) *Euripides and the Tragic Tradition*. Madison.

Missiou, A. (2011) *Literacy and Democracy in Fifth-Century Athens*. Cambridge.

Moles, J. (2001) 'A false dilemma: Thucydides' *History* and historicism', in S. J. Harrison (ed.), *Texts, Ideas, and the Classics*, 195–219. Oxford.

Momigliano, A. (1993) *The Development of Greek Biography*. Cambridge.
Morgan, T. (1998) *Literate Education in the Hellenistic and Roman Worlds*. Cambridge.
Morlet, S. (2020) 'Euripides in Greek Christian apologetics (2nd–5th c. AD)', in Schramm (2020), 351–66.
Morson, G. S. (2011) *The Words of Others*. New Haven.
Most, G. W. (1990) 'Canon fathers: literacy, mortality, power', *Arion* 1: 35–60.
Most, G. W. (2003) 'Euripide Ο ΓΝΩΜΟΛΟΓΙΚΩΤΑΤΟΣ', in M. Funghi (ed.), *Aspetti di lettaratura gnomica nel mondo antico*, 141–66. Florence.
Neymeyr, U. (1989) *Die christlichen Lehrer im zweiten Jahrhundert*. Leiden.
Norrick, N. R. (2009), 'Interjections as pragmatic markers', *Journal of Pragmatics* 41: 866–91.
Nünlist, R. (2009) *The Ancient Scholar at Work*. Cambridge.
Ober, J. and Strauss, B. (1990) 'Drama, political rhetoric, and the discourse of Athenian democracy', in J. Winkler and F. Zeitlin (eds), *Nothing to Do with Dionysos? Athenian Drama in Its Social Context*, 237–70. Princeton.
Oborn, E. (2005) *Clement of Alexandria*. Cambridge.
Ogden, D. (2001) *Greek and Roman Necromancy*. Princeton.
Olson, S. D. (2012) (ed.) *Athenaeus VIII: Book 15 and Indexes*. Cambridge.
Olson, S. D. (2017) (ed.) *Eupolis: Einleitung, Testimonia und Aiges-Demoi*. Heidelberg.
Orth, C. (2009) *Strattis: Die Fragmente*. Berlin.
Padel, R. (1974) 'Imagery of the elsewhere: two choral odes of Euripides', *Classical Quarterly* 24: 227–41.
Page, D. L. (1934) *Actors' Interpolations in Greek Tragedy*. Oxford.
Parker, L. P. E. (2007) (ed.) *Euripides:* Alcestis. Oxford.
Patzer, A. (1986) *Der Sophist Hippias als Philosophiehistoriker*. Munich.
Paulas, J. (2012) 'How to read Athenaeus' *Deipnosophists*', *American Journal of Philology* 133: 403–39.
Pearson, A. C. (1917) (ed.) *The Fragments of Sophocles*. Cambridge.
Pelling, C. B. (2008) 'Ion's *Epidemiai* and Plutarch's *Ion*', in A. Katsaros and V. Jennings (eds), *The World of Ion of Chios*, 75–109. Leiden.
Perlman, S. (1964) 'Quotations from poetry in Attic orators of the fourth century BC', *American Journal of Philology* 85: 155–72.
Pernigotti, C. (2003) 'Euripide nella tradizione gnomologica antica', in L. Battezzato (ed.), *Tradizione testuale e ricezione litteraria antica nella tragedia greca*, 97–112. Amsterdam.
Petersen, K. (2018) 'Shakespeare and *sententiae*: the uses of quotation in *Lucrece*', in Maxwell and Rumbold (2018): 46–59.
Petrovic, A. (2013) 'Inscribed epigrams in orators and epigraphic collections', in P. Liddel and P. Low (eds), *Inscriptions and Their Uses in Greek and Latin Literature*, 197–213. Oxford.
Pfeiffer, R. (1968) *History of Classical Scholarship: From the Beginnings to the End of the Hellenistic Age*. Oxford.

Pinto, P. M. (2013) 'Men and books in fourth-century BC Athens', in J. König et al. (eds), *Ancient Libraries*, 85–95. Cambridge.
Plett, H. F. (1991) *Intertextuality*. Berlin and New York.
Porter, J. I. (2016) *The Sublime in Antiquity*. Cambridge.
Race, W. H. (1992) 'How Greek poems begin', *Yale Classical Studies* 29: 13–38.
Rau, P. (1967) *Paratragodia*. Munich.
Regier, W. G. (2010) *Quotology*. Lincoln.
Revermann, M. (2006) 'The competence of theatre audiences in fifth- and fourth-century Athens', *Journal of Hellenic Studies* 126: 99–124.
Riedweg, C. (1987) *Mysterienterminologie bei Platon, Philon und Klemens von Alexandrien*. Berlin.
Romero-Trillo, J. (2013) 'Pragmatic markers', *Encyclopedia of Applied Linguistics*. Malden and Oxford.
Roselli, D. K. (2011) *Theater of the People: Spectators and Society in Ancient Athens*. Austin.
Rosen, R. M. (2006) 'Aristophanes, fandom and the classicizing of Greek tragedy', in L. Kozak and J. Rich (eds), *Playing around Aristophanes*, 27–47. Oxford.
Russell, D. A. (1964) (ed.) *Longinus: On the Sublime*. Oxford.
Russell, D. A. (1972) *Plutarch*. London.
Russo, J. (1997) 'Prose genres for the performance of traditional wisdom in ancient Greece: proverb, maxim, apophthegm', in L. Edmunds and R. Wallace (eds), *Poet, Public, and Performance in Ancient Greece*, 49–64. Baltimore.
Rutherford, R. B. (1989a) *The Meditations of Marcus Aurelius: A Study*. Oxford.
Rutherford, R. B. (1989b) (tr.) *Marcus Aurelius: Meditations*. Oxford.
Rutherford, R. B. (2012) *Greek Tragic Style*. Cambridge.
Said, E. (1975) *Beginnings: Intention and Method*. New York.
Schlegel, F. (1991) *Sämmtliche Werke*, ed. E. Böcking. Leipzig.
Schorn, S. (2004) *Satyros aus Kallatis: Sammlung der Fragmente mit Kommentar*. Basel.
Schramm, M. (2020) (ed.) *Euripides-Rezeption in Kaiserzeit und Spätantike*. Berlin and New York.
Scodel, R. (1999–2000) 'Verbal performance and Euripidean rhetoric', *Illinois Classical Studies* 24–5: 129–44.
Segal, C. P. (1992) 'Tragic beginnings: narration, voice, and authority in the prologues of Greek drama', *Yale Classical Studies* 29: 85–112.
Sellars, J. (2012) 'The *Meditations* and the ancient art of living', in van Ackeren (2012), 453–64.
Serafim, A. (2017) *Attic Oratory and Performance*. London.
Sider, D. (2007) 'Sylloge Simonidea', in P. Bing and J. Bruss (eds), *Brill's Companion to Hellenistic Epigram*, 113–30. Leiden.
Silk, M. S. (2000) *Aristophanes and the Definition of Comedy*. Oxford.
Sommerstein, A. H. (1996) (ed.) *Aristophanes: Frogs*. Warminster.
Sonnino, M. (2010) *Euripidis Erechthei quae exstant*. Florence.

Stählin, O. (1936) (ed.) *Clemens Alexandrinus*, Band IV. Leipzig.
Sternberg, M. (1982) 'Proteus in Quotation-Land', *Poetics Today* 3: 107–56.
Storey, I. C. (2003) *Eupolis, Poet of Old Comedy*. Oxford.
Storey, I. C. (2011) (ed.) *Fragments of Old Comedy*. Cambridge.
Telò, M. (2007) *Eupolidis* Demi. Florence.
Thomas, R. (1992) *Literacy and Orality in Ancient Greece*. Cambridge.
Too, Y. L. (2000) 'The walking library of Athenaeus', in Braund and Wilkins (2000), 111–23.
Too, Y. L. (2010) *The Idea of the Library in the Ancient World*. Oxford.
Torrance, I. (2013) *Metapoetry in Euripides*. Oxford.
Tronzo, W. (2009) (ed.) *The Fragment: An Incomplete History*. Los Angeles.
Turner, E. (1968) *Greek Papyri*. Oxford.
Turner, E. (1987) *Greek Manuscripts of the Ancient World*, 2nd edn, ed. P. J. Parsons. London.
Turyn, A. (1943) *The Manuscript Tradition of the Plays of Aeschylus*. New York.
Usher, M. D. (2007) 'Theomachy, creation and the poetics of quotation in Longinus chapter 9', *Classical Philology* 102: 292–303.
van Ackeren, M. (2012) (ed.) *A Companion to Marcus Aurelius*. Malden.
van den Hoek, A. (1996) 'Techniques of quotation in Clement of Alexandria', *Vigiliae Christianae* 50: 223–43.
Volonaki, E. (2017) 'Euripides' *Erechtheus* in Lykourgos' *Against Leokrates*', in A. Fountoulakis, A. Markantonatos and G. Vasilaros (eds), *Theatre World*, 251–68. Berlin and New York.
Warren, J. (2007) 'Diogenes Laertius, biographer of philosophy', in J. König and T. Whitmarsh (eds), *Ordering Knowledge in the Roman Empire*, Cambridge: 133–49.
West, M. L. (1982) *Greek Metre*. Oxford.
White, S. (2020) 'Diogenes Laertius and philosophical lives', in De Temmermann (2020), 279–96.
Whitmarsh, T. J. G. (2001) *Greek Literature and the Roman Empire*. Oxford.
Wilkins, J. M. (1993) (ed.) *Euripides: Heracleidae*. Oxford.
Wilkins, J. M. (2008) 'Athenaeus the navigator', *Journal of Hellenic Studies* 128: 132–52.
Wilson, P. (1996) 'Tragic rhetoric: the use of tragedy and the tragic in the fourth century', in M. S. Silk (ed.), *Tragedy and the Tragic*, 310–31. Oxford.
Woodward, C. (2001) *In Ruins*. London.
Worman, N. (2008) *Abusive Mouths in Classical Athens*. Cambridge.
Wright, M. E. (2012) *The Comedian as Critic*. London.
Wright, M. E. (2013) 'Poets and poetry in later Greek comedy', *Classical Quarterly* 63: 603–22.
Wright, M. E. (2016a) *The Lost Plays of Greek Tragedy. 1: Neglected Authors*. London.
Wright, M. E. (2016b) 'Euripidean tragedy and quotation culture: the case of *Stheneboea* F661', *American Journal of Philology* 138: 601–23.
Wright, M. E. (2016c) 'Gnomic φεῦ', *Greek, Roman, and Byzantine Studies* 56: 585–93.

Wright, M. E. (2019) *The Lost Plays of Greek Tragedy. 2: Aeschylus, Sophocles and Euripides*. London.

Yunis, H. (2003) (ed.) *Written Texts and the Rise of Literate Culture in Ancient Greece*. Cambridge.

Zeegers-Vander Vorst, N. (1972) *Les citations des poètes grecs chez les apologistes chrétiens du IIe siècle*. Louvain.

Zuntz, G. (1965) *An Inquiry into the Transmission of the Plays of Euripides*. Cambridge.

Index

Achaeus 21
actors and acting 26, 31, 43, 75, 80, 124–6, 129–32, 161, 185
adaptation and alteration 87–8, 102–3, 118, 120–1, 191
Adorno, T. 22, 176
Adrastus 36
Aelian 60
Aeschines 61, 125–32, 174, 183, 191
  Against Timarchus 126–32
Aeschylus 6, 24, 29, 36, 40, 55, 57, 74, 82, 99, 109, 146, 156, 174, 178, 180, 190, 192
Aesop 187
Agathon 49, 176–7, 181
Alcaeus 22, 176
Alcidamas 175
Alexander the Great 135
Alexis 76, 77, 185
ambiguity 25–7, 31–2, 33, 38, 114, 117, 120–1, 128
Amphis 74
Amphitryon 36
Anaxagoras 146, 149, 156, 193
Anaxandrides 74
Anaximenes of Lampsacus 60–1
anecdotes 58, 66, 112, 135, 138–9, 141, 151, 157–9, 166, 189; see also *chreiai*
anthologies 4, 12–13, 14–19, 32, 43–4, 50–2, 56, 61, 64, 66–71, 72, 82, 96, 99, 103, 104, 113–14, 130, 133, 134, 152–3, 155, 168, 174, 181, 182, 183
Antigonus 151, 156
Antiphanes 19, 74, 87–8, 175
Antisthenes 67, 102, 167
Apollonides 179
apostrophe 41–5, 51, 69, 71, 104, 181
Arcesilaus 160–2
Archilochus 105
Archippus 77
Aristides 173
Aristippus 157–9
Aristodemus 138

Ariston 187
Aristophanes 6, 17, 58, 67–8, 71, 72, 73–4, 76, 77, 80–1, 101, 150–1, 154, 161, 166, 174, 175, 179, 182, 185, 186, 187, 188, 193
  Acharnians 73, 81, 151, 179
  Birds 56, 179, 182, 186
  Clouds 68, 81, 138, 175, 179, 183, 184
  Frogs 6–7, 17, 67–8, 73, 76, 77, 79, 80, 81, 101, 151, 161, 174, 175, 177, 182, 184, 185, 187
  Knights 175, 186
  Lysistrata 179
  Peace 66, 73, 76, 81, 185
  Thesmophoriazusae 71, 73, 76, 55, 150, 151, 173, 174, 177
  Wasps 81, 173, 174, 179, 188
  Wealth 179
Aristophanes of Byzantium 59
Aristotle 6, 11–12, 13, 22, 62, 65–6, 88, 124, 125, 127, 139–40, 154, 174, 175, 180, 181, 183, 190, 192
  Poetics 15
  Politics 65–6
  Problems 192
  Rhetoric 11–12, 49–50, 124–5, 127, 180, 181, 186, 190, 192
Aristoxenus 151, 153, 156
Arrighetti, G. 152
Arsenius 184
art 104–9
Athenaeus, *Deipnosophistae* 55, 61, 64, 65, 68, 132, 133–43, 146, 175, 184, 185, 190, 191, 192, 193
Athenagoras 112
attribution, problematic cases of 87, 104, 109, 111, 112, 141, 182, 183, 184, 185, 189
audience 7, 10, 20, 24–7, 31, 41–2, 43, 44–5, 58, 67, 68, 74–5, 76–80, 88–9, 105–6, 112, 123, 124, 128, 142, 161, 174, 185
Aulus Gellius 16, 55–6, 113, 174

Index

Austin, J. L. 123
authorship and authority 2, 6, 8, 10, 13, 20–3, 24–7, 46, 68, 84, 87, 100, 103, 104, 120–1, 126, 135, 136, 145, 168, 190, 192, 194
Axionicus 74

Bacchylides 115, 176, 179
Barthes, R. 22–3, 103
Bartlett's Dictionary of Quotations 16
Basil, Saint 112
Bayard, P. 53–4
Bellerophon 5–6, 8, 25–6, 129–30
biblical quotation 14, 112–21
bibliocosm 142
biography 4, 58, 141, 145–71, 189, 192–3
Bion 141, 158
books 6, 10–11, 13, 14–19, 24–6, 36, 41, 51, 55, 76, 92–8, 133, 138, 142, 176, 180, 185, 186; *see also* readers and reading habits
Bourdieu, P. 106–7

Caecilius, *On the Sublime* 104, 107
Callimachus, *Pinakes* 138
Calliphanes 134
Carcinus 82, 174
cento 85
Chaeremon 82, 174, 176–7
Chamaeleon 138, 151
Charmus 136–7
chorus 34, 36, 38, 41, 43, 50, 57, 66, 148–9, 179
chreiai 96, 158–9, 187, 194
Christianity 4, 91, 112–21, 189
Chrysippus 99, 187
Churchill, W. 186
Cicero 33, 59, 145, 162–5, 166, 171, 177, 194
    Ad Atticum 164, 194
    Ad Familiares 163, 194
    Ad Quintum fratrem 194
classic status 21, 67–8, 74, 91, 100, 107, 110, 112, 120–1, 127, 135, 136, 185
Cleanthes 102, 115
Clearchus 137–8
Clement of Alexandria (Titus Flavius Clemens) 18, 61, 70, 91, 112–21, 152, 168, 175, 186, 189–90, 193
    Paedagogus 112, 113, 114, 116
    Protrepticus 112, 114, 115, 116, 117, 119, 193
    Stromateis 70, 112–19, 175, 183, 186, 189, 193
closure 33–5, 36
code-switching 164
comedy 6, 8, 9, 26, 31, 58, 67–8, 73–89, 134, 136, 138, 140, 146, 147, 148, 154, 156, 182, 184, 191
Compagnon, A. 120, 173, 174, 177, 180
competitive quotation 17, 106–7, 127–8, 130–2, 135, 143, 158, 187, 188, 194
Crantor 159–62
Cratinus 17, 73, 174, 185
Culler, J. 42, 180
cultural capital 106–7, 121, 122, 188
Cypria 137

dates of performances 6, 7, 67–8, 76–7, 147, 153–4, 173, 185, 193
decorative *versus* illustrative quotations 109–10, 111–12, 135, 140
deductive method of interpretation 147–54, 192
Deinolochus 74
Demetrius of Phaleron 96
Democritus 166, 167
Demosthenes 104, 105, 109, 125–32, 174, 175, 183, 190–1
    On the Crown 132
    On the False Assembly 130–2
dialogue 41, 42, 62, 102, 118, 146–7, 153–5
Didymus 59
Diocles 159
Diogenes Laertius 62, 112, 145, 156–62, 171, 187, 189, 190, 193–4
    Life of Aristippus 157–9
    Life of Crantor 159–62
Diogenes of Sinope 194
Dio of Prusa (Dio 'Chrysostom') 29, 33, 57, 59, 95, 176, 177, 182
Dionysius of Halicarnassus 57
Dionysius of Syracuse 157–8, 159
Diphilus 74, 83–5, 86–7, 173, 186
Douris of Samos 153

education 14–15, 21, 29, 43, 62, 65, 91–122, 128, 160–1, 171; *see also* schools

ekphrasis 105–6
elegy 93, 156
Empedocles 166
epic 137, 147, 156; *see also* Homer
Epicharmus 56
Epictetus 166, 194, 195
Epicurus 167
epigraphs 4, 24–7, 31
epigram 93, 156
Eriphus 177, 186
Eubulus 74, 76, 77, 185
Eupolis 77–80, 185
  Demes 77–80, 185
Euripides (*passim*): admired by ancient critics 29, 59, 193; anticipates readers' responses 21–3, 29, 41, 51–2; and Athenian public 147–9; biography 135, 145–55, 192–3; contrasts with other tragedians 29–30, 52, 135, 156; controversies and scandals 58, 66–7; favourite of Aristophanes 73–4, 76; halitosis 146; heterodox views 115; as love poet 161; orthodox views 49; 'philosopher of the stage' 119, 121, 129, 135; popularity surges in fourth century 73–4, 76, 129, 161, 185; prologues 6–7, 24–7; as rhetorician 124–5; skill at depicting emotions 108–9, 124, 135, 160–1; status as classic 2, 7, 20–1, 29–30, 67–8, 74, 100, 107–8, 110, 112, 135, 151–2, 159–60, 185; status within the early Church 112–21, 190; views on women 150
(works cited):
Aegeus 92, 122
Aeolus 1, 39–40, 62–72, 76, 81, 102–3, 138, 174, 176, 177, 179, 180, 183, 185
Alcestis 34, 45, 92, 115, 177, 179, 181, 192
Alcmene 181
Alcmeon I or II 56, 62, 179
Alcmeon in Corinth 57, 180, 182
Alexandros 57, 62, 116, 176, 180, 181, 182, 188
Alope 71
Andromache 34, 50, 77, 92, 137, 177, 178, 179, 180, 181, 192, 194

Andromeda 62, 76, 160–1, 177, 180, 181, 190, 192, 194
Antigone 6, 43, 77, 177, 181, 182
Antiope 39, 56, 59, 60, 83–4, 110, 115, 116, 117, 167, 169, 179, 180, 181, 182, 183, 186, 190
Archelaus 6, 43, 101, 177, 180, 181, 184, 192
Auge 62, 112, 156, 176, 177, 189
Bacchae 34, 92, 114, 117–19, 136, 141, 157–8, 177, 178, 179, 189, 193
Bellerophon 48, 60, 61, 62, 76, 160, 167, 169, 180, 181, 182, 183
Chrysippus 103, 114, 167, 180
Cresphontes 58, 178, 180
Cretans 60
Cretan Women 136, 140
Cyclops 178
Danae 39, 56, 179, 180, 181, 192
Daughters of Pelias 58
Dictys 40, 71, 179, 180
Electra 92, 103, 111–12, 159, 178, 179, 180, 189
Erechtheus 50–2, 61, 126, 179, 181, 182, 183
Eurystheus 136
Hecuba 11–12, 34, 37, 50, 56, 92, 177, 178, 179, 180, 190, 191
Helen 34, 48, 76, 92, 177, 178, 179, 181, 182, 184, 189
Heracleidae 31–2, 36, 176, 177, 178, 179, 180, 181
Heracles 34, 36, 110, 136, 179, 181
Hippolytus 1, 38, 42–3, 47, 56, 57, 77, 92, 100, 123, 139–40, 141, 177, 178, 179, 180, 184, 189, 190, 192, 193, 194
Hippolytus Veiled 116, 180, 181
Hypsipyle 6, 62, 76, 92, 101–2, 122, 167, 169, 177, 178, 185
Ino 55, 92, 93, 94–5, 98, 122, 179, 180
Ion 34, 115, 164, 178, 179, 181, 194
Iphigenia at Aulis 77, 103, 114, 178, 179, 190
Iphigenia among the Taurians 84, 106, 115, 116, 157, 178, 180, 190
Ixion 46, 58
Licymnius 56, 181, 182, 192

Medea 34, 37, 58, 77, 92, 114, 136, 159, 164, 177, 178, 179, 181, 182, 190, 193, 194
Melanippe I or II 49, 56, 71, 180
Melanippe Captive 79
Melanippe the Wise 57, 58, 61, 150, 177, 179, 182, 183, 184, 193
Meleager 56, 60, 177, 179, 182, 184, 190
Oedipus 77, 116–17, 177, 189
Oeneus 58, 62, 79, 190
Orestes 1, 32–3, 38, 76, 88, 106, 108–9, 115, 116, 159, 174, 176, 177, 178, 179, 182, 185, 186, 190, 193
Palamedes 156, 180, 193
Peleus 43, 180
Peliades 177, 180, 182
Phaethon 57, 108–9, 156
Philoctetes 56, 57, 60, 164, 179, 180, 181, 182, 190, 193, 194
Phoenician Women 34–5, 36, 45, 48, 50, 86, 92, 93–4, 95–6, 97–8, 100, 116, 137, 178, 179, 180, 181, 184, 187, 193, 194
Phoenix 32, 61, 81, 129–31, 174, 176, 177, 180, 191
Phrixus I or II 56, 177, 181, 185
Phrixus II 47, 182
Polyidus 179, 185
Rhesus 178
Sciron 136, 177
Scyrians 62, 177, 179
Stheneboea 3–4, 5–13, 20, 23–7, 31, 49, 61, 63, 76, 81–2, 85, 110–11, 129, 173, 174, 177, 184, 185, 190
Suppliant Women 36, 45, 46, 159, 167, 176, 177, 178, 179, 180, 181, 184, 194
Syleus 57, 182
Telephus 58, 76, 92, 122, 177, 185, 190
Temenus (or *Temenidae*) 57, 179, 182
Theseus 179
Thyestes 46, 180, 190
Women of Troy 92, 137, 149, 178, 181, 190, 193, 194
unidentified plays (*incertae fabulae*, 'incert. fab.') 39, 49, 61, 62, 70, 101, 109, 111, 114, 119–20, 147–8, 149, 150, 154–5, 163–4, 167, 179, 180, 181, 183, 186, 188, 189, 193, 194
Euripidophilia 88, 129

Eusebius 112, 193
Eustathius 64

florilegium, see anthologies
fortune (*tyche*) 33, 39, 97, 104
fragments 1, 2, 5, 19–20, 22, 30, 44, 53–72, 114, 122, 124, 136, 166
framing devices 4, 21, 29–52, 71, 76, 80, 86

Genette, G. 24–7
genre 11, 67, 73, 97, 136, 166, 174
gnomai, see maxims
'gnomic pointing' 41, 180
gods 26, 33, 46–7, 63, 93, 112–21, 149–50, 178
Gregory of Nazianzus 68, 184

half-quotation 69, 109, 111, 164, 184
hedgehogs 30
Hegelochus 185
Heracles 34–5, 45
Heraclides of Pontus 153
Hermippus 151, 156
Hermogenes 5, 190
Herodas 186
Herodian 194
Herodotus 104, 174, 176
Hesiod 17, 18, 99, 105, 116, 175
Higbie, C. 106
Hippias of Elis 18, 175
Hippolytus 43
Holmes, S. 147, 186
Homer 2, 18, 21, 91, 92, 93, 94, 99, 100, 104, 108, 110, 113, 121, 122, 126–7, 129, 137, 150, 156, 159, 163, 187, 189, 191
humour 8–10, 67–8, 73, 77–80, 81, 86, 89, 135, 136, 137–8, 139–40, 141, 165
hypotheses 5, 19, 31, 63, 154

incomplete quotation 69–70
interpolation 112, 178
intertextuality and allusion 31, 73, 75, 165
'invisible' quotations 71, 76–80, 89, 140, 184, 185, 193
Iolaus 31–2, 36
Ion of Chios, *Epidemiai* 138–9, 192
Isaiah 116

Iser, W. 23
Isocrates 174, 175, 186, 189

Jacob, C. 134
Jesus 112, 117, 118, 119, 120
Jocasta, 36, 45, 50, 86
jokes, *see* humour
Jude 116
Justin, martyr 61

Kannicht, R. 5, 63
knowledge of texts 4, 6, 8, 10, 12–13, 53–72, 75, 76–80, 84, 88–9, 91, 98, 104–5, 108, 110, 113, 117, 122, 123, 130, 133–5, 137, 142–3, 146, 152–3, 158, 160, 162, 163–5, 168–9, 182, 183, 187, 189, 194
König, J. 133
Konstan, D. 103
Kristeva, J. 73

Larensis 133, 134, 139, 140, 142
Larochefoucauld, F. de La, *Maximes* 166
lawcourts 4, 11, 123, 124–32, 142–3, 169
letters 162–5, 194
lexicography 55, 71
Libanius 190
libraries 4, 105, 133, 138, 142, 154
literacy 10, 15, 75, 91–8, 122, 128, 174, 185
Livre d'Écolier, Un (Guéraud and Jouguet) 92–8
Logothetes, Ioannes 5, 61, 183
Longinus (author of *On the Sublime*) 59, 60, 77–8, 91, 103–12, 152, 183, 185, 187, 193, 194
Longinus, Cassius 104–5
Lucian 16, 33, 107, 132, 161, 174, 177, 189
  Ignorant Book-Collector, The 107
  On the Writing of History 161
Lycurgus 16, 74, 126, 174, 183
  Against Leocrates 126, 174, 183
Lynceus 135, 138
lyric poetry 20, 42, 132, 149, 156; *see also* Alcaeus, Bacchylides, Pindar, Sappho, Simonides

Machon 66–7
Macrobius 60, 132
Marcus Aurelius 145, 165–71, 194–5

Matthew, Saint 116, 119
maxims (*gnomai*) 8, 9–10, 11–12, 20, 24, 29–30, 32, 33, 36, 37–41, 42, 44, 47, 48, 51, 55, 59, 63, 64–5, 68–71, 80–8, 91, 92, 93–7, 99, 104, 122, 124, 135, 150, 157, 159, 163–4, 174, 176–7, 186, 187
memory 6, 8, 15, 16, 19, 21, 41, 51, 53–4, 61, 62, 72, 81, 110, 113, 122, 125, 133–4, 146, 160, 167, 170, 171, 187, 191
Menander 9–10, 11, 56, 77, 81–2, 85, 87, 91, 92, 99, 173, 174, 175, 177, 183, 186
  Aspis ('*Shield*') 9–10, 81–2, 175, 177
  Epitrepontes 173, 183
  Monostichoi 87, 186
metaphors 101, 106, 107, 113, 119, 138, 169, 180, 187, 189, 191, 194, 195
metapoetics 33, 48–9, 51, 71, 73, 132
metre 30, 36, 41, 80, 93, 185
mimesis 98–9
Miltiades 77–8
miscellanies 112–13, 189; *see also* Aulus Gellius
misquotation 95, 96, 97–8, 114, 160, 194
Mnesitheus 136
monologues 31–2, 36, 45, 61, 126
Morson, G. S. 3, 20, 24, 26, 46, 194
mystery-cult 118–19

necromancy 119–20
Nicander 136
Nicoboule 135
Nicophon 136
Nicostratus 9, 74, 85, 177
nostalgia 133, 147
notebooks 99, 134, 162, 166, 168, 187, 188
Numenius of Heracleia 138

Oedipus 35, 116–17
Olympiodorus 59
opening lines 3–4, 5–13, 20, 23–7, 31–3, 36, 55, 63–4
orality 11, 15, 72, 81
Orestes 116–17
Orion 63, 180, 183
Oxford Dictionary of Quotations 16

Pacuvius 59
Palladas 194
papyri 5, 16, 18, 41, 63, 78–9, 92–8, 146–55, 180, 183, 186–7, 189, 191, 192, 193
parabasis 192
paradox 49
paratexts 4, 24–7
parody and paratragedy 10, 31, 58, 66, 67–8, 73–5, 76, 84–6, 88, 131, 136, 138, 165, 182, 185–6
Pascal, B., *Pensées* 166
performance 10, 19, 24–5, 31, 33–4, 36, 41, 58, 72, 73, 74–5, 76, 80, 106, 123–43, 170, 190
pheu (interjection) 37–41
Philemon 49, 56, 74, 77, 147, 150, 181, 193
Philippides, 8–9, 74
Philo of Alexandria 57, 182
Philochorus of Athens 152
philosophy 4, 22, 85, 96, 98–100, 132, 141, 146, 147, 156–62, 164, 165–71
Philoxenus 87–8
Phocylides 175
Phrynichus 139
Photius 62
Pindar 99, 149, 175
Plato 15, 59, 66, 88, 91, 96–7, 104, 111, 132, 150, 156–7, 158, 159, 166, 167, 174, 175, 179, 181, 183, 184, 186, 187, 188
Pliny the Elder 113
Pliny the Younger 164
Plutarch 6, 12–13, 16, 55, 57–8, 62, 67, 68, 69, 91, 95–6, 98–103, 104, 120–1, 125, 127, 132, 152, 159, 174, 175, 181, 182, 183, 184, 187, 188, 189, 190, 191, 192, 193, 194
  Life of Alexander 151
  Life of Demosthenes 125, 183
  Life of Pompey 159
  How The Young Man Should Study Poetry 67, 98–103, 104, 127, 159, 184
Pollux 192
Porphyry 60, 64
priamel 24
prologues 4, 5–9, 23–7, 31–3, 63, 64, 176, 183

proverbs 8, 10, 13, 32, 34, 47, 69, 70, 88, 92, 111, 164, 165, 188
Pyrrhon 157

Quintilian 29, 91, 97, 124, 176, 186
'quotationality' 20, 24, 27, 30, 33, 45, 59, 78, 104, 110, 135
quotation marks 4, 29–52, 140, 165, 177
quotation-spotting 7, 8, 75, 78–80, 82, 85, 88–9, 134, 140, 141, 157–8, 165, 191

readers and reading habits 2, 3, 4, 9, 13, 14–19, 20–1, 22, 25, 27, 29, 30–1, 36, 41, 44, 53–72, 76, 80–88, 89, 99, 103, 113, 133–4, 163–4, 166, 168–9, 174
rhetoric 4, 11–12, 15, 43, 60–1, 65–6, 91, 103–4, 117, 124–32, 158, 190–1
Rhetoric to Alexander 60–1, 190
rhyme 30, 45, 177, 181
Rutherford, R. B. 166

Sannyrion 185
Sappho 22, 176
Satyrus, tragic actor 125
Satyrus of Callatis, *Life of Euripides* 145–55, 156, 171, 191, 192–3
Schlegel, F. 19–20, 22, 23, 30, 176, 177
scholia 29, 56, 57, 58–9, 62, 66, 111, 152, 176, 182, 183, 184, 185, 188, 192, 193
scholarship in antiquity 4, 16, 31, 58–9, 63–4, 96, 103, 135–6, 138, 145, 151–4, 156, 176, 182, 187, 192–3; *see also* scholia
schools 4, 11, 61, 91–122, 186–7, 190
Schorn, S. 147, 148, 150, 192
Sellars, J. 170, 195
Semus 136
Seneca the Younger 164, 174, 186, 189, 192, 195
Serenus 66–7, 184
Sextus Empiricus 62, 68, 184, 186
Shakespeare, William 1, 50–1, 111, 194
Simonides 17, 139
slaves 9–10, 174
Socrates 14, 17, 112, 134, 146, 149, 156, 193
Solon 157

sophistic movement 18, 19, 117, 124
Sophocles 24, 27, 29, 36, 40, 55, 57, 74, 99, 109, 110, 115, 131, 135, 139, 146, 156, 158–9, 169, 176, 177, 178, 179, 180, 189, 192, 193, 194
Sotion 158
source references (or lack thereof) 72, 101–2, 108, 115, 116–17, 129–30, 134, 135, 136, 138, 139, 140–1, 153, 159, 164, 166–7, 168, 186, 189
speech acts 123
Stesimbrotus of Thasos 192
stichomythia 50, 102, 187
Stobaeus, Ioannes (John of Stobi), 12, 16–17, 52, 55, 61, 62, 64–5, 66, 67, 68–71, 95, 152, 168, 176, 177, 180, 181, 182, 183, 184, 186, 187, 188, 189, 193
Strabo 57, 64, 182
Strattis 74, 76, 85–6, 185
style 30, 32–3, 37–41, 45, 60–1, 109, 124, 146, 151, 160, 190
Symmachus 58, 183
symposia 4, 11, 36, 123, 132–43, 146, 169, 191

Terentianus, Postumius Florus 104, 105, 106, 108, 109
testimonia 57–8, 64
textual criticism 63–4, 67, 96, 102, 192
Theagenes of Rhegium 192
Theodorus Metochites 177
Theognis 17
Theophilus 112, 174

Theopompus 87
Theophrastus 96, 138, 160–1, 184
Theseus 36, 43, 45
Thucydides 174, 181
Timachidas of Rhodes 138
Timarchus 126–7, 130, 132
transmission of texts 3, 30, 64, 122
'triangulated address' 42, 44
turn-indicators 40, 41, 47, 179
Tzetzes, Iohannes 57

Ulpian 134
unity 22, 27, 30

Valerius Maximus 29, 176
value 106–7, 110, 112, 123; *see also* classic status
Vitruvius 176, 190
voice 2, 13, 20, 22, 25–7, 32, 45–6, 47–8, 100, 121, 126, 130, 145, 149–51, 152, 154–5, 164–5, 168, 181, 190, 192

Warren, J. 161
Wilde, O. 186
wisdom, traditional 1, 8, 11, 12, 17, 18, 20, 26–7, 32–3, 34, 46, 47–8, 49, 113, 142, 168, 181; *see also* proverbs

Xenarchus 77
Xenocles 21
Xenophon 14–15, 17–18, 51, 132, 174, 175, 179, 181, 186, 191

Zeno 102, 141, 159

www.ingramcontent.com/pod-product-compliance
Lightning Source LLC
Chambersburg PA
CBHW052112300426
44116CB00010B/1632